5/98

 St. Louis Community College

Forest Park
Florissant Valley
Meramec

Instructional Resources
St. Louis, Missouri

THIRD EDITION -
REVISED AND ENLARGED

CARIBBEAN
REEF FISHES

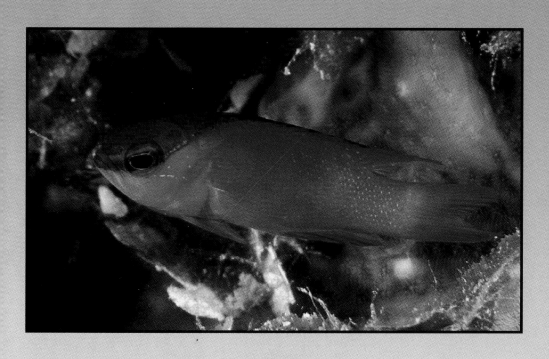

H-932

JOHN E. RANDALL

TO HELEN

© 1996 by T.F.H. Publications, Inc.

Distributed in the UNITED STATES to the Pet Trade by T.F.H. Publications, Inc., One T.F.H. Plaza, Neptune City, NJ 07753; distributed in the UNITED STATES to the Bookstore and Library Trade by National Book Network, Inc. 4720 Boston Way, Lanham MD 20706; in CANADA to the Pet Trade by H & L Pet Supplies Inc., 27 Kingston Crescent, Kitchener, Ontario N2B 2T6; Rolf C. Hagen Inc., 3225 Sartelon St. Laurent-Montreal Quebec H4R 1E8; in CANADA to the Book Trade by Vanwell Publishing Ltd., 1 Northrup Crescent, St. Catharines, Ontario L2M 6P5 ; in ENGLAND by T.F.H. Publications, PO Box 15, Waterlooville PO7 6BQ; in AUSTRALIA AND THE SOUTH PACIFIC by T.F.H. (Australia), Pty. Ltd., Box 149, Brookvale 2100 N.S.W., Australia; in NEW ZEALAND by Brooklands Aquarium Ltd. 5 McGiven Drive, New Plymouth, RD1 New Zealand; in Japan by T.F.H. Publications, Japan—Jiro Tsuda, 10-12-3 Ohjidai, Sakura, Chiba 285, Japan; in SOUTH AFRICA by Lopis (Pty) Ltd., P.O. Box 39127, Booysens, 2016, Johannesburg, South Africa. Published by T.F.H. Publications, Inc.
MANUFACTURED IN THE
UNITED STATES OF AMERICA
BY T.F.H. PUBLICATIONS, INC.

TABLE OF CONTENTS

INTRODUCTION

The primary purpose of this book is to provide for the identification of the 327 most common fishes that one might observe while snorkeling or diving on reefs of the Caribbean Sea or over adjacent sand flat or seagrass environments. Many of these species are very colorful, and a number of them are popular aquarium fishes.

Nearly all of these Caribbean fishes occur also in Bermuda, southern Florida, the Bahamas, and along the coasts of the Guianas and Brazil. Some range into the Gulf of Mexico and north of Florida along the Atlantic seaboard as well.

Many of the smaller reef and inshore fishes such as the two families of stargazers, the wormfishes, the cusk-eels, and most of the gobies, blennies, clinids, pipefishes, clingfishes, cardinalfishes, and burrowing eels have not been included. The majority of these fishes are either not seen by the average underwater observer or elicit little interest because of their small size and/or drab color. A more comprehensive volume which will include all of the shallow–water and surface-dwelling species of the West Indies and many references is in preparation by the author.

The species are arranged in approximate phylogenetic sequence, beginning with the cartilaginous fishes (sharks and rays). General discussions of the families (headings ending in "IDAE") precede the species accounts except those families containing only a single western Atlantic species. Brief remarks are sometimes made in family or species accounts of fishes which are not formally discussed because they are inconspicuous, rare, or generally absent from the reef habitat.

Species headings begin with the common name in boldface type. Most of these names are from *Common and Scientific Names of Fishes from the United States and Canada,* Fifth Edition, Special Publication No. 20 of the American Fisheries Society by C. R. Robins et al. (1991). The scientific name of each of the fishes appears in italics below the common name and to the left, followed by the author or authors who gave the fish its name and the year the name was published. It will be noted that some authors' names appear in parentheses; these marks indicate that the author originally described his species in a different genus (first word of the two-part scientific name) than the one in which it is now classified. Most of the known fishes have one or more obsolete scientific names which are called *synonyms* (names proposed for a species after the original one). They also have different common names in different parts of the distribution. It would be impractical to attempt to list all of the invalid scientific names and common names for each species in a work of this scope.

The discussions of the species begin with a listing of the most important external characteristics that provide for the identification of the fish, commencing with the number of fin rays, lateral-line scales, and gill rakers when of diagnostic value. In some cases the ranges given for the various counts and proportional measurements are not as broad as they might be because too few specimens have been examined. The distinguishing characteristics are followed by remarks on size (total length in inches) and distribution.

When the distribution is cited as tropical western Atlantic, this implies that the fish occurs in southern Florida, Bermuda, the West Indies, usually the southern Gulf of Mexico, and the continental shores of the Caribbean Sea south to Brazil. When a range is given from a locality of north latitude to one in the south, such as Massachusetts to Brazil, it is understood that the species has been found or can be expected from intervening areas such as the Gulf of Mexico and the West Indies.

A surprising number of tropical Atlantic fishes range north to New England, but most of these are strays, and many are juveniles that probably do not survive their first winter there. The Gulf Stream is responsible for sweeping the larval stages of these fishes from southern breeding areas to northern latitudes.

All of the fishes for which there are species accounts are illustrated. The photographs of fishes after removal from the sea were taken mostly by the author in the Virgin Islands or Puerto Rico by a technique described in a short paper [Randall, *Copeia*, 1961(2): 241-242]. Underwater photographs without a credit line were taken by the author in the Bahamas and various Caribbean localities.

Two illustrations are given for some of the fishes because of marked differences between juveniles and adults or between the two sexes. Sexual differences in color are particularly important for the wrasses and parrotfishes (see introductory discussions of these families).

The total length is given in the caption for each of the fishes that was collected and photographed; weight is also listed for many of the larger specimens. It is important to record the size of illustrated specimens because body and fin proportions may change, as well as color, when a fish grows. A juvenile fish, for example, will have a larger eye relative to the size of its head or body length. The locality from which a photographed fish was collected is also given in the figure caption.

Mention is made in some family and species discussions of the possibility of being poisoned by eating certain fishes, even when fresh. The resulting illness is known as *ciguatera*. Among the usual symptoms are weakness, particularly of the legs, diarrhea, confusion of the sensations of heat and cold, and unpleasant tingling sensations of the hands and feet. Severe cases have terminated in coma and death.

Eating the viscera of the puffers (Tetraodontidae) will also produce a serious toxemia with a notably higher rate of fatality. There seems to be no relationship between tetraodon poisoning and ciguatera. The puffers produce the toxin themselves, whereas the fishes which cause ciguatera appear to acquire their toxicity via their feeding. The basic poisonous organism is a benthic dinoflagellate, *Gambierdiscus toxicus.* The toxin is passed on to plant-feeding animals and thence to carnivorous forms when they feed on the herbivores. The larger the fish, the more apt it is to be poisonous. The worst offenders are the barracuda, amberjack, most of the jacks of the genus *Caranx,* large moray eels, some of the larger groupers (especially the genus *Mycteroperca)* and snappers of the genus *Lutjanus* (particularly the Dog Snapper and Cubera Snapper). These fishes feed heavily on reef fishes. The Queen Triggerfish, which feeds mainly on sea urchins, and the Hogfish, which is primarily a mollusk-feeder, have also, on occasions, caused ciguatera.

The incidence of ciguatera is greater at some West Indian islands than others and is often confined to certain reef sectors. Presumably these sectors are regions where the conditions for the growth of the dinoflagellate are optimal. One should make inquiry of local fishermen to determine the possible existence of reefs harboring poisonous fishes before attempting to eat any of the potentially dangerous species.

There is no truth to the popular statement that a silver coin will turn black if cooked with the flesh of a fish that can cause ciguatera (at least if the fish is fresh). The belief that flies will avoid a toxic fish is also a misconception.

Some persons have fed suspected fishes to cats or dogs before attempting consumption themselves. These animals are sensitive to ciguatera toxin and display such symptoms as sluggishness, gastro-intestinal distress, and lack of muscular coordination, especially of the hind limbs. Cats are prone to regurgitate toxic fish, so should be confined during the testing period. Although symptoms generally appear within four or five hours, one should observe the test animal for 12 hours to be certain the fish is safe to eat. Since the liver and internal organs of a poisonous fish contain a much greater concentration of toxin than the muscle tissue, it is advisable to feed viscera to test animals. Mongooses have been extensively used for feeding tests in experimental work on ciguatera in the Hawaiian Islands.

Still another type of fish poisoning known from the Caribbean and other littoral tropical waters is *clupeid poisoning,* named for the herring family. The threadfin herring and species of *Harengula,* which are schooling plankton-feeding fishes, have produced this illness when eaten. It is more often fatal than ciguatera. Fortunately, the incidence is very low.

Fishes which can cause serious injury to man because of venomous spines or a proclivity to bite are discussed under family or species headings. The most important groups with venomous spines are the stingrays and the scorpionfishes, and those feared for biting are the sharks, moray eels, and barracudas. The danger from morays and barracudas is generally exaggerated.

Ichthyological terminology is unavoidable in a handbook of fishes if adequate information is to be provided for the positive identification of species. Names of the external parts of fishes should be learned to enable the reader to fully utilize the descriptive remarks in species accounts. The following diagram and definitions of the most important scientific terms are therefore presented. A glossary is given at the back of the book just before the index.

METHODS OF COUNTING AND MEASURING FISHES

Whereas fishermen understandably want to express the length of their catch as the maximum or **total length** (and it is this length which is given in the species accounts herein for the size attained by each species of fish), ichthyologists usually use the **standard length**. This is the straight-line measurement from the tip of the upper jaw (with jaw not protracted) to the base of the caudal (tail) fin. The latter point is also the end of the vertebral column. On small fishes it can sometimes be seen by holding the tail up to a bright light. Usually it is determined by bending the caudal fin upward and noting where a wrinkle occurs at the base. Standard length is preferred because the ends of caudal fin rays are often bent or missing on preserved specimens in museums. It may be very difficult or even impossible to measure externally on some fishes such as jacks with scutes along the side of the tail or tunas with a keel at this location. Then **fork length** is generally taken. It is the length from the tip of the upper jaw to the end of the middle caudal rays.

Various proportional measurements are important in distinguishing species of fishes. These are usu-

ally expressed as the number of times a small measurement is contained within a larger one. Standard length is most often used as a basis for the larger measurements, and **head length** (tip of upper jaw to membranous end of gill cover) for the smaller measurements, such as the **interorbital space** (least width between eyes on top of head). Some proportional measurements, such as the diameter of the eye in the head length, often change a great deal with age and are less useful than more stable measurements unless the actual length of specimens is stated.

Proportional measurements may show considerable variation even among specimens the same size. For example, the **depth** of the body (maximum vertical height of a fish discounting the fins) will be greater in a fish which has just consumed a large meal or is heavy with roe than one which has been living in a region of limited food. Therefore these measurements are usually given as a range to include the normal variability. In general, measurements of the young are omitted because they often extend the range to the point where it is no longer useful to distinguish related species.

The fins of bony fishes are supported by **rays** which are of two fundamental types, spines and soft rays. The **spines** are uniserial, not segmented and never branched; they are usually stout and rigid with sharp tips. The **soft rays** are biserial (two lateral components joined in the mid-line) and show segmentation (which can be seen as dark transverse lines); they are flexible and often branched. By tradition,

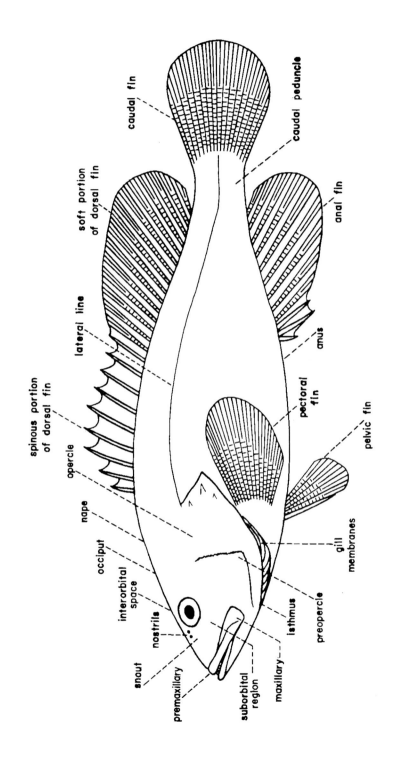

counts of spines are given in Roman numerals and those of soft rays in Arabic numerals. A comma is used to separate the spine and soft-ray counts of a single fin. A dash between two sets of fin-ray counts indicates a separation to two fins (usually applies to the dorsal fin).

Collectively, the dorsal, anal and caudal fins are termed **median fins.** The **pectoral fins** (one on each side of body behind gill opening) and **pelvic fins** (two fins side by side on lower edge of body, usually approximately below the pectorals) are referred to as the **paired fins.** The pelvic fins are sometimes called ventral fins. The counts of the pectoral fins include the short splint-like uppermost ray except when very rudimentary (as on the filefishes).

In making counts of spines, care should be taken to include the very small initial spines that are often present in dorsal and anal fins. Difficulty may be experienced in deciding whether to count the last two soft rays of the dorsal or anal fins as one or two when they are close together. If two rays share the same basal element, they are here counted as one. If each has its own basal support, regardless of spacing, they are counted separately.

The shape of the caudal fin (more specifically the shape of the terminal or posterior border of the fin) is often used in diagnoses of fishes. The following descriptive terms are usually employed, most of which are obvious: **rounded** (convexly curved); **truncate** (vertical and straight, the corners almost square); **emarginate** (concavely curved); **lunate** (deeply concavely curved; usually used for a fin that is sickle-shaped); **double emarginate** (biconcave); **pointed** (rounded but with the middle caudal rays ending in a point); **lanceolate** (excessively pointed); **forked** (inwardly angular); and **rhomboid** (outwardly angular).

Lateral-line scales (the single series of pored scales along the side of the body of most bony fishes) are counted from the level of the upper end of the gill opening to the base of the caudal fin. Often a few pored scales extend posterior to the base of the caudal fin, but they are not included in the count. The lateral line on some fishes is **interrupted,** *i.e.* divided into two distinct portions, the first usually on the upper anterior part of the body and the second mid-posteriorly.

Scales above the lateral line are those in a diagonal row between the lateral line (not including any lateral line scales) and the origin of the dorsal fin; **scales below the lateral line** are those in a diagonal row below the lateral line to the origin of the anal fin. The latter two counts have not been used much in the present book because differences in scale counts are usually reflected in the count of the lateral line alone and because difficulty is often experienced in deciding whether to include small scales that are often found basally at the origin of the dorsal or anal fins.

Lateral scale rows (near-vertical rows of scales between upper end of gill opening and base of caudal fin) are counted on some species in which the lateral line is absent or obscure.

Sometimes the number of scales around the **caudal peduncle** (posterior part of body between the ends of the dorsal and anal fins and the base of the caudal fin) is a useful distinguishing character. This count is called the **circumpeduncular scales.**

The scales of most bony fishes are either **ctenoid** (the exposed surface and edge of the scales with small sharp projections called ctenii, and hence slightly rough to the touch) or **cycloid** (without ctenii and therefore smooth to the touch).

The number of **gill rakers** are often useful in distinguishing related species of fishes. They are projections on the inner front edge of a gill arch (bony support for the gills), hence on the opposite side of the red gill filaments where the gaseous exchange of respiration takes place. They serve as a sieve to retain food organisms that might otherwise pass out the gill opening with the respired water. Fishes which feed on small organisms, especially planktonic forms, tend to have numerous long gill rakers in contrast to species which feed on large prey. Some fishes such as many barracudas have no gill rakers. Counts are made of the rakers on the first (outermost) gill arch. Usually there is an obvious angle in the gill arch such that counts of the gill rakers can be made above and below the angle. The **upper-limb gill rakers** are those above the angle, and the **lower-limb gill rakers** are those below the angle, *including* the one at the angle. A "plus" sign is used to separate upper- and lower-limb counts. The counts, in general, include the small rudimentary gill rakers which may be present at the ends of the gill arch. The rudiments are not counted in some species, particularly when coalesced (in which case mention is made of their omission).

The **branchiostegal rays** are occasionally of diagnostic value. They are the slender bony supports for the gill membranes on the ventroposterior part of the head at the edge of the gill opening. The more primitive teleost fishes tend to have a greater number of branchiostegal rays than the fishes which are evolutionarily more advanced.

The dentition of fishes is fundamental in their classification. Teeth may be present or absent on the jaws (the upper jaw consists of two bones, the **premaxilla** at the front and the **maxilla** to the side), the **vomer** (median bone at the front of the roof of the mouth), the **palatines** (paired bones to the side of the roof of the mouth) or the tongue. They may vary significantly in number, size and shape. Long pointed teeth are called **canines;** short pointed ones are termed **conical;** very small conical teeth in several rows are usually designated **villiform;** flattened chisel-like teeth are **incisiform;** and broad low rounded teeth are **molariform.**

The terminology for the color markings of fishes is more-or-less standardized as follows: a **bar** is a vertical marking with straight sides and a **stripe** is comparable but horizontal; a **band** is usually diagonal or curved (if curved, it is so described); a **line** is a very narrow linear marking of any orientation; a **spot** is well-defined and usually round or nearly so; a **blotch** is more obscure, with poorly defined margins; an **ocellus** (or ocellated spot) is a spot with a ring of another color around it (in fishes the spot is usually dark and the ring pale).

CARTILAGINOUS FISHES
(CHONDRICHTHYES)

This class of fishes includes the sharks (Selachii or Squaliformes), the rays and skates (Batoidei or Rajiformes) and the chimaeras (Chimaeriformes), a small bizarre deep-water group. The sharks and rays (collectively subclass Elasmobranchii) are characterized principally by a cartilaginous skeleton (which may be hardened through calcification, but is nevertheless not bone) and five to seven gill slits on each side. Many species have a small opening in front of the gill slits called a spiracle which is a vestigial gill cleft. When scales are present, they are not overlapping plates but consist of small tubercles known as placoid scales or dermal denticles (these give the coarse texture to shark skin). Typically the tail has a long upper and short lower lobe (the heterocercal caudal fin), in contrast to the symmetrical or homocercal tail of the higher bony fishes. There is no swimbladder to offset the weight of the body. To maintain a position in mid-water, a shark must keep swimming; the pectoral fins are held to the side and their slight inclination provides the necessary lift; possibly there is a hydrofoil effect as well. Rather than increase the absorptive surface of the digestive tract through lengthening of the tract, sharks and rays have resorted to the so-called spiral valve in the intestine. Fertilization is internal; the intromittent organ of the male develops as a pair of elongate appendages called claspers on the inner edges of the pelvic fins. Adult males are easily distinguished externally by the presence of claspers. The majority of sharks and most of the rays (but not the skates) give birth to living young. The teeth of sharks are common in fossil marine deposits. They reveal that most genera of living sharks were in existence in the Cretaceous Period which began 135 million years ago.

Figure 1. Nurse Shark (*Ginglymostoma cirratum*), 5 feet 3 inches, 52 pounds, St. John, Virgin Islands.

Figure 2. Nurse Shark (*Ginglymostoma cirratum*), Andros, Bahamas.

NURSE SHARKS
(ORECTOLOBIDAE)

Nurse Shark

Ginglymostoma cirratum (Bonnaterre, 1788).   Figures 1 & 2

A long barbel on front edge of each nostril; small mouth with seven to 12 functional rows of small teeth; caudal fin with a long upper but no lower lobe; dorsal fins posterior on body; grayish brown, the young with widely scattered small black spots. Reported to reach a maximum length of 14 feet. Littoral on both sides of the tropical and subtropical Atlantic and in the eastern Pacific. Seen more frequently in shallow water on West Indian reefs than any other shark. Often observed lying on the bottom. Although popularly believed to be harmless, the nurse shark has on occasions bitten divers when provoked, and when it bites, it may hang on with bulldog tenacity. Feeds on fishes and sundry invertebrate animals.

REQUIEM SHARKS
(CARCHARHINIDAE)

This is the largest family of sharks. At least 18 species of the family occur in Caribbean waters; most are dangerous to man. The six species discussed are the most common ones that might be observed in inshore waters. During daylight hours, however, even these sharks are infrequently encountered. At night the picture is different, for sharks, in general, are nocturnal. Some species such as the feared Tiger Shark may then invade very shallow water to feed. Even by day, a shark can be lured inshore to take a fish struggling on the end of a fisherman's line or spearfisherman's spear. As many experienced spearfishermen know, it is the low frequency vibration from the struggling fish that attracts sharks initially, and not the blood which does not diffuse rapidly enough in the sea to account for the speed with which sharks can appear. Once in

Figure 3. Caribbean Reef Shark (*Carcharhinus perezii*), Long Island, Bahamas.

the area, a shark may be further stimulated by body fluids released from a wounded fish, and a dangerous situation results. Spearfishermen are well advised not to retain their catch in close proximity to their person when in the sea.

The common names "Sand Shark" and "Mako" are often erroneously applied by laymen to any of several species of *Carcharhinus* in the tropical western Atlantic. The name Sand Shark belongs with *Carcharias taurus*, a coastal species with brown spots on the body and slender protruding teeth, which ranges from the Gulf of Maine to Texas. The Mako, *Isurus oxyrinchus*, is a fast-swimming offshore species with a very pointed snout, slender prong-like teeth, a nearly symmetrical caudal fin with a keel laterally at the base, and blue on the back. Related to the Mako is the White Shark, *Carcharodon carcharias*, the most dangerous fish in the sea. It also has a caudal fin with the lower lobe nearly as large as the upper and a strengthening ridge at the base. In contrast to the Mako, its teeth are triangular with serrate cutting edges. Fortunately, it is also principally a temperate species and is known from very few records from the Caribbean.

The reader interested in more information on sharks and the shark hazard is referred to *Sharks and Survival*, edited by P. G. Gilbert and published by D. C. Heath and Co., Boston (1963).

Bull Shark

Carcharhinus leucas (Valenciennes, 1841).
Figure 4

No interdorsal ridge; 12 or 13 teeth on each side of jaws not counting the small centrals; teeth serrate; vertical height of second dorsal fin about 4% of total length; lower posterior margin of second dorsal fin shorter than vertical height of fin; snout broadly rounded and short, its length before mouth 4 to 6.6% of total length. Grows to a length of at least 10 feet. An inshore

Figure 4. Bull Shark (*Carcharhinus leucas*), 6 feet 11 inches, Miami, Florida. Photo by Samuel H. Gruber.

species occurring along continental shelves in all warm seas; appears to be absent from most islands of the West Indies. Will penetrate fresh water (known, for example, from Lake Nicaragua). A dangerous shark.

Blacktip Shark

Carcharhinus limbatus (Valenciennes, 1841).
Figure 5

No interdorsal ridge on back; 14 to 16 upper and 13 to 15 lower teeth on each half of jaws; teeth serrate (the lowers finely); vertical height of second dorsal fin 3.1 to 3.4% of total length; lower posterior margin of second dorsal fin about equal to vertical height of fin (about 1.5 times greater than vertical height in another species of shark with black-tipped fins, *C. brevipinna);* snout in front of mouth about 7 to 8% of total length; fins black-tipped (these markings more evident on young). Probably does not exceed 7 or 8 feet in length. Circumtropical.

Figure 5. Blacktip Shark (*Carcharhinus limbatus*), female with embryos, 5 feet 10 inches, St. John, Virgin Islands.

Figure 6. Caribbean Reef Shark (*Carcharhinus perezii*), female with embryos, 6 feet 6 inches, St. John, Virgin Islands.

Caribbean Reef Shark

Carcharhinus perezii (Poey, 1876).
Figures 3 & 6

A low median ridge on back between dorsal fins; 12 or 13 teeth on each half of upper jaw and 11 or 12 on each half of lower, excluding one or two small central teeth; edges of teeth entirely serrate (serrations fine on lower teeth); vertical height of second dorsal fin 2.9 to 3.2% of total length; posterior margin of second dorsal fin only slightly greater than vertical height of fin; length of snout before mouth about 5.6 to 7.1% of total length. Reaches at least 9 feet. Because of difficulty in the identification of sharks of the genus *Carcharhinus*, the exact distribution of this species is not known. It is perhaps the most common member of the genus found in the inshore waters of West Indian islands. Capable of lying motionless on the bottom like the Nurse and Lemon Sharks. *C. springeri* is a synonym.

Tiger Shark

Galeocerdo cuvier (Peron & LeSueur, 1822).
Figure 7

Short blunt snout; long caudal fin (upper lobe about 2.5 times longer than the lower lobe); coarsely serrate teeth with a prominent notch in the outer edge; 11 or 12 teeth in the outer functional row on each side of jaws (disregarding small central tooth); gray to grayish brown with dark spots that often fuse to bars (markings may be faint or absent on large individuals). There are unofficial reports of lengths to 30 feet, but the largest reliably measured was 18 feet; it was caught in Cuba. The world's record for anglers is a 13-foot 10.5-inch individual that weighed 1780 pounds. Found in all tropical seas. Feeds on a wide variety of marine animals, including sea turtles which it can apparently cut into pieces with its saw-like teeth. Also well known as a scavenger, and indigestible items such as

Figure 7. Tiger Shark (*Galeocerdo cuvier*), 9 feet 2 inches, 260 pounds, Grand Bahama Island.

tin cans are occasionally found in their stomachs.

Lemon Shark

Negaprion brevirostris (Poey, 1868).

Figure 8

Second dorsal fin nearly as large as first; snout short and broadly rounded; central triangular portion of teeth smooth-edged; usual color of back yellowish brown. Attains a maximum length of about 11 feet. Ranges from North Carolina (during summer months) south to Brazil. A common inshore species which will enter brackish and even fresh water. Capable of resting motionless on the bottom. A hardy species readily transported and maintained in captivity, hence popular for experimental work. Has been known to attack man.

Figure 8. Lemon Shark (*Negaprion brevirostris*), 2 feet 1 inch, 2.7 pounds, St. John, Virgin Islands.

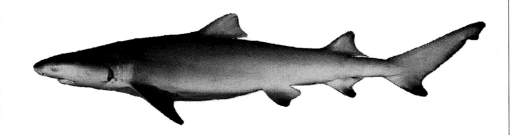

Figure 9. Sharpnose Shark (*Rhizoprionodon porosus*), 2 feet 11 inches, 6.3 pounds, St. John, Virgin Islands.

Sharpnose Shark

Rhizoprionodon porosus (Poey, 1861).
Figure 9

Labial furrow running forward on each side of corner of mouth for a distance more than half the diameter of the eye; body slender, the depth contained about 6 times in standard length; snout relatively long, its length in front of mouth 7.2 to 8.9% of total length. A small species, it attains a length of about 3.5 feet. Littoral in the western Atlantic from about 24° N to 35° S. The related *R. terraenovae* ranges from Yucatan to the Bay of Fundy, and *R. lalandei* from Panama to Brazil. The latter has short pectoral fins which do not reach a vertical at the middle of the base of the first dorsal fin.

HAMMERHEAD SHARKS
(SPHYRNIDAE)

These sharks are well named for their distinctive shape. The eyes are at the ends of the lateral projections of the head, and the nasal apertures are also widely spaced. Presumably this gives the hammerheads greater ability to swim to the sources of attractive visual and olfactory stimuli. It has also been postulated that the broadly expanded head serves as a forward plane which makes them more maneuverable than other sharks.

Eight species of the genus *Sphyrna* occur in the western Atlantic, of which five are known from the Caribbean. The two which are most apt to be found over inshore reefs are discussed below. The "Bonnethead" (*S. tiburo*), a small species with a shovel-shaped head (front very rounded when viewed from above), is characteristic of turbid continental-shelf waters.

The larger hammerheads have a sinister reputation; several well-authenticated attacks on man have been attributed to them.

Scalloped Hammerhead

Sphyrna lewini (Griffith & Smith, 1834).
Figure 10

Front margin of head slightly convex and unmistakably indented in mid-line; teeth smooth-edged; prenarial grooves well developed; lower posterior edge of second dorsal fin about twice as long as verti-

Figure 10. Scalloped Hammerhead (*Sphyrna lewini*), 9 feet 1 inch, 240 pounds, Grand Bahama Island.

cal height of fin. Grows to a length of about 10 feet. Circumtropical. *S. diplana* is a synonym.

Great Hammerhead

Sphyrna mokarran (Rüppell, 1835).

Figure 11

Head distinctly hammer-shaped, the anterior contour with a median indentation, but otherwise relatively straight (except in young); teeth serrate from tip to base; inner narial grooves absent; lower posterior edge of second dorsal fin about as long as vertical height of fin; pelvic fins falcate. The largest of the hammerheads, it attains at least 18 feet. Circumtropical.

Figure 11. Great Hammerhead (*Sphyrna mokarran*), 2 feet 7.5 inches, 4.3 pounds, Trinidad.

STINGRAYS
(DASYATIDAE)

Like other rays, the stingrays have broadly expanded pectoral fins, and the head is not well defined (head, body, and pectorals are collectively termed the disc). The gill openings are entirely ventral. Respiratory water enters the gill chamber through a small hole behind each eye known as the spiracle. There is no rayed dorsal fin, and the tail is slender, tapering, often long and usually armed basally with one or two serrate venomous spines. Wounds from these spines are extremely painful and can be serious. The teeth are nodular to pointed and occur in numerous close-set rows.

Stingrays of this family are usually seen lying on the bottom, often partially buried in the sand. Char-acteristically, they feed by excavating broad depressions in the sediment to expose various invertebrate animals, but they also manage to capture fishes. They are live-bearing like most sharks. The family is represented in the Caribbean by five species of *Dasyatis*, two of *Urotrygon* and one each of the genera *Himantura* and *Urolophus*.

Southern Stingray

Dasyatis americana Hildebrand & Schroeder, 1928.   Figures 12 & 13

Disc rhomboid, the snout not projecting; midline of back from head to base of tail with a row of tubercles; a short row of two to 12 small tubercles in middle of disc on either side of central row; tail without tubercles; venomous spine within a spine's length of base of tail; lower surface of tail with a well-developed mid-ventral cutaneous

Figure 12. Southern Stingray (*Dasyatis americana*), Belize.

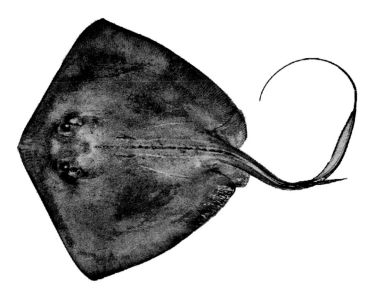

Figure 13. Southern Stingray (*Dasyatis americana*), length without tail 20.5 inches, St. John, Virgin Islands.

fold which originates below front of spine; gray to dark brown or olivaceous dorsally. Reaches a width of at least 5 feet. Ranges from New Jersey to Brazil. The most common species of the genus in the West Indies.

Yellowspotted Stingray

Urolophus jamaicensis (Cuvier, 1817).
Figures 14 & 15

Disc nearly round, slightly longer than broad; tail shorter than disc and bearing a distinct caudal fin at

Figure 14. Yellowspotted Stingray (*Urolophus jamaicensis*), length with tail 14.75 inches, Exumas, Bahama Islands.

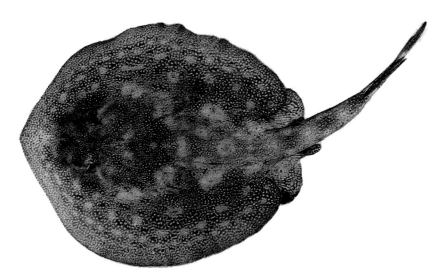

Figure 15. Yellowspotted Stingray (*Urolophus jamaicensis*), Long Island, Bahamas.

end (in contrast to *Dasyatis)*; venomous spine near end of tail; a mid-dorsal region of small tubercles running from head to base of spine; color variable, but usually with yellow spots. A small species which probably does not exceed 2.5 feet in total length. Recorded from Jamaica, Hispaniola, Cuba, the Bahamas, Florida, Yucatan and Trinidad; not known from Puerto Rico or the Lesser Antilles.

EAGLE RAYS
(MYLIOBATIDAE)

Like the dasyatid rays, the eagle rays are broadly flattened. Their body is thicker, however, and the head is more conspicuously marked off from the pectoral region; the eyes and spiracles occur on the sides of the head. The teeth are flat and pavement-like. The tail is slender and much longer than the disc and has a small dorsal fin anteriorly.

Venomous spines may or may not be present.

Three species occur in the Caribbean; only the Spotted Eagle Ray is commonly observed over reef areas.

Spotted Eagle Ray

Aetobatis narinari (Euphrasen, 1790).
Figure 16

Width more than twice length of disc (excluding head and pelvic fins); tail about 3.5 times longer than body and bearing one to five serrate venomous spines at the base; head with a flattened rostral projection— a feature which has given rise to a second common name, "Duck-billed Ray;" color dark with white spots on young, rings and spots on adults. Large adults may reach 7.5 feet in width and an estimated weight of 500 pounds. Found inshore in all tropical and warm temperate seas. Feeds primarily on mollusks and can be destructive to species of commercial importance such as clams and the Queen Conch. More active

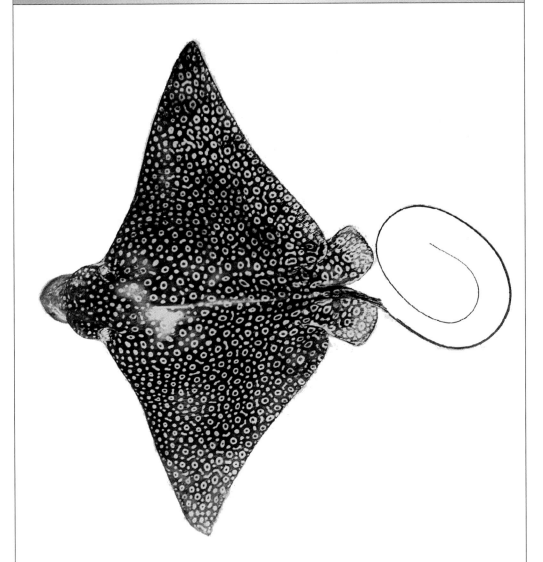

Figure 16. Spotted Eagle Ray (*Aetobatis narinari*), length without tail 3 feet, 76 pounds, St. John, Virgin Islands.

than dasyatid rays, it is usually encountered in motion; sometimes observed to leap into the air. Gives birth to an average of about four young at one time which vary from 7 to 14 inches in width.

ELECTRIC RAYS
(TORPEDINIDAE)

The electric rays, sometimes called "torpedo rays," are soft-bodied bot- tom-dwelling fishes which have a pair of large electric organs with which they can shock their prey and probably also deter preda- tors. These rays have a broad ta- pering tail ending in a distinct caudal fin and bearing two dorsal fins. Of the seven western Atlantic species, only *Narcine brasiliensis* is apt to be seen in shallow water in the Caribbean.

Figure 17. Lesser Electric Ray (*Narcine brasiliensis*), length with tail 11.75 inches, Trinidad.

Lesser Electric Ray

Narcine brasiliensis (Olfers, 1831).

Figure 17

Disc almost circular; snout about twice as long as width of interorbital space; mouth straight and narrow, the width about .85 of interorbital space; teeth in seven or eight functional rows; color may be uniform grayish brown, but usually there are dark blotches, and there may be dark irregular rings, especially in the young. Attains a total length of about 18 inches. The kidney shaped outline of the electric organ may be seen readily on each side of the disc on the ventral side. Although contact with this ray is said to produce a shock strong enough to knock a man down, most reports indicate much lesser effects. Ranges from North Carolina to northern Argentina, but appears to be absent in the West Indies north of Tobago. May occur in very shallow water on sandy bottom.

BONY FISHES (OSTEICHTHYES)

As the name implies, this class of fishes is characterized by a bony skeleton (except in degenerate forms), in contrast to the cartilage of sharks and rays. There is a single gill opening on each side. When scales are present, they are usually thin and overlapping. The soft (nonspinous) rays of the fins are segmented. Most species lay numerous small eggs; few are viviparous. The Osteichthyes is traditionally divided into two subclasses, the Choanichthyes (lobefin fishes such as lung fishes and *Latimeria*) and the Actinopterygii (ray-fin fishes). The latter is divisible into three superorders, the Chondrostei, the Holostei, and the Teleostei, in which the great majority of living fishes are classified.

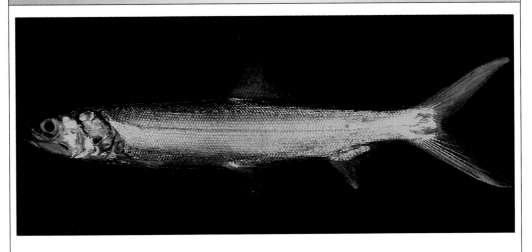

Figure 18. Ladyfish (*Elops saurus*), 13 inches, St. John, Virgin Islands.

LADYFISHES AND TARPONS
(ELOPIDAE)

These fishes are the most primitive of living teleosts. The pectoral fins are low on the body and the pelvic fins abdominal (*i.e.* relatively posterior) in position. There is an elongate bony plate between the branches of the lower jaw. The mouth is large, but the teeth small. The branchiostegal rays (supports for the gill membranes ventrally on the head) are numerous (23 to 35); the caudal fin is deeply forked. The late larval stage, called the "leptocephalus," is transparent and ribbon-like, similar to that of eels.

The elopids are carnivorous, feeding primarily on a variety of fishes and crustaceans. Neither of the Caribbean species is valued for food, but both are prized as game fishes.

Ladyfish

Elops surus Lin naeus, 1766.   Figure 18

Dorsal rays 21 to 26; last ray of dorsal fin not filamentous; pelvic fin rays 14 or 15; lateral-line scales 103 to 120; body elongate, the depth about 6 in standard length; mouth nearly at tip of snout; silvery. Attains a maximum length of about 3 feet. Although one of its common names is "Tenpounder," it is doubtful if it ever attains this weight. Ranges from Massachusetts to Rio de Janeiro. Common in the West Indies in its typical habitat of shallow brackish lagoons; rarely seen over reefs. Prone to leap when caught. A study of larvae has revealed two species of *Elops* in the western Atlantic (David G. Smith, pers. comm.). With a type locality of "Carolina," the name *saurus* may not apply to ladyfish in the Caribbean.

Tarpon

Megalops atlanticus Valenciennes, 1846.
Figure 19

Dorsal rays 13 to 16, the last prolonged as a filament; pelvic rays 10; scales large, those of the lateral line numbering 41 to 48; body notably compressed and not highly elongate, the depth about 4 in standard length; mouth opens dorsally; back dark, the sides silvery (individuals from rivers or turbid brackish areas

Figure 19. Tarpon (*Megalops atlanticus*), 14.4 inches, 3.5 pounds, St. John, Virgin Islands.

may be yellowish). Reaches at least 8 feet in length and a weight of 350 pounds. The world record for hook and line is 283 pounds, from Lake Maricaibo, Venezuela. Widely distributed on both sides of the tropical and subtropical Atlantic. Has been known to migrate as far north as Nova Scotia during warm months. Appears equally at home in salt or fresh water and is capable of existing in an oxygen-poor environment by virtue of its ability to take atmospheric air into a lung-like air bladder. Famous for its spectacular leaps when hooked. Juveniles have been found in shallow brackish pools isolated from the sea except during the highest tides or storms. They feed on copepods, aquatic insects, and small fishes. Adults prey mainly on crabs, shrimps, and a variety of fishes.

BONEFISHES
(ALBULIDAE)

The bonefishes are also primitive, having the pectoral fins low on the body and the pelvics abdominal in position, no spines in the fins, and a leptocephalus larva. They are known in the literature in the western Atlantic by two species, only one of which is discussed below. The other, *Albula nemoptera* (sometimes classified in the genus *Dixonina*), is rare; it is readily distinguished from *A. vulpes* by the prolonged last dorsal and anal rays. James B. Shaklee (pers. comm.) has discovered another species of *Albula* in the western Atlantic.

Bonefish

Albula vulpes (Linnaeus, 1758). Figure 20
Dorsal rays 18 to 20; pelvic rays 9; snout long; body only slightly

Figure 20. Bonefish (*Albula vulpes*), 19.5 inches, 2.6 pounds, St. Thomas, Virgin Islands.

compressed and moderately elongate, the depth about 4.5 in standard length; mouth small and ventral in position; teeth small; branchiostegal rays 13 or 14; silvery. Attains 20 pounds and a length of about 3 feet. Once believed to be a circumtropical species, the bonefish is now known to be confined to the Atlantic Ocean. Lives on sand or mud flats; it may occur in such shallow water that a fin may project above the surface. Characteristically it feeds by nosing into the sediment for various subsurface invertebrates such as small clams. Highly prized as a game fish. Although the Bonefish is tasty, it is not often eaten because of the numerous small bones in its flesh.

Figure 21. Dwarf Herring (*Jenkensia lamprotaenia*), Belize.

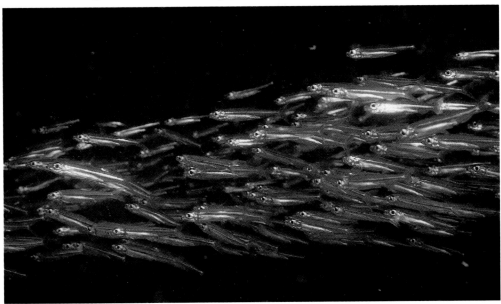

HERRINGS
(CLUPEIDAE)

The herrings are small schooling silvery fishes which feed primarily on plankton. They are moderately elongate and compressed. There is a single dorsal fin; the pectoral fins are low on the body and the pelvics generally lie beneath the dorsal fin; the species discussed below have 8 pelvic rays; the caudal fin is forked. There is no lateral line. Except for *Jenkinsia*, the mid-ventral scales on the chest and abdomen are compressed to form a sharp edge (these scales are called ventral scutes).

Although at least 15 species of clupeids occur in the Caribbean Sea, only those of the genera *Harengula, Opisthonema,* and *Jenkinsia* are apt to be encountered in clear shallow water. On rare occasions *Harengula* and *Opisthonema* have caused serious illness (clupeid poisoning) when eaten.

False Pilchard

Harengula clupeola (Cuvier, 1829).

Figure 22

Anal rays 17 to 20; ventral scutes 29 to 32; scales adherent; inner edge of palatine bones without pointed teeth at the front; a small round blackish spot slightly behind gill opening at level of eye. Attains 5.5 inches. Appears to have the

Figure 22. False Pilchard (*Harengula clupeola*), 4.5 inches, St. John, Virgin Islands.

Figure 23. Red-Ear Sardine (*Harengula humeralis*), 4.3 inches, Puerto Rico.

same distribution as *H. humeralis* and sometimes schools with it.

Red-Ear Sardine

Harengula humeralis (Cuvier, 1829).
Figure 23

Anal rays 16 to 19; ventral scutes 25 to 29; scales easily detached; inner edge of palatines (bones laterally in roof of mouth) with a row of pointed teeth at front; snout and end of lower jaw dusky orange-yellow; a prominent orange spot at upper end of gill opening; upper part of body with brassy stripes. Reaches a length of about 8.5 inches. Occurs in the Florida Keys, West Indies, and the coast of Yucatan to Venezuela.

Dwarf Herring

Jenkinsia lamprotaenia (Gosse, 1851).
Figures 21 & 24

Dorsal rays 10 to 13 (17 to 21 for other clupeids herein); anal rays 12 to 16; a broad silvery band on side of body separated from the green of the back by an iridescent blue-green line; some dusky pigment on tips of jaws, dorsally on snout and postorbital part of head, in a narrow double mid-dorsal band on body, and on edges of scales of back. Attains only 2.5 inches. Known from Florida, the Bahamas and throughout the Caribbean. Appears to be the most abundant small schooling fish in clear shallow water in the West Indies. Feeds on zooplankton, and in turn is fed upon by many carnivorous inshore fishes and roving predaceous fishes. A study now in progress will distinguish other western Atlantic species closely related to *lamprotaenia*.

Thread Herring

Opisthonema oglinum (LeSueur, 1817).
Figure 25

Anal rays 20 to 25; ventral scutes 32 to 36; last ray of dorsal fin greatly prolonged; tips of dorsal fin and caudal lobes dusky; usually a dark blotch behind upper end of gill opening. Reported to reach a length of 12 inches. Ranges from Massachusetts to southern Brazil.

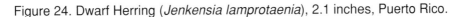

Figure 24. Dwarf Herring (*Jenkensia lamprotaenia*), 2.1 inches, Puerto Rico.

Figure 25. Thread Herring (*Opisthonema oglinum*), 5.2 inches, Puerto Rico.

ANCHOVIES
(ENGRAULIDAE)

Like the herrings, the anchovies are small zooplankton-feeding schooling fishes. They are silvery in color or have a lateral silvery stripe. They share the morphological features listed above for the clupeids. They are distinctive in their blunt projecting snout and very large shark-like mouth. Twenty-eight species are known from the Caribbean. Only the one most prone to occur inshore over reefs is discussed below.

Dusky Anchovy

Anchoa lyolepis (Evermann & Marsh, 1902).
Figure 26

Dorsal rays 12 to 15; anal rays 19 to 23; pelvic rays 7; origin of anal fin under or posterior to base of last dorsal ray; length of snout of adults about equal to eye diameter; lateral silvery band as wide as eye; tip of snout and dorso-posterior part of head dusky. Reaches nearly 3 inches. Gulf of Mexico and Caribbean Sea from the shore to depths as great as 180 feet.

Figure 26. Dusky Anchovy (*Anchoa lyolepis*), 2.5 inches, St. John, Virgin Islands.

St.Louis Community College

ITLE: Reef fish identification : Florid
ARCODE: 300080005537883
UE DATE: 04-07-08

ITLE: Caribbean reef fishes / John E. R
ARCODE: 300080002978608
UE DATE: 04-07-08

TLE: Sea turtles : a complete guide to
RCODE: 300080005643786
E DATE: 04-07-08

Figure 27. Sand Diver (*Synodus intermedius*), Bonaire.

LIZARDFISHES
(SYNODONTIDAE)

The lizardfishes have a reptile-like head, a large mouth with numerous slender sharp teeth in the jaws, a cylindrical body, a single relatively high dorsal fin of 10 to 13 rays, an adipose fin (small fleshy fin on back between dorsal and caudal fins), and large pelvic fins with 8 or 9 rays; there are no spines.

They are usually found on sand or mud bottoms; they can partially bury in the sediment with facility. They are voracious carnivores and generally feed by darting upward for their prey which usually consists of small fishes.

Five species of *Synodus*, four of *Saurida* and the monotypic *Trachinocephalus* are known from the Caribbean Sea. *Saurida*, which is distinctive in having two bands of teeth on each side of the roof of the mouth and numerous teeth showing laterally when the jaws are closed, is rarely found in shallow water. *Synodus poeyi* is also a deeper water species; *S. saurus* is rare in the Caribbean.

Galliwasp

Synodus foetens (Linnaeus, 1766).
Figure 28

Lateral-line scales 56 to 65; 4.5 or 5.5 scales between lateral line and dorsal fin; anal fin base longer than or equal to dorsal base (shorter on other species of *Synodus*); anterior dorsal rays extending slightly beyond tips of all but the most posterior rays when fin depressed. Attains 18 inches. Known from Massachusetts to Brazil. Occurs on mud or sand bottoms from the shore to 600 feet.

Figure 28. Galliwasp (*Synodus foetens*), 12.3 inches, St. John, Virgin Islands.

Sand Diver

Synodus intermedius (Spix, 1829).

Figures 27 & 29

Lateral-line scales 45 to 52; 3.5 scales between lateral line and dorsal fin; anterior dorsal rays not extending beyond tips of more posterior rays when fin depressed; a blackish blotch on shoulder girdle which is largely hidden by gill cover (absent on other *Synodus*). Reaches 18 inches. Ranges from North Carolina to Brazil; the most common lizardfish in the West Indies. Al-though usually seen on sand, it will come to rest on the hard bottom of reefs. Not infrequently taken by trolling a lure at the surface over shallows.

Rockspear

Synodus synodus (Linnaeus, 1758).

Figure 30

Anal rays 8 to 10 (10 to 13 on other species); lateral-line scales 54 to 59; 4.5 scales between lateral line and dorsal fin; anterior dorsal rays not extending beyond tips of more

Figure 29. Sand Diver (*Synodus intermedius*), 14.8 inches, Puerto Rico.

Figure 30. Rockspear (*Synodus synodus*), 4.8 inches, Curaçao.

posterior rays when fin depressed; posterior edge of scale-like supraorbital bone smooth (serrate on preceding two species); a small black spot usually present just behind tip of snout. Largest specimen, 13 inches, from St. Helena. Occurs on both sides of the Atlantic; on the western side known from the Gulf of Mexico and West Indies to Uruguay.

Snakefish

Trachinocephalus myops (Forster, 1801).
Figure 31
Anal rays 14 to 16; lateral-line scales 54 to 58; anal fin base about 1.3 to 1.5 times longer than dorsal base; interorbital region deeply concave; snout very short, its length always less than eye diameter; an oblique black spot at upper end of gill opening; alternate stripes of pale blue (with dark edges) and yellow on body in life. Attains 15 inches. Occurs in the Indo-Pacific region as well as both sides of the Atlantic. Recorded from bottoms of sand, shell, rock and mud from the shore to nearly 1300 feet.

Figure 31. Snakefish (*Trachinocephalus myops*), 6.4 inches, Puerto Rico.

CONGER EELS
(CONGRIDAE)

The Congridae is one of about 20 families of true eels of the Order Anguilliformes (older name, Apodes). Collectively these families share the following characteristics: an elongate body, no pelvic fins, no distinct caudal fin (median fins usually continuous around tip of tail), no spines in fins, scales reduced or absent, gill opening small, numerous vertebrae and a leptocephalus larval stage. The congers have strong jaws; they may have stout teeth but they usually do not have long canines like most morays; the lateral line is present; the anterior nostrils terminate in a short tube, and the posterior nostrils are free from the confines of the mouth.

The family is divisible into two subfamilies, the Heterocongrinae (garden eels) which are extremely elongate burrowing forms with pectoral fins reduced or absent and an oblique mouth with projecting lower jaw, and the Congrinae with well-developed pectoral fins and a near-horizontal mouth.

Figure 32. Manytooth Conger (*Conger triporiceps*), 12.3 inches, Puerto Rico.

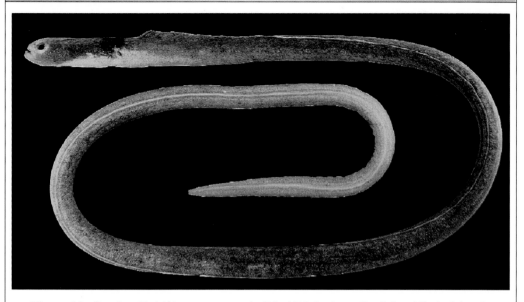

Figure 33. Garden Eel (*Heteroconger halis*), 15.8 inches, St. John, Virgin Islands.

CONGER EELS
(CONGRINAE)

Manytooth Conger

Conger triporiceps Kanazawa, 1958.
Figure 32

Pectoral rays 14 to 17; depth of body 18 to 22 in length; gray, the margins of the fins distinctly black. Florida and the West Indies to Brazil. Taken by the author in West Indian reef areas from 10 to 180 feet. *C. esculentus* differs in having a stouter body (depth about 14 in length) and 18 or 19 pectoral rays.

GARDEN EELS
(HETEROCONGRINAE)

Garden Eel

Heteroconger halis (Böhlke, 1957).
Figures 33 & 34

Pectoral fins small (longest ray one-third or less of eye diameter),

Figure 34. Garden Eels (*Heteroconger halis*), Bahamas.

immediately behind gill opening; depth of body 50 to 70 in length; eye large, about 4 to 6 in head; snout short, its length 7 to 8 in head; mouth oblique; dark brown, with about the posterior fourth of the body distinctly paler. Largest specimen collected, 19 inches. Florida and the West Indies. Lives in groups in sand, each eel in its own permanent burrow. Approximately the anterior three-fourths of the body emerges for capturing zooplankton from the passing water mass; the feeding action results in the body undergoing odd but graceful movements. With the approach of danger, the eels withdraw deep into their burrows.

SNAKE EELS
(OPHICHTHIDAE)

The snake eels are named for their long near-cylindrical muscular bodies and burrowing habits. Erroneous reports of sea snakes from the West Indies are probably the result of sightings of snake eels. Many ophichthiids have no pectoral fins, and a few completely lack median fins. The tip of the tail of most genera is sharp and without a caudal fin (true of the four species discussed below). The posterior nostrils are inside the mouth or on or just above the upper lip; the branchiostegal rays overlap midventrally (a characteristic unique to this family).

Snake eels do not live in permanent burrows like the garden eels but move readily in the bottom sediment, apparently either forward or backward. Most appear to remain completely buried, at least by day, but a few species may occasionally

Figure 35. Spotted Snake Eel (*Ophichthus ophis*), Bonaire.

Figure 36. Sharptail Eel (*Myrichthys breviceps*), 12.9 inches, Puerto Rico.

be seen with head emerged from the sand or moving freely over reefs or adjacent habitats by day.

Sharptail Eel

Myrichthys breviceps (Richardson, 1848).
Figures 36 & 37

Differs from the following species primarily in color; dark olive to purplish brown, shading to whitish ventrally, with three rows of diffuse pale spots containing yellow centers; small yellow spots on head. Reaches at least 3 feet. Bermuda, Florida Keys and the Caribbean Sea. Usually seen in sand or seagrass beds, but may be observed in reef areas. *Myrichthys acuminatus* (Gronow) is a synonym.

Figure 37. Sharptail Eel (*Myrichthys breviceps*), Bonaire.

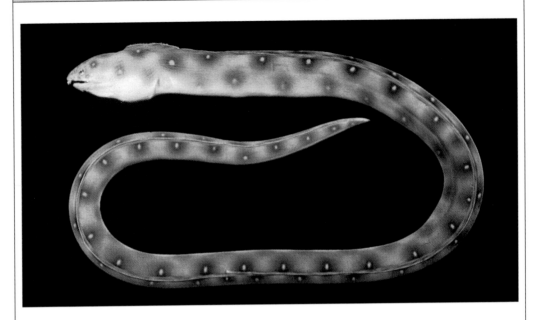

Figure 38. Goldspotted Snake Eel (*Myrichthys ocellatus*), 25.3 inches, St. John, Virgin Islands.

Goldspotted Snake Eel

Myrichthys ocellatus (LeSueur, 1825).
Figure 38

Depth of body 28 to 33 in length; origin of dorsal fin just behind occipital part of head; pectoral fins small, their length about 14 in head (from snout to gill opening); yellowish or greenish tan, shading to yellowish white ventrally, with two rows of round blackish spots, none sharply defined, and most with small bright yellow centers. Reaches a length of about 3 feet. Bermuda, West Indies, Brazil and islands of the tropical eastern Atlantic. Feeds primarily on crabs. *Myrichthys oculatus* (Kaup) is a synonym.

Shrimp Eel

Ophichthus gomesii (Castelnau, 1855).
Figure 39

Depth of body about 20 to 30 in length; origin of dorsal fin above or in advance of tips of pectoral fins; two rows of teeth on vomer which converge posteriorly; light brown shading on lower side to white; median fins edged with blackish; pectoral fins dusky; pores on head rimmed with blackish. Probably attains 2.5 feet. Known from southern Brazil, Gulf of Mexico, Florida Keys, Cuba, Puerto Rico and South Carolina.

Spotted Snake Eel

Ophichthus ophis (Linnaeus, 1758).
Figures 35 & 40

Depth of body 24 to 28 in length; origin of dorsal fin over posterior tips of pectoral fins; one row of teeth on vomer (median bone at front of roof of mouth); tan, shading ventrally to white, with two rows of dark brown spots on upper half of body and a row of smaller spots on lower side; head with small dark spots and a transverse dark band on top

Figure 39. Shrimp Eel (*Ophichthus gomesii*), 23 inches, Puerto Rico.

behind eyes. Reaches 4.5 feet. Re-corded from Cuba, Florida, Bermuda, Curaçao and Brazil. Specimens collected by the author from Curaçao and Puerto Rico were first noted with their heads protruding diagonally from the sand; they had eaten octopuses and fish. Fishermen fear this eel as much as the larger morays.

Figure 40. Spotted Snake Eel (*Ophichthus ophis*), 45.8 inches, 3.25 pounds, Klein Curaçao.

MORAYS
(MURAENIDAE)

The morays are a well-known group of eels with stout muscular somewhat compressed bodies, no pectoral fins, and awesome dentition. Most have long canine teeth, some of which are inwardly depressible; the occipital region of the head is elevated due to development of strong muscles which close the lower jaw; the anterior nostrils are tubular at the front of the snout and the posterior nostrils lie above or in front of the eyes; the dorsal and anal fins (when not vestigial as in *Uropterygius)* are confluent with a short caudal fin around tip of tail; the anus is usually near the middle of the body.

Typically the morays are reef-dwellers and are observed more often by divers than any other eels. There are generally many more on a reef, however, than may be seen at any one time by day, for they hide in holes and crevices. They are regarded as nocturnal; however, few species actively forage at night. Morays with long fang-like teeth feed mainly on fishes. They are prone to bite if provoked but are not apt to leave their hiding places to attack swimmers. The flesh of large morays may be poisonous to eat.

Chain Moray

Echidna catenata (Bloch, 1795). Figure 42

Depth of body 13 to 17 in length; teeth short and blunt; dark brown

Figure 41. Spotted Moray (*Gymnothorax moringa*), Long Island, Bahamas.

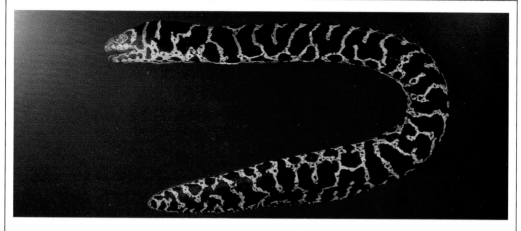

Figure 42. Chain Moray (*Echidna catenata*), 17.5 inches, Trinidad.

with narrow irregular bright yellow bands containing small dark brown spots, these bands primarily vertical and often interconnected, thus dividing the dark ground color into large roundish or subquadrate blotches. Largest specimen, 2 feet 4 inches. Tropical Atlantic. Common in the West Indies where it is often found beneath rocks in surprisingly shallow water. Feeds mainly on crabs.

Viper Moray

Enchelycore nigricans (Bonnaterre, 1788).
Figure 43

Body relatively slender, the depth 17 to 29 in length; head 7 to 9 in length; snout 5.2 to 6 in head; eye 1.5 to 2.1 in snout; posterior nostril slit-like, except in young; jaws curved, only the tips making contact when closed; teeth biserial in upper jaw, uniserial at sides of lower jaw; brown, faintly mottled with darker brown. Attains at least 2.5 feet. Tropical Atlantic.

Figure 43. Viper Moray (*Enchelycore nigricans*), 29.5 inches, St. John, Virgin Islands.

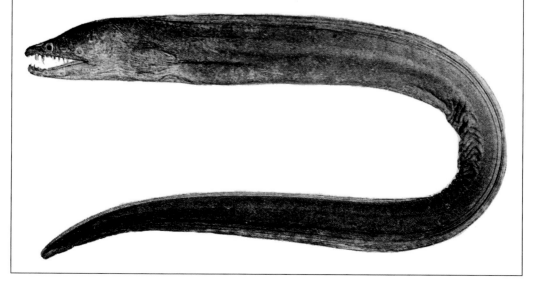

Figure 44. Green Moray (*Gymnothorax funebris*), 33 inches, 3.3 pounds, Puerto Rico.

Green Moray

Gymnothorax funebris Ranzani, 1840.

Figures 44 & 45

Similar in morphology to the spotted moray. Differs in often having two instead of one row of teeth on the vomer, in larger maximum size, and in the nearly uniform green color. Juveniles may be olivaceous or dark brownish gray. The green color of this moray is due to a blending of dark gray-blue skin color and overlying yellow mucus. Reliable records to 6 feet 2.5 inches in length

Figure 45. Green Moray (*Gymnothorax funebris*) and Neon Goby (*Gobiosoma oceanops*), Belize.

Figure 46. Goldentail Moray (*Gymnothorax miliaris*), 9.3 inches, Puerto Rico.

and a weight of 27 pounds. There are unauthenticated reports of larger individuals. Known from the tropical western Atlantic. The closely related *Gymnothorax castaneus* occurs in the tropical eastern Pacific Ocean. Also recorded from the Cape Verde Islands.

Goldentail Moray

Gymnothorax miliaris (Kaup, 1856).

Figures 46 & 47

Depth of body 12 to 15 in length; head 7 to 8.5 in length; snout about 5.7 in head; eye 1.7 to 2 in snout; teeth biserial on most of upper jaw and front half of lower jaw, the inner

Figure 47. Goldentail Moray (*Gymnothorax miliaris*), Belize.

teeth largest (but still relatively small for a moray); dark brown with numerous yellow dots, smallest on head and largest toward end of tail where they are irregular and variously confluent (on most individuals the tip of the tail is entirely yellow). Attains a maximum length of about 20 inches. Caribbean Sea to Bermuda. A yellow moray with irregular black markings was described as *G. flavopicta*; it is now known to be one of the color forms of *G. miliaris*.

Spotted Moray

Gymnothorax moringa (Cuvier, 1829).
Figures 41 & 48
Depth of body 12 to 21 in length (smaller individuals more slender); head (measured to gill opening) 5.9 to 7.3 in length; snout 4.5 to 5.8 in head; eye 1.5 to 2.2 in snout; about 24 upper and 22 lower teeth in one row on each half of jaws except for mid-side of upper jaw where one or two depressible canines may be found in an inner second row; large needle-like canine teeth at front of jaws alternating with one or two smaller canines; a single median row of short canine teeth on vomer; pale yellow dorsally, whitish ventrally, with numerous dark brown spots of variable size, most of which on the body are confluent; edge of median fins pale (may be largely obscured by dark spots except posteriorly). Attains about 4 feet. Brazil to Florida, including the Gulf of Mexico; also known from Bermuda and St. Helena. The most common moray in shallow water in the West Indies.

Figure 48. Spotted Moray (*Gymnothorax moringa*), 20.6 inches, St. John, Virgin Islands.

Purplemouth Moray

Gymnothorax vicinus (Castelnau, 1855).

Figure 49

Also similar in dentition and body form to the spotted moray. Color variable but usually yellowish, densely mottled with brown spots of different intensity, most of these conjoined, thus restricting the yellow to an incomplete and often faint reticulum (some individuals are nearly uniform brown); anal fin and posterior part of dorsal fin with a white edge and a broad submarginal blackish zone; snout and lower jaw light lavender brown; roof of mouth pale lavender; floor of mouth dark purplish; corner of mouth with a small dark brown patch; iris yellow. Attains about 4 feet. A shallow-water species known through the tropical Atlantic.

FROGFISHES
(ANTENNARIIDAE)

The pediculate fish family Antennariidae, popularly known as frogfishes, is an odd group of sedentary fishes, most of which inhabit shallow tropic seas. They are among the most amorphous of fishes. The body is compressed, in contrast to the related goosefishes which are depressed. The first dorsal spine is located anteriorly on the snout; typically it is modified into a bait or lure (slender stalk and lure collectively termed the illicium); the second and third dorsal spines are separate and covered by skin (rarely embedded); a fourth free dorsal spine is completely embedded. The pectoral fins are limb-like with an "elbow" joint proximal to the rays; the pelvic fins, of 5 rays, are jugular. The gill open-

Figure 49. Purplemouth Moray (*Gymnothorax vicinus*), 21.3 inches, St. John, Virgin Islands.

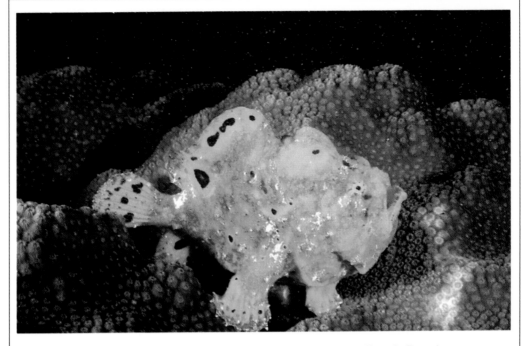

Figure 50. Longlure Frogfish (*Antennarius multiocellatus*), Bonaire.

ing is restricted to a small round opening which is usually on the posterior basal part of the pectoral appendage or just behind it. The mouth is large, highly oblique to vertical, the lower jaw projecting; the upper jaw is protractile. There are small conical teeth in bands on the jaws, vomer, palatines and tongue. The skin is thick and loosely attached to the body; although it may be smooth, it is usually prickly or warty; there are often membranous filaments or flaps, their development varying among individuals. The lateral line has a curious ridged structure. The soft dorsal and anal fins are not preceded by spines; the anal fin is notably shorter than the soft dorsal; the caudal fin is rounded, with 9 rays.

The frogfishes are sluggish and may remain in the same position on the bottom for long periods. They are often colored like their surroundings and consequently exhibit great individual variation in coloration. Some have patches of pale pink that look exactly like coralline red algae. The two sexes are said to be of different color in some species.

Most species feed on fishes, characteristically by attracting them with the illicium, the end of which may resemble a normal item of food such as a worm or worm tentacles; it can be enticingly wriggled just above the frogfish's cavernous mouth. When the prey (which can be of greater length than the frogfish) approaches the bait, it may be suddenly engulfed. Frogfishes do not have to angle to feed (the illicium of some species is rudimentary); they may merely lie in wait for prey to come near; they have also been observed in aquaria to actively stalk fishes and crustaceans. They are voracious and are therefore not good aquarium fishes if one values the other resident fishes of the tank.

Some species have been observed to distend themselves with water (or air if held out of water) when roughly handled.

Forty-one species are known in the family, classified in 12 genera (Pietsch and Grobecker, 1987). Seven are recorded from the western Atlantic; six occur in the Caribbean. The best known is the Sargassumfish *(Histrio histrio)*, a pelagic species of all warm oceans that lives in floating *Sargassum* weed which it resembles. None of the benthic species are very common; the two most often collected are discussed below. The largest of the remaining species (to 17 inches) is *Antennarius ocellatus* which is characterized by branched fin rays (except upper and lower caudal rays), 13 dorsal soft rays, 8 anal rays, usually 12 pectoral rays, an illicium which is slightly shorter than the second dorsal spine, a large ocellated black spot basally on soft dorsal fin, one on about mid-side of body and usually one on the caudal fin. Two other Caribbean species also have the illicium shorter than the second dorsal spine; both are small species, rarely exceeding 3 inches. One is *A. bermudensis* which is distinctive in having the dorsal and anal fins end over the base of the caudal fin (hence there is no caudal peduncle), 11 or 12 dorsal soft rays, 7 anal rays, 9 or 10 pectoral rays and a large ocellated black spot at the base of the soft dorsal fin, as much on the body as on the fin. The other is *A. pauciradiatus* which is a pale species with a distinct caudal peduncle, 12 dorsal soft rays, 7 anal rays, and usually 9 pectoral rays.

Until recently another *Antennarius, A. tenebrosus,* was recognized from the Caribbean. It was based on a single 4-inch specimen from Cuba, no longer extant, which was described in 1853. It resembled *A. multiocellatus* but was distinguished from it mainly by the simple form of the illicium. Recent studies have shown that the illicium may be aberrant or damaged (perhaps fishes attracted to the "bait" sometimes succeed in severing it), so a classification based on this feature alone might be in error if the illicium is atypical. *A. tenebrosus* is now regarded as a synonym of *A. multiocellatus.*

Longlure Frogfish

Antennarius multiocellatus (Valenciennes, 1837). Figures 50-52

Dorsal rays I-I-I-11 or 12 (usually 12, none or the last one or two branched); anal rays 6 or 7 (usually 7, all branched); pectoral rays 10, all unbranched; pelvic rays 5, only the last branched; illicium slender and long, the second dorsal spine contained about 1.7 to 2.2 in its length, the tip membranous and lobate, sometimes with filaments; length of caudal peduncle (measured from rear base of dorsal fin) contained about 1.7 in least depth of peduncle; the common color phase light (of various hues, often drab yellowish, but may be bright yellow or rust red) with ocellated black spots in the following characteristic locations: basally on soft dorsal fin between eighth and tenth rays; mid-basally on anal fin; three (sometimes four) of smaller size forming a triangle in middle of caudal fin; a

Figure 51. Longlure Frogfish (*Antennarius multiocellatus*), 7.3 inches, St. John, Virgin Islands.

small one beneath pectoral fin and another on side above fin; a small one at base of posterior flap of skin of third dorsal spine; there may be other scattered small blackish spots, especially in median fins; bony part of illicium often with dark cross bands; a second phase is black with the tips of the rays of the paired fins pale and a whitish blotch dorsally

Figure 52. Longlure Frogfish (*Antennarius multiocellatus*), 4.7 inches, Maiquetia, Venezuela.

on the caudal peduncle (this may be visible on light-phase individuals but is less obvious on them because it is not as contrasting). Probably does not exceed 6 inches. Black-phase individuals as small as 1.2 inches have been collected by the author. Tropical western Atlantic. The most common member of the genus on West Indian reefs. May occur in such shallow water that it is driven ashore during storms. Feeds mainly on fishes, but also ingests crustaceans.

Splitlure Frogfish

Antennarius striatus (Shaw & Nodder, 1794). Figures 53 & 54

Dorsal rays I-I-I-12 (last two or three rays branched); anal rays 7 (all branched); pectoral rays 11 (rarely 10, none branched); pelvic rays 5 (only the last branched); stalk of illicium slightly longer than second dorsal spine, the bait bifid, large and worm-like; length of caudal peduncle (measured from rear base of dorsal fin) about 1.4 in least depth of peduncle; median fins relatively large; two primary color phases, the most common light to medium gray, brown or reddish with irregular black spots and short black bands on body and head (some radiating from eye) and large black spots on fins; second color phase (originally named *A. nuttingi*) black except for bait which is whitish. Attains about 7 inches. Circumtropical; in the western Atlantic from New Jersey to Rio de Janeiro. Occurs in different habitats including mud bottoms. The stomachs of five specimens that contained food consisted only of fish remains.

Figure 53. Splitlure Frogfish (*Antennarius striatus*), 2.6 inches, Puerto Rico.

Figure 54. Splitlure Frogfish (*Antennarius striatus*), 5.9 inches, Puerto Rico.

BATFISHES
(OGCOCEPHALIDAE)

The batfishes, along with the frogfishes and 13 related families of deepsea fishes, are grouped together in the order Lophiiformes (Pediculati). All are exceedingly bizarre, and some are grotesque.

The batfishes are characterized as follows: head very broad and depressed, the snout often elevated and protruding; body slender, varying from slightly depressed to slightly compressed; no spines in fins; spinous dorsal reduced to a short illicium (rarely obsolete) with a bulbous or lobate bait; illicium retractile into a triangular rostral cavity; soft dorsal and anal fins small; paired fins well developed, the pelvics jugular, of 5 rays, and broadly separated; pectorals often with a prominent peduncular portion containing an "elbow" joint; mouth not large, the upper jaw anterior to lower and protractile downwards; teeth villiform; gill opening very small, slightly behind and above base of pectoral fin; head and body covered with bony tubercles and spinules; lateral line present but difficult to trace; no swimbladder.

The ogcocephalids include shallow-water and deep-sea representatives. Fourteen species are known from the western Atlantic, ten in the genus *Ogcocephalus* and one each in three other genera.

Three species of *Ogcocephalus* occur in the Caribbean Sea and two others incorporate the Bahamas within their range. The author has encountered only *O. nasutus* and *Halieutichthys aculeatus* in relatively shallow water of the Caribbean. The head region of the latter species is flat and nearly circular, its pectoral fin peduncles are attached to the body by a membrane, and the ventral parts of the head and body are without scales or tubercles; it was taken only on mud bottoms.

Figure 55. Redbellied Batfish (*Ogcocephalus nasutus*), St. Croix, Virgin Islands.

Redbellied Batfish

Ogcocephalus nasutus (Valenciennes, 1837).   Figures 55 & 56

Dorsal rays 4; anal rays 4; pectoral rays 13; caudal rays 9; depth at anus about 6.5 to 7 in standard length; head and body with conical tubercles (sometimes termed bucklers), better developed dorsally (those ventrally are small and numerous and not aligned in two main rows, as in the genera *Zalieutes* and

Figure 56. Redbellied Batfish (*Ogcocephalus nasutus*), dorsal view, 10.2 inches, St. John, Virgin Islands.

Malthopsis); rostrum prominent, variable in length, with a large median tubercle; recess for illicium at anterior base of rostrum; pectoral fin peduncles well separated from body, with a distinct "elbow"; distal ends of pectoral fin rays with fleshy pads on the ventral side; mouth small; villiform teeth in broad bands in jaws and on vomer and palatines; brown dorsally, light red or reddish ventrally; dark spots, when present, restricted to shoulder region and axillae (none on sides of head, pectoral peduncles, or posteriorly on sides of body; markings, when present posteriorly, form a reticulum). Attains about 11 inches. Southeast Florida and Bahamas, south through the Caribbean Sea to the Amazon. A sluggish fish which may be caught by hand. Occurs on flat bottoms of sand, coral rubble, seagrass or mud; not common. Stomach contents have consisted primarily of mollusks, crabs, fishes, polychaete worms and algae.

CLINGFISHES
(GOBIESOCIDAE)

The clingfishes are a highly specialized family of small fishes which are usually classified in an order by themselves, the Gobiesociformes (or Xenopterygii). They are characterized chiefly by a large complex ventral sucking disc below the junction of the head and body, the anterolateral edge of which is formed on each side by the four pelvic rays (the last ray with a membranous attachment to the lower pectoral base); the bones of the pelvic and pectoral girdles have been modified for support of the disc; regions of the disc have flattened dermal papillae, the patterns of which are useful in classification of some species.

The family is distinguished further as follows: head depressed; general configuration varying from elongate to tadpole-shaped; no scales; head and body with a heavy coat of mucus; lateral-line system present, the pores well developed on head but difficult to see on body; mouth terminal or ventral, the lips usually large, the upper jaw slightly protractile; dentition variable; anterior nostrils tubular; posterior nostrils usually tubular; median fins without spines; all fin rays unbranched; a single posterior dorsal fin; caudal fin usually rounded; no swimbladder.

Most of these curious fishes live on rocky bottom in shallow water, frequently in the intertidal zone. They adhere strongly to the substratum with their thoracic sucking disc (which can be as long as one-third the total length of the fish) and are thus able to live in regions of strong wave action and current. A few such as *Gobiesox nudus* of the Caribbean Sea ascend streams and rivers. Some live in close association with other animals, a West Indian example being the common *Acyrtus rubiginosus* which may be found inshore beneath the sea urchin *Echinometra*. The slender *Acyrtops beryllinus*, also of the tropical western Atlantic, occurs in turtle grass beds; it is usually green with small pale spots.

Little is known of the biology of most clingfishes. Some, at least, are carnivorous.

The family consists of about 100 species, of which ten are recorded from the Caribbean Sea, four in the large genus *Gobiesox*. Two common species, one in the genus *Arcos*, and one in *Tomicodon*, are discussed below.

Tadpole Clingfish

Arcos macrophthalmus (Günther, 1861).
Figure 57

Dorsal rays 7 or 8; anal rays 6 or 7 (first ray in dorsal and anal fins usually not externally visible but here included in counts); pectoral rays 23 to 25; caudal rays 10; head and anterior part of body very broad and highly depressed, the length of the head about 2.2 in standard length, and the width about 2.3 in standard length; body compressed posteriorly; disc 2.5 to 2.7 in standard length; anus much closer to disc than anal fin; subopercular spine well developed; conical teeth in upper jaw in one row at sides and several rows at front, the outer row at front enlarged; four to six protruding incisiform teeth at front of lower jaw, the median pair notably large; small conical teeth behind incisors leading laterally to larger teeth, one of which is nearly a canine; lower lip divided into fleshy lobes; a broad membranous flap at lower pectoral base; posterior edge of anterior nostrils with a broad branched dermal flap. The 3.5-inch illustrated specimen (the largest collected) was colored in life as follows: head brownish red; body purplish anteriorly, shading to yellowish brown posteriorly; head and body spotted and barred with brown. West Indies. Found in very shallow water along rocky shores which may be exposed to surf. The depressed body permits entry into narrow cracks or crevices. The stomach contents of ten adult specimens from the Virgin Islands and Tobago consisted of limpets (the most common food item, the shells largely intact), crabs and crab megalops, chitons, isopods, amphipods, fishes, polychaete worms, and in one, the proboscis of a peanut worm. The protruding incisiform teeth of the lower jaw are probably useful in detaching limpets and chitons from rocks.

Figure 57. Tadpole Clingfish (*Arcos macrophthalmus*), dorsal view, 3.4 inches, St. John, Virgin Islands.

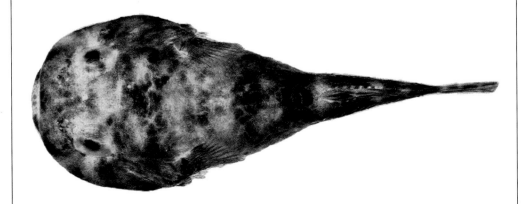

Figure 58. Hourglass Clingfish (*Tomicodon fasciatus*), dorsal view, 1.2 inches, St. Thomas, Virgin Islands.

Hourglass Clingfish

Tomicodon fasciatus (Peters, 1860).

Figure 58

Dorsal rays 7 to 9; anal rays 6 to 9 (first two dorsal and anal rays, though not externally visible in adults, are included in counts); pectoral rays 20 to 22; caudal rays 8; head not very wide but depressed, the length 2.8 to 3.6 in standard length, and the width 3.8 to 5.5 in standard length; body depressed anteriorly, the depth 6.6 to 8.4 in standard length, and compressed posteriorly, the width at end of dorsal fin about half the depth; disc 4 to 5 in standard length; anus usually a little closer to anal fin origin than posterior edge of disc; subopercular spine poorly developed; eight to ten trifid incisiform teeth in upper jaw, six to eight in lower, and one or two canines at each end of both jaws, all in one row; dermal flap on margin of anterior nostrils minute or absent; color variable but usually with broad transverse dark bars on back that tend to be hourglass-shaped, and narrow dark bars on the sides. A collection of four specimens from Puerto Rico aptly demonstrated the variability in color: one was black, white and olive; one olive and white; one red and olive; and the last pink and black. Largest specimen, 1.6 inches. Caribbean Sea. Lives on rock substratum close to shore. A southern subspecies has been named from Brazil.

PEARLFISHES
(CARAPIDAE)

The pearlfishes (Fierasferidae of the older literature) are very elongate fishes allied to the cusk eels (Ophidiidae). They have a short head with a bluntly rounded snout, usually a large oblique mouth, the upper jaw preceding the lower. Teeth are present in the jaws and on the vomer and palatines; those on the upper jaw are the smallest and those on the vomer usually the largest. There are no scales. There is a very long tapering tail, the median fins confluent at the slender tip, and no caudal fin. There are no pelvic fins or pelvic girdles; pectoral fins are present or absent. The anus of adults is located in the throat region. The late larval stage, which is exceedingly elongate, is called the "tenuis"; it may be attracted to a light at night. Many species live commen-

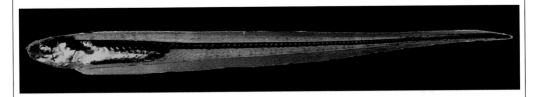

Figure 59. Pearlfish (*Carapus bermudensis*), 4.1 inches, Puerto Rico.

sally in various bottom-dwelling invertebrates, particularly sea cucumbers. Other host animals include clams, starfishes, sea urchins and tunicates. Some species are known to feed on the reproductive organs and respiratory tree of the sea cucumbers in which they live. Others leave their hosts and forage for food outside, apparently primarily, if not entirely, at night. One Indo-Pacific carapid is reported to eat the tenuis larvae or small adults of its own species on occasions (apparently when competition for host sea cucumbers is great). Carapids enter sea cucumbers through the anal opening. The head of the fish first approaches the opening, the body is then bent into a loop, and the fish slips in rapidly tail first. The name pearlfish is derived from species found inside living pearl oysters. The body is often transparent, giving rise to another common name, "glass eel."

Pearlfish

Carapus bermudensis (Jones, 1874).
Figure 59

Head 7 to 8 in total length; body elongate, the depth of adults about 10 to 17 in total length; pectoral fins pointed, about 1.7 in head; anus anterior to base of pectoral fins; two to four large conical teeth on vomer; transparent with indistinct orange blotches; a row of interconnected copper blotches anteriorly on body; head coppery with iridescence; peritoneum shows through as silvery with pale-centered dark pigment cells; vertebral column visible, also with dark pigment cells. Reaches 6 inches. Bermuda, Florida to Brazil, and the West Indies. Has been taken from nine different sea cucumbers, including *Actinopyga agassizii* and *Holothuria mexicana*. One may have to open many sea cucumbers to find a single fish. *Carapus bermudensis* is the only shallow-water species of the family in the western Atlantic; it is a close relative of *C. acus* of the eastern Atlantic.

TOADFISHES
(BATRACHOIDIDAE)

The toadfishes are bottom-dwelling inshore fishes, mostly of warm seas, which are classified in an order by themselves, the Batrachoidiformes (or Haplodoci). They are not among the most attractive of fishes, most are drab-colored. They have robust bodies, depressed anteriorly and compressed posteriorly. The head is large and depressed, the eyes toward the top and directed more upward than to the side. The mouth is large, oblique, the lower jaw preceding the upper; the jaws are strong and the teeth stout. The gill opening is restricted to the side of the body just in front of the pectoral base. There are small cycloid scales or none at all. The fins, in general, are fleshy; there are two dorsal fins, the first of two or three short stout spines; the pelvic fins of I,2 or I,3 rays are jugular in position (in front of gill openings); the caudal fin is broadly rounded.

The family of ten genera and 33 species is divided into three subfamilies: the Batrachoidinae which is characterized chiefly by having subopercular spines and three solid dorsal spines; the Porichthyinae with two solid dorsal spines and no subopercular spines; and the Thalassophyrninae which is distinctive in the possession of two hollow dorsal spines and a hollow opercular spine which are associated with poison glands.

Some of the Batrachoidinae have scales. One of the most common Caribbean representatives is the "sapo" *(Batrachoides surinamensis)*, a fish of shallow mud or sand bottoms which can attain 18 inches in length; it has 28 to 29 dorsal soft rays and 24 to 26 anal soft rays. The related *B. manglae*, recently described from Venezuela, has 22 or 23 dorsal soft rays and 20 anal soft rays. Among the scaleless genera of the subfamily are *Amphichthys* (the common species is discussed below), *Opsanus* (the only West Indian member of the genus, O. *phobetron*, was recently described from Bimini and is considered a glacial relict), and *Sanopus*, which includes *S. barbatus* from Panama and *S. astrifer* from Belize, the

latter described in 1965.

The Porichthyinae is further distinguished by having canine teeth and several (often four) lateral lines. The best known species is *Porichthys porosissimus* (sometimes classified in *Nautopaedium*) which occurs inshore in continental waters on sand or mud bottoms from Virginia to Argentina.

The Thalassophyrninae, known as the venomous toadfishes, is represented by two genera, the Pacific *Daector* and *Thalassophryne* with six species, of which two are known in the Caribbean and one is confined to the Amazon. With their hollow spines, these fishes have the most highly developed venom apparatus in the fish world. Other venomous fishes have only grooved spines at best.

The toadfishes are carnivorous, feeding mainly on crustaceans and mollusks; some species are known for their voracity. They may bite when handled.

Sapo Bocon

Amphichthys cryptocentrus (Valenciennes, 1837).   Figure 60

Dorsal rays III-28 or 29; anal rays 23 to 25; pectoral rays 22 or 23; two lateral lines, the upper with about 36 pores; depth of body 4 to 5.3 in standard length; head broad and depressed, the width about equal to or slightly less than the length, and the depth about 1.6 to 1.8 in the length; opercle with two diverging spines; subopercle with one spine; no venomous spines; mouth large, the maxilla reaching to or beyond posterior edge of eye; small conical teeth in approximately two irregular rows at front of upper jaw; lower

Figure 60. Sapo Bocon (*Amphichthys cryptocentrus*), 9.5 inches, Trinidad.

jaw, vomer and palatines with a row of short stout nodular teeth which are nearly incisiform, the lower jaw with a short outer row of stout conical teeth at the front; eyes on top of head, about an eye diameter apart; no scales; head, especially anteriorly, with scattered fleshy protuberances, some with branches; axil of pectoral fins with an elongate patch of glandular lamellae (of unknown function); dark brown or yellowish brown above, whitish ventrally; pores of lateral lines distinct as pale dots; young with faint dark bars. Largest specimen collected by author, 15 inches, from Isla Cubagua, Venezuela. Panama to Brazil; not found in the West Indies except those islands on or near the continental shelf. Common on rocky bottom in shallow water. In spite of its ugly appearance it is readily sold in the fish markets of the southern Caribbean.

Sapo Caño

Thalassophryne maculosa Günther, 1861.
Figure 61

Dorsal rays II-17 to 20 (the dorsal spines hollow and venomous); anal rays 16 to 19; pectoral rays 14 to 16

Figure 61. Sapo Caño (*Thalassophryne maculosa*), 3.8 inches, Isla Cubagua, Venezuela.

(usually 15), head broad, the width about equal to length; opercle with a single hollow spine (also venomous); mouth size and dentition similar to *Amphichthys;* no scales; short fleshy protuberances at base of lips; a single lateral line on body, dorsal in position, the pores elongate; dark spots and irregular blotches on head and body, variable in size and position; ground color of young lighter, in general, than adults, so dark markings more conspicuous. Largest specimen, 7.2 inches. Colombia to Trinidad and Tobago, including Aruba and Curaçao. Common at Isla de Margarita and Isla Cubagua, Venezuela. Occurs on sandy bottom from the shore to 600 feet; may bury in sand with only the eyes showing. Wounds from the venomous spines have caused severe pain and illness that persisted as long as one week. *T. quadrizonatus* and *T. wehekindi* are synonyms. The related *T. megalops,* known only from Colombia and Panama at depths of 250 to 600 feet, has the same dorsal and anal ray counts as *maculosa* but 13 to 15 (usually 14) pectoral rays; it lacks the well-defined dark spots and has a larger eye, on the average, than *maculosa.*

NEEDLEFISHES
(BELONIDAE)

The needlefishes are distinctive in having slender bodies and highly elongate pointed jaws with numerous needle-like teeth. The fins are soft-rayed; the dorsal and anal fins are posterior in position; the pelvics are abdominal and have 6 rays; the pectorals are short. The lateral line runs very low on the body. The nostrils are in a deep cavity.

These fishes live at the surface and are protectively colored for this mode of life by being green or blue on the back and silvery white on the sides and ventrally. They are carnivorous and feed mainly on small fishes. The eggs of most species are large and have adhesive filaments with which they can be attached to floating objects.

Needlefishes tend to leap and skitter at the surface, and some persons have been injured when accidentally struck by them, particularly at night when the fishes may be confused by a light.

Figure 62. Houndfish (*Tylosurus crocodilus*), Belize.

Figure 63. Keeled Needlefish (*Platybelone argalus*), 13.5 inches, St. Thomas, Virgin Islands.

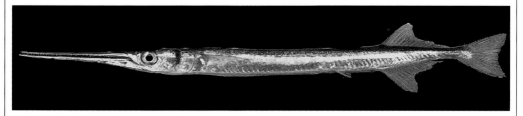

Figure 64. Redfin Needlefish (*Strongylura notata*), 10 inches, Bimini, Bahama Islands.

Keeled Needlefish

Platybelone argalus (LeSueur, 1846).
Figure 63
Dorsal rays 12 to 15; anal rays 17 to 20; predorsal scales 107 to 128; gill rakers present (absent in *Strongylura* and *Tylosurus*); caudal peduncle with a lateral keel, the lateral line passing ventral to it; least depth of caudal peduncle about half the width; opercles not scaled; caudal fin moderately forked; origin of dorsal fin over base of sixth or seventh anal ray. Attains a maximum length of about 20 inches. Circumtropical.

Redfin Needlefish

Strongylura notata (Poey, 1861). Figure 64
Dorsal rays 12 to 15; anal rays 12 to 15; predorsal scales 76 to 117; maxilla concealed under preorbital bone; origin of the dorsal fin approximately over the anal fin origin; both left and right gonads present; anterior lobe of dorsal fin and upper lobe of caudal fin orange-red; a broad region of deep greenish blue on head along upper margin of preopercle. In most other respects, similar to *timucu*. Recorded from Cuba, the Bahamas, Jamaica, Florida, and Yucatan.

Timucu

Strongylura timucu (Walbaum, 1792).
Figure 65
Dorsal rays 15 to 17; anal rays 16 to 20; predorsal scales 120 to 185; caudal peduncle without a lateral keel, the least depth about equal to the width; maxilla exposed posteriorly; opercles scaled; caudal fin emarginate, the lower lobe a little longer than upper; origin of dorsal fin over sixth or seventh anal ray; left and right gonads present; gray-green on back, silvery on sides, the two regions separated by a silvery

blue-green stripe that is more apparent posteriorly. Attains about 18 inches. Florida through the West Indies to Brazil. Enters fresh water. The closely related *S. marina* (differs in having 213 to 304 predorsal scales and only one gonad is present) is absent from the West Indies but overlaps the range of *timucu* along the continental shores of the Caribbean and in Florida.

Houndfish

Tylosurus crocodilus (Peron & LeSueur, 1821).   Figures 62 & 66

Dorsal rays 21 to 23; anal rays 18 to 22; predorsal scales 240 to 290; caudal peduncle with a darkly pigmented lateral keel into which the lateral line terminates; least depth of caudal peduncle about equal to width; opercles not scaled; caudal fin forked, the lower lobe much longer than the upper; origin of dorsal fin slightly posterior to origin of anal fin; green on back; silvery white on sides; teeth and bones green. Grows to a length of 5 feet. Worldwide in the tropics. The related *T. acus*, which is blue on the back, is rarely found inshore. It differs in having 23 to 26 dorsal rays, 20 to 23 anal rays, 320 to 390 predorsal scales, a narrower head (3.4 to 4.8% of standard length, in contrast to 5 to 6.8% for *crocodilus*), longer jaws, and more consistently vertical teeth.

HALFBEAKS
(HEMIRAMPHIDAE)

The halfbeaks are grouped in the same order (Beloniformes) as the needlefishes and flyingfishes. They share the same general characteristics as given above for the needle-

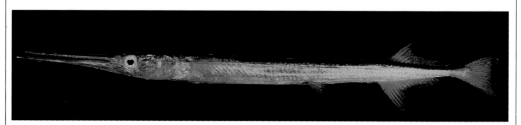

Figure 65. Timucu (*Strongylura timucu*), 12.5 inches, St. John, Virgin Islands.

Figure 66. Houndfish (*Tylosurus crocodilus*), 22.8 inches, Puerto Rico.

Figure 67. School of halfbeaks *(Hemiramphus balao)* from St. Croix, Virgin Islands.

fishes except for the scales and the jaws. The scales are relatively large; the upper jaw is short and triangular in shape when viewed from above; typically the lower jaw is much prolonged (and often tipped with red). The disparity in jaw length is the feature by which the halfbeaks are best known and for which they are named; however there are members of the family which do not have a long lower jaw. The one species from the Caribbean is *Chriodorus atherinoides* which has been recorded only from southern Florida, the Bahamas, Cuba and Yucatan.

The halfbeaks are also prone to leap and skitter at the surface. Although their bodies are somewhat compressed laterally, their bellies tend to be flattened which may be an adaptation enabling them to skip like a flat stone thrown parallel to the surface of the water. One offshore species, the very

elongate flying halfbeak *(Euleptorhamphus velox)*, is exceptional in having long pectoral fins which it can extend during leaps and glide like a flyingfish. Some authors classify the halfbeaks in the same family as the flyingfishes.

Only two species of halfbeaks are apt to be sighted in clearwater reef areas of the Caribbean, both in the genus *Hemiramphus. Hyporhamphus*, represented by the Caribbean species *unifasciatus* and *roberti*, is distinguished from *Hemiramphus* by having scales on the snout, the dorsal fin origin over the anal fin (in advance of anal in *Hemiramphus)*, and a less deeply forked caudal fin.

Balao

Hemiramphus balao LeSueur, 1823.
Figure 67-68

Dorsal rays 11 to 15 (usually 13 or 14); anal rays 10 to 13 (usually 11 or 12); lateral scale rows about 53;

Figure 68. Balao (*Hemiramphus balao*), 9.8 inches, Culebra, Puerto Rico.

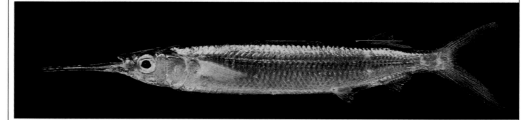

Figure 69. Ballyhoo (*Hemiramphus brasiliensis*), 11 inches, Puerto Rico.

pectoral fins greater than distance from origin of fins to front edge of nasal cavities; back bluish gray; upper lobe of caudal fin and front of dorsal fin bluish violet (rarely faintly reddish). Reaches about 15 inches. New York to the Caribbean Sea and south to Brazil; also Bermuda and the tropical eastern Atlantic. More inclined to range offshore than the ballyhoo.

Ballyhoo

Hemiramphus brasiliensis (Linnaeus, 1758).
Figures 69

Dorsal rays 12 to 15 (usually 13 or 14); anal rays 11 to 15 (usually 12 or 13); lateral scale rows (from gill opening to base of caudal fin) about 53; pectoral fins short, their length less than the distance from origin of these fins to front edge of nasal cavities; greenish on back; upper lobe of caudal fin and front of dorsal fin orange-yellow. Attains a total length of about 15 inches. A com-

mon inshore species ranging from Massachusetts to the south, throughout the West Indies and Gulf of Mexico, to Brazil; also known in tropical West Africa. Feeds principally on floating pieces of seagrass, in part on small fishes.

SILVERSIDES
(ATHERINIDAE)

The silversides are small fishes which usually have a silvery stripe along the side. In general, they occur in small schools in inshore waters, and some penetrate fresh water. In contrast to the small schooling fishes of the herring and anchovy families, which have a single dorsal fin and the pectoral fins low on the body, the silversides have two dorsal fins (the first consisting of a few slender spines), and the pectorals are inserted about half way up the side of the body. The pelvic fins, of I,5 rays, are somewhat posterior in position. There is no lateral line. The mouth is moderately large, the teeth small, and the gill rakers numerous.

Typically these fishes feed on small animals of the plankton; they may be attracted to a light at night; four species are recorded from the West Indies, but only two are common in shallows over sand, seagrass or reefs. Several others are known from continental shores and tributaries of the Caribbean.

Although traditionally grouped with the mullets and barracudas, one recent study suggests that the silversides are more closely related to the halfbeaks and their allies.

Reef Silversides

Allanetta harringtonensis (Goode, 1877). Figure 70

Dorsal rays V to VII-I,8 to 10; scales 42 to 45; mid-side of lower jaw with a prominent elevated region, its height about 2.7 in jaw length; width of head about 1.8 in head length; green on back, silvery white below (with bluish reflections), with a silvery stripe on side, the upper edge of which is bordered by an iridescent blue-green line. Attains about 3 inches. Bermuda, Florida, West Indies and southwest Gulf of Mexico to Colombia.

Hardhead Silversides

Atherinomorus stipes (Müller & Troschel, 1848). Figure 71

Dorsal rays IV to VI-I,8 to 10; scales 37 to 41; mid-side of lower jaw only slightly elevated; head broad, the width about 1.6 in head length; greenish on back, with a silvery stripe about as wide as pupil extending from upper pectoral base to mid-base of caudal fin. Attains at least 3.5 inches. Known from Florida to Brazil. The most common silversides inshore in the West Indies.

Figure 70. Reef Silversides (*Allanetta harringtonensis*), 2.1 inches, Puerto Rico.

Figure 71. Hardhead Silversides (*Atherinomorus stipes*), 2.9 inches, St. John, Virgin Islands.

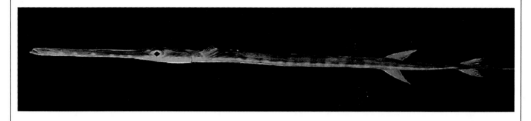

Figure 72. Cornetfish (*Fistularia tabacaria*), 15.5 inches, St. John, Virgin Islands.

CORNETFISHES
(FISTULARIIDAE)

Cornetfish

Fistularia tabacaria Linnaeus, 1758.
Figure 72

Dorsal and anal rays 13 to 16; no scales; body very elongate (depth about 30 in standard length) and depressed (depth about 1.7 in width); snout long and tubular, terminating in a small oblique mouth, the lower jaw preceding upper; teeth minute; caudal fin forked with a very long median filament; greenish brown to brownish gray, shading ventrally to light gray; a mid-dorsal row of light blue spots running from head to dorsal fin; a lateral row of pale blue spots becoming a solid line on about posterior half of body; two lateral rows of light blue spots on snout. Said to attain a length of 5 to 6 feet exclusive of the caudal filament. Littoral in the tropical Atlantic. Not common; most often seen swimming above seagrass beds. Limited data suggest that it feeds primarily on fishes.

TRUMPETFISHES
(AULOSTOMIDAE)

Trumpetfish

Aulostomus maculatus Valenciennes, 1842.
Figures 73 & 74

Dorsal rays IX to XII-24 to 28 (each spine a separate fin); anal rays 25 to 28; body with small ctenoid scales (bony fishes previously discussed have had cycloid scales); body elongate, the depth about 15 in standard length and compressed, the width about 1.7 in depth; snout long and tubular, the lower jaw projecting anterior to upper and bearing a barbel; no long filament from middle of caudal fin; usual color brown or reddish brown, with lengthwise pale lines, scattered small black spots, and a black streak on the upper jaw; however there is a yellowish color phase with the upper half of the head bright yellow and another with the upper half of the head purple. Attains a maximum length of about 30 inches. A single tropical Atlantic species. A common reef fish which often aligns itself vertically in the water; when among gorgonians it may be difficult to detect. Feeds on small fishes and shrimps; has been observed to dart directly down on its prey from a vertical pose above the bottom. Its prey is sucked in by a pipette-like action. Fishes seemingly larger than the narrow tubular snout have been found in the stomach. The membranous floor of the snout, however, is elastic and provides for the passage of large prey through the snout.

PIPEFISHES AND SEA HORSES
(SYNGNATHIDAE)

The syngnathids are small fishes whose bodies are encased in rings of bony armor. Like the cornetfishes and the trumpetfishes, which are classified in the same order, they have long tube-like snouts (a few exceptions) and small mouths. They ingest their food (usually small crustaceans) by a rapid intake of water, much as one would use a pipette. They have small gill openings, special tufted gills, a primitive kidney, no spines in fins, no pelvic fins, and a single dorsal fin. The dorsal, anal, pectoral, and caudal fins are usually present, but some species lack one or more of these fins as adults. Perhaps the most unique feature of

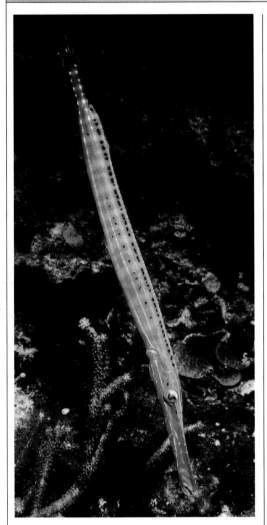

Figure 73. Trumpetfish (*Aulostomus maculatus*), St. Croix, Virgin Islands.

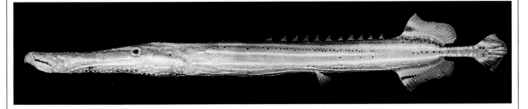

Figure 74. Trumpetfish (*Aulostomus maculatus*), 23.4 inches, St. John, Virgin Islands.

Figure 75. Slender Sea Horse (*Hippocampus reidi*), St Croix, Virgin Islands.

the family is the ventral brood pouch of the male fish in which the young are reared after the eggs are laid by the female.

Sea horses are distinctive in the vertical orientation of the body, horizontal orientation of the head, and a prehensile tail lacking a caudal fin.

Pipefishes and sea horses are slow-swimming and can often be caught by hand. With the exception of *Syngnathus pelagicus*, which lives in floating sargassum seaweed, all are shore fishes (maximum depth record, 600 feet). Twenty pipefishes and three sea horses are known from the Caribbean Sea and Bahamas. In general they are not abundant, and most are so small and protectively colored that they are rarely noticed by underwater observers. Accounts of one representative pipefish and one sea horse are presented in the following pages.

Slender Sea Horse

Hippocampus reidi Ginsburg, 1933.

Figures 75 & 76

Dorsal rays 15 to 18 (usually 17); trunk rings usually 11; tail rings usually 35 or 36; trunk slender; coronet (prominence on top of head) moderately developed in young, but low in adults; tubercles on back also becoming low in adults. Attains a height of at least 4 inches (nearly 6 inches in total length if stretched out). Known only from Bermuda and the Caribbean Sea.

Figure 76. Slender Sea Horse (*Hippocampus reidi*), 3.8 inches high, Curaçao.

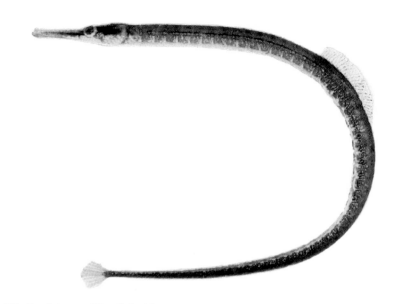

Figure 77. Caribbean Pipefish (*Syngnathus caribbaeus*), 7.4 inches, St. John, Virgin Islands.

H. hudsonius differs in having 18 to 21 (usually 19 or 20) dorsal rays, a broader trunk, and better developed coronet and tubercles on adults. The dwarf sea horse, *H. zosterae*, has 11 to 14 dorsal rays, usually 10 trunk rings and 31 to 33 tail rings.

Caribbean Pipefish

Syngnathus caribbaeus Dawson, 1979.

Figure 77

Dorsal rays 27 to 32; rings of trunk (region from gill opening to anus) 16 to 18; tail rings 32 to 35; head 7 to 8.3 in standard length; pectoral fins 4.6 to 7.2 in head; snout 1.7 to 2.2 in head; adult females flat-bellied. Attains at least 8.5 inches, which is unusually large for a tropical pipefish. Caribbean Sea to Surinam on sandy or weedy bottoms. Previously named *S. rousseau*, but recently the holotype was shown to be a specimen of the earlier-named *S. pelagicus*.

FLASHLIGHTFISHES
(ANOMALOPIDAE)

The Anomalopidae is a family of six species classified in five genera (*Anomalops*, *Parmops* and *Photoblepharon* in the Indo-Pacific region and *Kryptophanaron* and *Phthanophaneron* in the New World) which is placed in the order Beryciformes (along with the squirrelfish family Holocentridae). The family name is derived from the Greek meaning "abnormal eye" in reference to the unique light organ located just below and partly covering the lower part of the eye. The light is produced by a symbiotic bacterium. The fish provides the medium in its light organ for the bacterium to grow, and the bacterium produces the light as a byproduct of metabolism. Flashlightfishes are nocturnal, hiding deep in recesses in reefs by day and emerging only on moonless nights. Their light organs can

Figure 78. Atlantic Flashlightfish (*Kryptophanaron alfredi*), Puerto Rico.

be turned on and off by raising an eyelid–like black curtain *(Photoblepharon)*, rotating the entire light organ downward and internally *(Anomalops)*, or both *(Kryptophanaron)*. Apparently the species of *Kryptophanaron* and *Phthanophaneron* use the eyelid for rapid blinking, and rotation when they want the light off for long periods. The light enables flashlightfishes to see the small planktonic animals on which they feed, to confuse predators (after blinking the light off, the fish rapidly change direction), and for communication.

Atlantic Flashlightfish

Kryptophanaron alfredi Silvester & Fowler, 1926   Figure 78

Dorsal rays IV-II,14; anal rays II,10; pectoral rays 16 or 17 (usually 16); pelvic rays I,6; scales small and ctenoid, but pores in lateral line large, 32 to 34; gill rakers 6 to 7 + 18 to 20; small villiform teeth in bands in jaws; body depth 2.2 to 2.5 in standard length; eye large, about 3.0 in head; caudal fin forked; black, the head and fin rays darkest; lateral line and ventral scutes white. Attains 5 inches. Reported from the Greater Antilles, Bahamas, Cayman Islands, Virgin Islands, Curaçao, and the Bay Islands off Honduras. Occurs in the depth range of 80 to at least 165 feet. The related *K. harveyi* was discovered in 1976 in the Gulf of California.

SQUIRRELFISHES
(HOLOCENTRIDAE)

The holocentrids are very spiny reef fishes with large eyes and red color. They have moderately large mouths but small teeth. The scales are coarsely ctenoid. All Atlantic species have I,7 pelvic rays and IV anal spines; there are 18 or 19 principal caudal rays.

Their beryciform relatives are deep-water residents, and it is probable that their ancestors were too. Thus it is not surprising that squirrelfishes are nocturnal. They feed mostly on crustaceans. They are retiring by day, usually hiding in crevices or beneath ledges of reefs.

The family has been divided into two subfamilies, the Holocentrinae and the Myripristinae. Formerly the Holocentrinae contained only the genus *Holocentrus*. Recently it has been split into several genera which include *Holocentrus*, *Neoniphon* and *Sargocentron* (recently shown to be an older name than *Adioryx*) in the Atlantic; some authors prefer to retain these as subgenera of *Holocentrus*. All have a long stout spine on the cheek at the angle of the preopercle which is lacking in the Myripristinae. At least some species have a toxin associated with the preopercular spine, for puncture wounds from it can be very painful (although not as much as the venomous spines of scorpionfishes).

The swimbladder of the Holocentrinae is a tubular structure extending the entire length of the body cavity. Only in *Holocentrus ascensionis* and H. *rufus* does it make contact with the skull. In the Myripristinae, which includes the genera *Myripristis*, *Ostichthys*, *Plectrypops* and *Corniger*, the swim bladder is constricted at its anterior third to form two more-or-less separate chambers; the front of the anterior section has two antero-lateral projections which extend to the

Figure 79. Blackbar Soldierfish (*Myripristis jacobus*), St. Croix, Virgin Islands.

auditory region of each side of the cranium.

Four western Atlantic species are not included among the species accounts below. One is *Sargocentron bullisi* which is similar to *S. coruscum* but has 14 pectoral rays, 39 to 43 lateral-line scales, a slightly deeper body, and no large black spot at the front of the dorsal fin; it was described from specimens taken in from 150 to 360 feet. A related species, *Sargocentron poco*, was recently named from one specimen from shallow water in the Bahamas and has also been collected at Grand Cayman Island. This species has XI, 13 dorsal rays, 14 pectoral rays, 37 to 40 lateral-line scales, 18 to 20 gill rakers, a black spot on dorsal fin between first and fourth spines, and no dark pigment in axil of pectoral fins. The two other omitted species are *Ostichthys trachypomus* and *Corniger spinosus*. These very spiny holocentrids normally occur at depths greater than 300 feet.

Squirrelfishes are good to eat, but most Atlantic species are too small to have much value as food.

SQUIRRELFISHES
(HOLOCENTRINAE)

Longjaw Squirrelfish

Holocentrus ascensionis (Osbeck, 1765).
Figure 80

Dorsal rays XI, 14 to 16; anal rays IV, 10; pectoral rays 15 to 17; lateral-line scales 46 to 51; maxilla reaching to or beyond center of eye; preopercular spine 16 to 20 in standard length: length of caudal peduncle (measured horizontally from rear base of dorsal fin to base of

Figure 80. Longjaw Squirrelfish (*Holocentrus ascensionis*), St. Croix, Virgin Islands.

Figure 81. Squirrelfish (*Holocentrus rufus*), Bonaire.

caudal fin) 5.1 to 6.3 in standard length; this and the following species differ from other species of the subfamily Holocentrinae by having direct contact between the divided forward end of the swimbladder and the paired posterior auditory parts of the cranium. The color is light silvery red with a faint striping on the body; interspinous membranes of dorsal fin without distinct white areas near tips. Largest collected by the author, 13.6 inches, from Venezuela. Bermuda and New York to southern Brazil; also islands of the tropical middle and eastern Atlantic.

Squirrelfish

Holocentrus rufus (Walbaum, 1792).
Figure 81
Dorsal rays XI,14 to 16; anal rays IV,9 to 11; pectoral rays 15 to 17; lateral-line scales 50 to 57; maxilla usually not reaching center of eye;

preopercular spine 12 to 17 in standard length; length of caudal peduncle 4.7 to 5.9 in standard length; similar in color to *H. ascensionis*, but each interspinous membrane of dorsal fin with a white spot near margin (spots indistinct or absent on last two membranes). Reaches at least 12.5 inches. Known from Bermuda, Florida and throughout the Caribbean. Seems to be more abundant on well-developed coral reefs than *ascensionis*.

Longspine Squirrelfish

Neoniphon marianus (Valenciennes, 1829).
Figure 82
Dorsal rays XI,12 to 14; anal rays IV,9; pectoral rays 14; lateral-line scales 45 to 47; head pointed, the lower jaw projecting notably anterior to upper; third anal spine exceedingly long, reaching posterior to caudal base when depressed; silvery red

Figure 82. Longspine Squirrelfish (*Neoniphon marianus*), Bonaire.

Figure 83. Reef Squirrelfish (*Sargocentron coruscum*), night photo, Bonaire.

with lengthwise orange stripes on the body. Attains a maximum length of about 7 inches. West Indies. Rare in shallow water, but appears to be the most common squirrelfish in the depth range of 100 to 200 feet or more.

Reef Squirrelfish

Sargocentron coruscum (Poey, 1860).

Figure 83

Dorsal rays XI, 12; anal rays IV, 8; pectoral rays 13; lateral-line scales 41 to 45; depth of body 3.1 to 3.7 in standard length; maxilla usually reaching to or beyond center of eye; body with alternate stripes of red and silvery white; spinous dorsal fin red, white at tips, with a large black spot between the first three or four spines; axil of pectoral fins pale. Attains 5 inches. Bermuda, Florida and the West Indies.

Dusky Squirrelfish

Sargocentron vexillarium (Poey, 1860).

Figure 84

Dorsal rays XI, 13; anal rays IV, 9 (rarely 8 or 10); pectoral rays usually 15; lateral-line scales 40 to 44; depth of body 2.5 to 2.8 in standard length; maxilla usually not reaching center of eye; similar in color to *coruscus*, but with more dusky pigment in the red bands on the body, only an ill-defined dusky red region at front of dorsal fin, and deep red in axil of pectoral fins (blackish in preserved specimens). Rarely exceeds 5 inches, but has been recorded to nearly 7 inches in Bermuda. Bermuda, Florida and the West Indies, where it is the most common inshore squirrelfish.

Figure 84. Dusky Squirrelfish (*Sargocentron vexillarium*), night photo, Roatan, Honduras.

SOLDIERFISHES
(MYRIPRISTINAE)

Blackbar Soldierfish

Myripristis jacobus Cuvier, 1829.

Figures 79 & 85

Dorsal rays X-I,14; anal rays IV,13; pectoral rays 15; lateral-line scales 34 to 36; no large spines on head; a pair of bony tubercles bearing spinules anteriorly on jaws; third anal spine not long, its length 1.7 to 2 in second anal soft ray; a broad blackish bar running from upper end of gill opening to pectoral base. Largest specimen collected by the author, 8.5 inches, from Trinidad. Occurs from northern Florida to Brazil and throughout the West Indies; also islands of the central and eastern Atlantic.

Cardinal Soldierfish

Plectrypops retrospinis (Guichenot, 1853).

Figure 86

Dorsal rays XII,14; anal rays IV,11; pectoral rays 16 or 17; lateral-line scales 32 to 35; depth of body 2.2 to 2.4 in standard length; lower edges of bones rimming lower edge of eye with prominent, forward-curving spines; lobes of caudal fin strongly rounded; entirely bright red. Probably does not exceed 5 inches in total length. Caribbean Sea. A secretive species living by day in deep recesses in reefs.

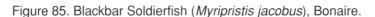

Figure 85. Blackbar Soldierfish (*Myripristis jacobus*), Bonaire.

Figure 86. Cardinal Soldierfish (*Plectrypops retrospinis*), 3.9 inches, St. John, Virgin Islands.

SCORPIONFISHES
(SCORPAENIDAE)

The scorpionfishes are carnivorous bottom-dwelling fishes of tropical and temperate seas which are named for the venomous spines possessed by many of the species. They are often found in rocky areas, and for this reason are sometimes called "rockfishes." Together with a few related families such as the searobins (Triglidae) they are classified in their own order, the Scorpaeniformes. The most conspicuous common feature of the group is a bony extension from the second suborbital bone which runs across the cheek from below the eye to the preopercle. This reinforcing bony plate has been called the suborbital stay, and the fishes with it are sometimes termed the "mail-cheeked" fishes.

Other general characteristics include a large head, large terminal mouth, small villiform teeth in jaws, on vomer and usually on the palatines, and a continuous dorsal fin which is often deeply notched. In addition to the usual two spines on the opercle and four or five on the preopercular margin, there are often many other spines and ridges on the head. Also there may be a variable number of fleshy flaps and cirri on the head and body of some species.

Many of the scorpionfishes spend much of their time lying almost motionless on the bottom. They are usually masterfully camouflaged and very difficult to distinguish from the marine growth around them. They prey upon small fishes and crustaceans that make the mistake of venturing near.

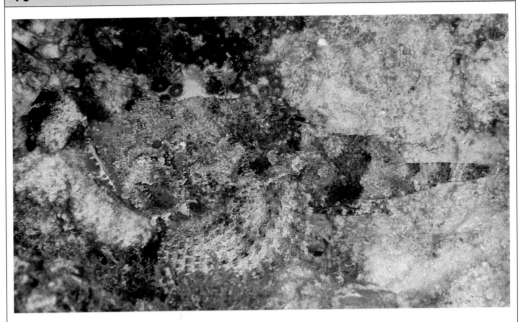

Figure 87. Spotted Scorpionfish (*Scorpaena plumieri*), St. Croix, Virgin Islands.

The Atlantic region is fortunate in not having any members of the genera *Synanceia* (stonefishes) or *Pterois* (lionfishes). Wounds from the spines of these scorpionfishes are very serious and may be fatal. Nevertheless great care should be exercised when in contact with Atlantic species, for extreme pain of long duration may result from deep puncture wounds by their spines.

The two genera which include shallow-water species in the Caribbean are *Scorpaena* (13 species in the region) and *Scorpaenodes* (two species). The three largest inshore species of *Scorpaena* and the most common *Scorpaenodes* are discussed.

In general, the larger species are highly valued as food.

Barbfish

Scorpaena brasiliensis Cuvier, 1829.
Figure 88

Dorsal rays XII,9; anal rays III,5; pectoral rays 18 to 20; lateral scale rows 50 to 58; preorbital with two spines; suborbital ridge usually with three spinous points; supraorbital tentacle may be well developed; first preopercular spine reaching to or beyond middle of opercle; usually two dark brown spots on body, one behind upper part of gill cover and the other posterior to pectoral fin; axil of pectoral fins pale with dark brown spots. Attains about 14 inches. Virginia to Brazil. More common in continental waters than insular; occurs from depths of a few feet to about 300 feet.

Grass Scorpionfish

Scorpaena grandicornis Cuvier, 1829.
Figure 89

Dorsal rays XII,9; anal rays III,5; pectoral rays 18 or 19 (usually 18); lateral scale rows 42 to 47; body moderately compressed, the width about 1.8 in depth; preorbital with

Figure 88. Barbfish (*Scorpaena brasiliensis*), 8 inches, St. John, Virgin Islands.

Figure 89. Grass Scorpionfish (*Scorpaena grandicornis*), 4.9 inches, St. John, Virgin Islands.

two spines; suborbital ridge with two or three spinous points; supraorbital tentacle notably well developed; first preopercular spine extending less than half the distance across opercle; no frontal spines (at anterior corners of occipital pit); mottled brown with three bars on caudal fin, the one at the base poorly defined; axil of pectoral fins pale on lower two-thirds, brown with white dots on upper third. Attains about 7 inches. Tropical western Atlantic. Common inshore in seagrass beds. Sometimes called "Lionfish."

Spotted Scorpionfish

Scorpaena plumieri Bloch, 1789.
Figures 87 & 90

Dorsal rays XII,9; anal rays III,5; pectoral rays 18 to 21; lateral scale rows 42 to 47; scales cycloid (true of other *Scorpaena);* body robust, the width about 1.4 in depth; individuals about 3 inches or longer with three preorbital spines (project downward over top of upper lip); suborbital ridge well developed, with three or four spinous points; first preopercular spine short, extending less than halfway to margin of opercle; occipital pit (a median prominent depression on top of head behind eyes) present (also found on the preceding two species); color variable but generally with a broad pale bar over much of caudal peduncle following an irregular broad dark bar; caudal fin with three dark bars, the first at base of fin. The most diagnostic color marking of adults is a large jet black area containing white spots in the entire axil of the pectoral fins. Juveniles are distinctive in color in lacking dark

Figure 90. Spotted Scorpionfish (*Scorpaena plumieri*), 6.4 inches, St. John, Virgin Islands.

Figure 91. Reef Scorpionfish (*Scorpaenodes caribbaeus*), 2.7 inches, Bimini, Bahama Islands.

pigment on the caudal peduncle. Reaches a length of about 17 inches. Eastern Pacific and Massachusetts to Rio de Janeiro in the Atlantic; also known from St. Helena and Ascension. A common shallow-water species of coral reefs or rocky bottom. When alarmed this fish spreads its pectoral fins so that the striking black and white axillary coloration is displayed—apparently as warning coloration.

Reef Scorpionfish

Scorpaenodes caribbaeus Meek & Hildebrand, 1928.   Figure 91

Dorsal rays XIII,9; anal rays III,5; pectoral rays 18 or 19; lateral scale rows 41 or 42; scales ctenoid; palatine teeth absent (present on *Scorpaena); no preorbital spines; suborbital ridge with four or five spinous points; no large supraor-

bital tentacle; no occipital pit; body so densely spotted with dark brown that spots not readily distinguishable; median fins and pectoral fins with small blackish spots; a broad blackish area posteriorly in spinous portion of dorsal fin; pectoral axil pale. Attains about 5 inches. Caribbean Sea. A common inshore reef fish, but rarely seen. The related *Scorpaenodes tredecimspinosus* has 17 pectoral rays and a suborbital ridge with three spinous points.

HELMET GURNARDS
(DACTYLOPTERIDAE)

Helmet Gurnard

Dactylopterus volitans (Linnaeus, 1758).
         Figures 92 & 93

Dorsal rays II-IV or V-8; first two dorsal spines free, located almost side by side; anal rays 6; base of pectoral fins horizontal, the fins divided into two sections, an anterior short part of 6 rays and a posterior part of 26 to 30 rays which is very long, reaching to caudal base in adults; pelvic fins I,4; lateral scale rows 60 to 69; scales with sharp keels; body moderately elongate, the depth in adults about 5.5 to 6.5 in standard length; head blunt, the top and sides encased in a bony shield which is deeply concave between eyes; a long keeled spine extending posteriorly from bony shield on nape to below mid-base of first dorsal fin; a long spine at angle of preopercle bearing a serrate keel; mouth small, low on head; jaws with a band of small nodular teeth, this band broader anteriorly; no teeth on roof of mouth; caudal fin emarginate with 8 principal rays, the ray tips exserted; two sharp keels basally on fin; color variable, but often yellowish brown; bright blue spots on pectoral fins. Largest collected by author, 13 inches, from the Bahamas. Both sides of the Atlantic; on the western side from Bermuda and Massachusetts to Argentina. The author has observed the Helmet Gurnard "walking" on the bottom with its pelvic fins and using the short anterior pectoral rays to scratch in the sand as if in search of food. When alarmed it spreads its long pectoral fins laterally. Reports of its leaping free of the surface and gliding on expanded pectorals must be false. It is a sluggish, heavy-bodied, bottom-dwelling fish. The young of about 2 inches are commonly taken at night lights; their pectoral fins are shorter than

Figure 92. Helmet Gurnard (*Dactylopterus volitans*), St. Croix, Virgin Islands.

Figure 93. Helmet Gurnard (*Dactylopterus volitans*), 13 inches, Nassau, Bahama Islands.

those of adults, reaching about half the distance to the base of the caudal fin. Limited data suggest that the food of adults consists primarily of benthic crustaceans, especially crabs; clams and small fishes may also be eaten. The Helmet Gurnard should not be confused with the Searobins (Triglidae) which are represented in the Caribbean by several species, most in the genus *Prionotus*. These fishes also have long pectoral fins which can be expanded laterally, but their bodies are more robust, their snouts are moderately long and tapering, and they lack dermal bone on the head; they "walk" on three pairs of detached lower pectoral rays.

SEAROBINS (TRIGLIDAE)

These unique fishes are grouped with the scorpionfishes and helmet gurnards in the large Order Scorpaeniformes. They are benthic; most occur in water greater than usual SCUBA-diving depths. They are characterized by a very bony head, usually with spines; two dorsal fins, the first with the spines fully joined by membrane; the lower two or three pectoral rays free of membrane; remaining typical part of pectoral fin long and may be extended fanlike to the side. These fish creep along the bottom on their pelvic fins and three lower pectoral rays, using the latter to probe for food. All searobins are carnivorous, feeding mainly on small crustaceans and mollusks. They are well known for making sounds which are produced by muscles attached to their very large swimbladder. The author has encountered only a single species of this family while diving in the Caribbean (see following account).

Bandtail Searobin

Prionotus ophryas Jordan & Swain, 1884
Figure 94

Dorsal rays VIII-13; anal rays 11; upper membranous part of pectoral fin with 14 rays, the fin broadly rounded and long, about 1.7 in standard length; lateral-line scales about 50; developed gill rakers 9; body depth about 4.5 in standard length; dorsal profile

Figure 94. Bandtail Searobin (*Prionotus ophryas*), St. Croix, Virgin Islands.

of head strongly concave from snout to upper level of eye, then nearly straight to origin of first dorsal fin; interorbital space deeply concave; preopercle with a stout spine preceded by a long ridge; opercle with two strong spines; a humeral spine and two pairs of small occipital spines present; a long filament on anterior nostril, and a fringed fleshy tentacle above eye; finely mottled reddish brown with irregular diagonal dark bars; caudal fin with three dark reddish brown bars, one at base, one in middle, and one at distal end of fin; fish from deeper water with red ground color. Attains 8 inches. North Carolina to Venezuela, Bahamas and Antilles. A specimen from the Bahamas was caught in 12 inches of water; another from the Gulf of Mexico was taken in 95 fathoms.

GROUPERS AND SEABASSES
(SERRANIDAE)

The Serranidae is one of the least specialized families of the largest order of fishes, the Perciformes. Most of the remaining fishes discussed in this book are perciforms. In general, they share the following characteristics: fins with spines; pelvic fin rays I,5 (but this number may be reduced) and located below or slightly anterior or posterior to pectoral base; caudal fin with not more than 17 principal rays (rays which extend to posterior edge of fin); maxilla not a part of the edge of the mouth (it forms part of the gape in many of the more primitive fishes) and no intermuscular bones (a favorable point to a person eating such a fish). The body of most groupers is robust; the mouth is large, and often the lower jaw projects anterior to the upper; the hind part of the maxilla is fully exposed on the cheek; there are bands of slender sharp depressible teeth in the jaws (these bands broader anteriorly) and usually a few stout fixed canines at the front of the jaws; the preopercular margin is nearly always serrate; and there are usually three flattened spines posteriorly on the opercle; the cheeks and opercles are scaled; the body scales are small and ctenoid (or secondarily cycloid); there are six or seven branchiostegal rays.

All of the serranid fishes are carnivorous, feeding mainly on fishes and crustaceans. Many are hermaphroditic; some such as species of *Serranus* and *Hypoplectrus* are both male and female at the same time; others such as the genera *Epinephelus*, *Cephalopholis* and *Mycteroperca* start out mature life as females and change over to males when they are larger.

Several species of groupers are known to migrate each year to a specific site for spawning. This makes them highly vulnerable to overfishing (see Nassau Grouper account below).

Some of the groupers and their allies are very drab in hue whereas others are strikingly colored. Many have considerable ability to alter the density of their color to match the bottom over which they may be swimming. A few exhibit very different color phases. In addition, many species display a marked difference in color with depth, those taken from deeper water having much more red. The same is true of some other groups of fishes such as the snappers.

Figure 95. Butter Hamlet (*Hypoplectrus unicolor*) spawning. Photo by Phil Lobel.

Groupers are among the most valuable food fishes of tropical seas. A few of the larger species which feed primarily on fishes, such as species of *Mycteroperca*, have been known to cause ciguatera when eaten.

The Serranidae treated in this volume are subdivided into four subfamilies, the Epinephelinae (groupers), the Serraninae (seabasses and hamlets), the Liopropominae (basslets), and the Grammistinae (soapfishes). These subfamilies are discussed below in this order.

GROUPERS
(EPINEPHELINAE)

Mutton Hamlet

Alphestes afer (Bloch, 1793).   Figure 96
Dorsal rays XI, 18 or 19; anal rays III, 9; snout short, 5.7 to 6.7 in head; eye relatively large, about 4 to 5.2 in head; a stout spine at angle of preopercle which is directed downward and forward (largely covered by skin); scales mostly cycloid; olivaceous or light brown, irregularly blotched and barred with dark brown, and densely spotted with orange. Attains about 1 foot. Tropical western Atlantic. Much more common in seagrass beds than on reefs.

Graysby

Cephalopholis cruentata (Lacepède, 1803).
Figure 97
Dorsal rays IX, 14; anal rays III, 8; pectoral rays usually 16; nostrils about equal in size or the posterior slightly larger; light gray or brown with numerous dark orange-brown dots over head, body and all fins; a row of four spots along back near base of dorsal fin which may be

Figure 96. Mutton Hamlet (*Alphestes afer*), 9.2 inches, St. John, Virgin Islands.

Figure 97. Graysby (*Cephalopholis cruentata*), Andros, Bahamas.

either white or black; outer part of interspinous membranes of dorsal fin orange. A small species which attains only about a foot in length. Tropical western Atlantic; one record from 240 feet off Texas. Relatively unafraid of divers. Most abundant where reefs have many ledges and caves. Often classified in the genus *Petrometopon*.

Coney

Cephalopholis fulva (Linnaeus, 1758).
Figure 98

Dorsal rays IX, 15 or 16; anal rays III,9; pectoral rays usually 18; color variable but usually orange-brown with numerous dark-edged blue dots on head, upper sides and lower part of dorsal fin; two dark spots dorsally on caudal peduncle and two on chin at edge of mouth. When viewed un-derwater the upper part of the fish is usually dark brown and the lower part below the level of the eye abruptly pale. One color phase is brilliant yellow but still has the characteristic pair of black spots on the caudal peduncle and the pair on the chin. Recorded to nearly 16 inches in Bermuda, but none of many examined by the author in West Indian localities exceeded 1 foot. Tropical western Atlantic. One of the most common groupers on West Indian reefs. Frequently taken on hook and line but not easily approached underwater.

Marbled Grouper

Dermatolepis inermis (Valenciennes, 1833).
Figures 99 & 100

Dorsal rays X or XI, 18 to 20; anal rays III,8 to 10; body deep, the depth

Figure 98. Coney (*Cephalopholis fulva*), Puerto Rico.

2.2 to 2.5 in standard length, and compressed, the width 2.2 to 2.9 in depth; no large canines in jaws; caudal fin rounded in young, emarginate in large adults; young are dark brown with scattered dark-edged white spots; adults are mottled brown with small black spots that tend to be arranged in rings. Largest examined by author, 32 inches in length and 20 pounds in weight, from 700 feet off Bimini. Tropical western Atlantic. Not common. A secretive species that tends to hide in crevices and caves in reefs.

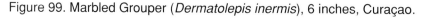

Figure 99. Marbled Grouper (*Dermatolepis inermis*), 6 inches, Curaçao.

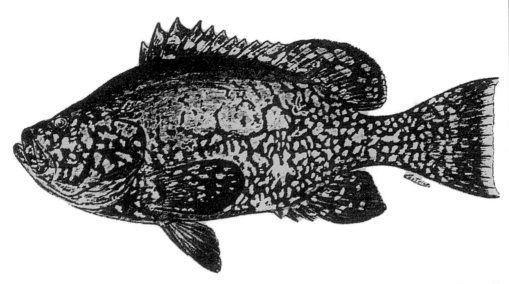

Figure 100. Marbled Grouper *(Dermatolepis inermis)*, adult (after Heemstra & Randall, 1993).

Rock Hind

Epinephelus adscensionis (Osbeck, 1771).
Figure 101

Dorsal rays XI, 16 or 17; anal rays III, 8; pectoral rays 18 or 19; scales usually not evident on maxilla; anterior nostrils about equal in diameter to posterior; light olivaceous with small scattered pale blotches, the entire head, body and fins spotted with orange-brown; a dark brown blotch on upper part of caudal peduncle; a series of five less intense dark blotches along back (blotches formed by groups of more heavily pigmented spots); no broad black-

Figure 101. Rock Hind (*Epinephelus adscensionis*), 13.3 inches, 1.3 pounds, Puerto Rico.

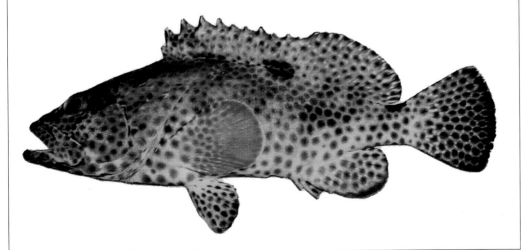

ish submarginal bands in median fins; tips of interspinous membranes of spinous dorsal fin yellow; outer edges of pectoral and caudal fins pale yellowish. Probably attains about 2 feet. Littoral in the tropical Atlantic, straying north on the western side to Massachusetts. Although it has been taken in 100 feet or more of water, it is most common in shallow water on rocky bottom. More at home in inshore rough water than the Red Hind. More wary than the Red Hind.

Red Hind

Epinephelus guttatus (Linnaeus, 1758).
Figure 102

Dorsal rays XI, 15 or 16; anal rays III,8; pectoral rays 16 or 17; small scales usually evident on maxilla; posterior nostrils larger than anterior; light yellowish green above,

shading to whitish below, with numerous small red spots on head, body and basally on fins; median fins olivaceous with scattered pale spots, the soft portions with a narrow pale edge and a broad blackish submarginal band; tips of interspinous membranes of dorsal fin yellow. Largest West Indian specimen, 26.5 inches (7.5 pounds). Tropical western Atlantic, ranging north to North Carolina. The most common species of the genus *Epinephelus* in the West Indies. Readily caught on hook and line and easily speared.

Jewfish

Epinephelus itajara (Lichtenstein, 1822).
Figure 103

Dorsal rays XI, 15 or 16; anal rays III,8; pectoral rays 19; third to eleventh dorsal spines about equal,

Figure 102. Red Hind (*Epinephelus guttatus*), St. Croix, Virgin Islands.

Figure 103. Jewfish (*Epinephelus itajara*), 5 feet 5 inches, 340 pounds, St. John, Virgin Islands.

much shorter than soft rays, the longest about 3.5 to 5 in head; mouth very large, the maxilla extending well beyond eye; eye small, its diameter ranging from 6 in head of a 6-inch specimen to 10 to 12 in head of adults; posterior nostrils about equal to or somewhat larger than anterior; brownish yellow with small dark brown spots on head, body and fins, and five irregular oblique bars on body (bars more evident on young than adults). World's record for anglers is a 7-foot 1.5-inch fish from Fernandina Beach, Florida, that weighed 680 pounds. Tropical Atlantic and eastern Pacific. Although common in Florida and parts of the Gulf of Mexico, it is not frequently encountered in the West Indies. The author has found fishes, hawksbill turtle, crabs, slipper lobsters and most often spiny lobsters in the stomachs. Highly esteemed as food. The age of a 6.5-foot Jewfish was estimated at 37 years. This huge species is not abundant anywhere, and its population can soon be reduced to critical numbers from angling and spearfishing. It has recently been designated a protected species in the U.S. Exclusive Economic Zone. Such protection should be extended to other areas of its range, particularly where the fish can be seen by sport divers.

Red Grouper

Epinephelus morio (Valenciennes, 1828).

Figure 104

Dorsal rays XI,16 or 17 (usually 16); anal rays III,9 (rarely 10); pectoral rays 16 to 18; second dorsal spine the longest, its length about 2.3 in head; interspinous membranes of dorsal fin not incised; posterior nostrils about equal to or slightly larger than anterior; reddish brown with scattered pale blotches; a few small dark dots around and below eye and on operculum; no black spot on caudal peduncle; median fins blackish outwardly with a narrow white margin; inside of mouth red and white; pupil green. Said to reach 50 pounds or more. The world record for hook

Figure 104. Red Grouper (*Epinephelus morio*), 16.8 inches, 2.4 pounds, St. John, Virgin Islands.

and line, 39 pounds, 8 ounces, is from Cape Canaveral, Florida. Bermuda and Massachusetts to Rio de Janeiro. Not common in the West Indies, but abundant in Florida and the Gulf of Mexico. Juveniles may be found in shallow water, but adults are usually taken from depths of 200 to 1000 feet.

Nassau Grouper

Epinephelus striatus (Bloch, 1792).

Figure 105

Dorsal rays XI,16 to 18 (usually

Figure 105. Nassau Grouper (*Epinephelus striatus*), Roatan, Honduras.

17); anal rays III,8; pectoral rays 17 to 19; third dorsal spine the longest, its length about 2.5 to 2.9 in head; interspinous membranes of dorsal fin deeply incised; posterior nostrils larger than anterior; light olive brown with a dark brown band running from snout through eye to origin of dorsal fin; two dark bands running from upper snout to nape; five somewhat irregular brown bars on body which may branch ventrally; a broad black saddle-like spot dorsally on caudal peduncle; black dots scattered around eye; fins except pelvics yellowish outwardly; inside of mouth red and white. Maximum weight reported as 55 pounds; however, the world angling record is 27 pounds, 8 ounces, from Bimini, Bahamas. Tropical western Atlantic, straying north to the Carolinas. One of the most important commer-cial fishes of the West Indies. The young are common in seagrass beds, and adults are primarily reef dwellers. Easily approached underwater. Large spawning aggregations have been reported during winter months at or near the time of new moon at various specific localities in the Caribbean, generally at 65 to 130 feet. Unfortunately, some of these populations have been essentially eliminated by overfishing. Effort should be made to preserve those that survive.

Comb Grouper

Mycteroperca acutirostris (Valenciennes, 1828). Figure 106

Dorsal rays XI, 15 to 17; anal rays III, 10 to 12; gill rakers 18 to 21 + 29 to 36 (all counted; none are obvious rudiments); caudal fin truncate in young, emarginate in larger indi-

Figure 106. Comb Grouper (*Mycteroperca acutirostris*), Bonaire.

viduals and concave in large adults; scales ctenoid; posterior nostrils larger than anterior in adults; body somewhat compressed, the width about 2.7 in depth; distinctively colored when young (see illustration), but adults less contrastingly marked. Largest Caribbean specimen, 27.5 inches. Known from Bermuda, northwestern Gulf of Mexico (where rare), Caribbean Sea and southern Brazil. The related *M. rubra* occurs in the eastern Atlantic and Mediterranean.

Black Grouper

Mycteroperca bonaci (Poey, 1861).
Figure 107

Dorsal rays XI,16 or 17 (usually 17); anal rays III,11 to 13; gill rakers 2 to 5 + 8 to 11. Similar to *venenosa*; differs in a slightly more elongate body on the average, the caudal fin usually truncate, usually one additional dorsal and anal ray, fewer developed gill rakers, and color, especially of the fins; the soft dorsal and anal fins have a broad outer blackish zone; a similar zone on caudal fin, followed by a narrow white margin; pectoral rays are brown, gradually becoming orange at the tips (there is no abrupt outer zone of yellow as on *venenosa*); gill rakers orange (pale pink on *venenosa* from shallow water). Frequently exceeds 50 pounds; maximum reported, 180 pounds, from Bermuda. Massachusetts and Bermuda to Brazil, including the Gulf of Mexico. Rare in Puerto Rico and the Virgin Islands but common in the Bahamas, Cuba, the Florida Keys and southern Caribbean.

Figure 107. Black Grouper (*Mycteroperca bonaci*), Belize.

White Grouper

Mycteroperca cidi Cervigon, 1966.

Figure 108

Dorsal rays XI, 14 to 17; anal rays III, 10 to 12; pectoral rays usually 16 (usually 17 on other species of *Mycteroperca* except *acutirostris*); gill rakers 9 to 13 + 18 to 23 (excluding rudiments); caudal fin slightly emarginate in young, more-or-less truncate in adults, with rays exserted; nostrils about equal in size below a length of about 1 foot (posterior nostrils become progressively larger than anterior with further growth); preopercular margin with an indentation above angle, as in *interstitialis, phenax* and *acutirostris;* individuals less than about 16 inches are greenish brown with irregular brown spots on sides of body; soft dorsal and anal fins with a white margin and broad dark submarginal zone; large individuals become plain light brown. Largest specimen, 3 feet 9 inches. Known from the coast of Venezuela and offshore islands where it is a common inshore species. Pale when first caught, giving rise to the common name "cuna blanca" (= white grouper).

Yellowmouth Grouper

Mycteroperca interstitialis (Poey, 1861).

Figure 109

Dorsal rays XI, 16 to 18; anal rays III, 11 or 12 (usually 12); gill rakers 4 to 6 + 11 to 15 (excluding rudiments); caudal fin distinctly emarginate, the rays exserted (tips of rays project beyond outline of fin); posterior nostrils of adults larger than anterior; corner of preopercle more angular than preceding species and with a distinct concave notch above; body slightly more compressed than previous species of the genus, the width about 2.5 in depth; light brownish gray with close-set

Figure 108. White Grouper (*Mycteroperca cidi*), 9.3 inches, Isla Cubagua, Venezuela.

Figure 109. Yellowmouth Grouper (*Mycteroperca interstitialis*), Andros, Bahamas.

small brown spots on upper half of body (some individuals nearly uniform brown); yellow around mouth; outer part of interspinous membranes of dorsal fin yellow. Largest reported, 27 inches, from Bermuda. Hook and line record, 8 pounds 2 ounces, from Tampa. Tropical western Atlantic; not common at most West Indian localities.

Scamp

Mycteroperca phenax Jordan & Swain, 1884. Figure 110

Dorsal rays XI, 15 to 18; anal rays III, 10 to 12 (usually 11); gill rakers 3 to 7 + 14 to 18 (excluding rudiments). Close to *interstitialis;* differs in the dorsal spines being more equal in height (tenth spine of *phenax* about 1.2 in fourth spine; tenth spine of *interstitialis* about 1.4 in fourth spine) and in color; the small brown spots on *phenax* occur on the fins and more ventrally on the body; also they are more inclined to join with others to form groups or short bands. Said to reach 2 feet in length. The world angling record is 28 pounds, from Port Canaveral, Florida. Massachusetts to the Gulf of Mexico and along the southern shore of the Caribbean Sea.

Tiger Grouper

Mycteroperca tigris (Valenciennes, 1833). Figure 111

Dorsal rays XI, 16 or 17; anal rays III, 10 or 11; gill rakers 2 or 3 + 5 to 9 (excluding rudiments); individuals larger than 20 inches with exserted caudal, soft dorsal and anal rays *(i.e.* ends of rays projecting, giving the fins a markedly irregular margin); posterior nostrils much

Figure 110. Scamp (*Mycteroperca phenax*), 10.8 inches, Isla de Margarita, Venezuela.

larger than anterior (in individuals larger than 8 inches); canine teeth notably large; about nine pale diagonal bars on back; head spotted and lower sides irregularly spotted. Small juveniles are bright yellow with a lengthwise black band (but diagonal pale bars still evident in the yellow of the back). Largest collected by the author, a 28-inch fish from Puerto Rico that weighed 13 pounds. The hook and line record is 11 pounds, 4 ounces, from Eleuthera, Bahamas. In Bermuda recorded to a length of nearly 40 inches. Known from Bermuda, Florida, the West Indies, southern Gulf of Mexico and Brazil.

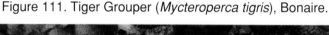

Figure 111. Tiger Grouper (*Mycteroperca tigris*), Bonaire.

Yellowfin Grouper

Mycteroperca venenosa (Linnaeus, 1758).
Figure 112

Dorsal rays XI,15 or 16; anal rays III,11; gill rakers 4 or 5 + 10 to 13 (excluding rudiments, *i.e.* those rakers broader than high); caudal fin slightly emarginate, the ends of the rays not projecting notably beyond margin of fin; nostrils about equal in size; scales mostly cycloid; preopercle broadly rounded, with only a very slight concavity above the angle; gray to olivaceous with subquadrate dark brown blotches arranged in approximate lengthwise rows; numerous small dark reddish or orange spots; posterior edge of pectoral fins abruptly and broadly orange-yellow. Reaches at least 3 feet in length. World record for hook and line, 34 pounds, 6 ounces, from Largo, Florida. Tropical western At-lantic. Its scientific name probably alludes to the toxic property of the flesh of occasional large individuals in regions where ciguatera is known.

Creole Fish

Paranthias furcifer (Valenciennes, 1828).
Figure 113

Dorsal rays IX,18 or 19, anal rays III,9; lateral-line scales 69 to 77; gill rakers 12 to 14 + 24 or 25; depth of body 3 to 3.4 in standard length; preopercular margin serrate; maxilla usually not reaching center of eye; caudal fin deeply forked; reddish brown, shading ventrally to pale salmon; a bright orange-red spot at upper base of pectoral fin; a series of three small widely-separated white spots along back above lateral line. Attains at least 10.5 inches. Littoral in the tropical Atlantic (the closely related *P. colonus*

Figure 112. Yellowfin Grouper (*Mycteroperca venenosa*), 70 feet deep, Conception Island, Bahamas.

Figure 113. Creole Fish (*Paranthias furcifer*), Bonaire.

occurs in the tropical and subtropical eastern Pacific). Common at depths of about 30 to at least 200 feet; usually seen as small schools several feet above reefs feeding on individual planktonic animals; with the approach of danger the fish descend to hide in the reefs.

SEABASSES AND HAMLETS
(SERRANINAE)

Some authors have regarded the various hamlets as color forms of a single species, *Hypoplectrus unicolor*. Although difficult to separate on any basis than color, they appear to be species. Evidence for this takes several lines. One is distribution. *H. gemma*, an apparent mimic of *Chromis cyanea*, occurs in southern Florida but not the West Indies. *H. indigo* and *H. gummigutta* do not range to the Lesser Antilles. Another distinction is ecological. *H. gummigutta*, for example, is usually found at depths of 100 feet or more.

Still another is behavioral. When the hamlets pair for spawning, the color of the pairs is nearly always the same. Phillip S. Lobel (pers. comm.) is recording the spawning sounds (which we cannot hear); his initial results suggest that he will be able to demonstrate different sounds for the different species.

Randall and Randall (1960) noted the superficial resemblance of the Yellowtail Hamlet *(Hypoplectrus chlorurus)* to the Yellowtail Damselfish *(Microspathodon chrysurus)* and suggested that the hamlet is mimicking the damselfish. In its guise of the harmless damselfish (which feeds mainly on benthic algae and detritus), the hamlet may be able to get closer to its prey of small crustaceans and fishes. Similarly, the Yellowbellied Hamlet *(H. aberrans)* and the Black Hamlet *(H. nigricans)* resemble adults of some of the damselfishes of the genus *Stegastes*.

Figure 114. Aguavina (*Diplectrum bivittatum*), 5 inches, Puerto Rico.

Aguavina

Diplectrum bivittatum (Cuvier, 1828).

Figure 114

Dorsal rays X,12; anal rays III,7; pectoral rays modally 15; lateral-line scales 54 to 75; preopercular margin with a single prominent lobe at angle, bearing large spines along its edge; second dorsal spine long, 1.2 to 1.6 in third spine; caudal fin slightly forked, the second upper principal ray often prolonged as a filament; upper half of body green-ish gray with two lengthwise dark stripes (or two irregular series of short double bars); cheek orangish with oblique pale blue lines; two blue-edged dark spots at upper edge of caudal base. Largest specimen, 6.5 inches. Florida, Gulf of Mexico, Caribbean Sea, and Brazil to 2°S. Occurs on sand or mud bottoms from the shore to depths of at least 350 feet. The related *D. radiale* from the southern Caribbean to Brazil (one record from the Virgin Islands

Figure 115. Sand Perch (*Diplectrum formosum*), 6.9 inches, Isla de Margarita, Venezuela.

Figure 116. Yellowbellied Hamlet (*Hypoplectrus aberrans*), 4.7 inches, St. John, Virgin Islands.

needs confirmation) differs in having modally 17 pectoral rays, a short second dorsal spine (1.7 to 2.1 in third spine) and in lacking a filament from the upper caudal fin lobe.

Sand Perch

Diplectrum formosum (Linnaeus, 1766).
Figure 115

Dorsal rays X,12; anal rays III,7; pectoral rays modally 16; lateral-line scales 46 to 55. Distinctive in having two prominent spinous lobes on the preopercular margin, one at the angle and one above; body with blackish bars and alternating bluish and orangish stripes. Reaches a length of 1 foot. Virginia to southern Brazil, possibly to Uruguay; known in the West Indies from Cuba, Bahamas, and islands of the southern Caribbean. Recorded from depths of 3 to 244 feet.

Yellowbellied Hamlet

Hypoplectrus aberrans (Poey, 1868).
Figure 116

Typical of the genus (see *H. puella*). Brown dorsally, with a bluish cast on the head, shading to yellow ventrally and posteriorly; fins yellow except spinous portion of dorsal which is bluish brown; lateral edge of pelvic fins usually blue; a faint dark spot often present on upper base of caudal peduncle; rarely a black spot may be seen on the snout. Occasional individuals are melanistic, the back and dorsal fin being darker and the yellow or orange color more restricted ventrally on the body. Largest, 4.8 inches. Florida Keys and Caribbean Sea, but not the Bahamas. Because of its similarity in color to adult damselfishes with yellow ventral color, such as *Stegastes planifrons*, this hamlet may be able to get closer to its prey.

Figure 117. Yellowtail Hamlet (*Hypoplectrus chlorurus*), Puerto Rico.

Yellowtail Hamlet

Hypoplectrus chlorurus (Cuvier, 1828).
Figure 117

Typical of the genus in morphology; dark brown, the caudal fin bright yellow. Attains 5 inches. West Indies, Venezuela and Texas. As noted above, this hamlet appears to be mimicking the Yellowtail Damselfish *(Microspathodon chrysurus).*

Golden Hamlet

Hypoplectrus gummigutta (Poey, 1852).
Figure 118

Similar to other species of the genus; depth 2.2 to 2.45 in standard length; pelvic fins usually not reaching anal fin, sometimes falling short of anus; brilliant orange-yellow with a large blue-edged black spot on snout. Attains 5 inches. Observed and collected by the author on only two occasions—at 130 feet in the Bahamas and 100 feet off the Dominican Republic. Otherwise known only from southern Florida, Cuba, Jamaica, and one individual from Puerto Rico.

Shy Hamlet

Hypoplectrus guttavarius (Poey, 1852).
Figure 119

Similar in morphology and size to *H. aberrans*; body and nape dark brown with a purplish iridescence; head, chest, abdomen and fins bright orange-yellow; a blue-edged black spot often present on snout; a blue line surrounding all but ventral part of eye, the anterior part extending ventrally across cheek. A rare species which has been taken only in the Florida Keys and six West Indian localities.

Indigo Hamlet

Hypoplectrus indigo (Poey, 1852).
Figure 120

Similar to *H. puella* and *unicolor,* differing in relatively short pelvic

Figure 118. Golden Hamlet (*Hypoplectrus gummigutta*), 5.1 inches, Dominican Republic.

Figure 119. Shy Hamlet (*Hypoplectrus guttavarius*), Bonaire.

Figure 120. Indigo Hamlet (*Hypoplectrus indigo*), Andros, Bahamas.

fins (usually just reaching anus or extending slightly beyond it) and color. Has the same basic barred pattern as *puella* but the overall color is mainly blue. Largest specimen, 5.5 inches. A rare species which has been collected only in Cuba, Haiti, Jamaica, the Bahamas, Florida and off Honduras. Observed by the author in the depth range of 40 to 130 feet.

Black Hamlet

Hypoplectrus nigricans (Poey, 1852).
Figure 121

Has the counts and basic body shape of the preceding species; differs in the long pelvic fins of adults (fins usually extend posterior to origin of anal fin and may reach base of fourth anal ray on some specimens), and in color. Typically dark bluish brown, the head and ventral part of the body more bluish. Reaches 6 inches. West Indies, where it is the largest species of the genus and moderately common in shallow water. May be a mimic of adults of the dark species of damselfishes of the genus *Stegastes*.

Barred Hamlet

Hypoplectrus puella (Cuvier, 1828).
Figure 122

Dorsal rays X,14 to 16; anal rays III,7; pectoral rays 14 (rarely 13); lateral-line scales 48 to 53; gill rakers 6 to 8 + 11 to 15; depth of body 2.1 to 2.43 in standard length; pelvic fins usually reaching origin of anal fin and occasionally to base of second anal spine; yellowish with a broad dark brown bar on front half of body which narrows ventrally, a smaller bar running from nape to and beyond pectoral base, and three narrow bars on posterior half of body; pale regions between bars

Figure 121. Black Hamlet (*Hypoplectrus nigricans*), Long Island, Bahamas.

Figure 122. Barred Hamlet (*Hypoplectrus puella*), Long Island, Bahamas.

with vertical blue lines; a dark bar running from eye to chest; a bright blue line encircling eye and continuing as an anterior border to dark bar below eye; bright blue spots on snout; three or four blue lines on operculum, one or two of which extend to chest; median fins yellowish, the soft portion of the dorsal with irregular diagonal blue lines. Small juveniles have two black spots at the caudal base, one above the other, with a squarish white blotch, edged in dusky, above each; larger juveniles develop a dark area anterior and adjacent to upper black caudal spot. Attains nearly 6 inches in west Florida but not quite 5 inches at Antillean localities. West Indies, Bermuda, Florida Keys and Gulf coast of Florida. The most common representative of the genus in the West Indies.

Butter Hamlet

Hypoplectrus unicolor (Walbaum, 1792).

Figures 95 & 123

Similar to *H. puella*, differing in the slightly deeper body on the average (depth 1.95 to 2.35 in standard length) and color; yellowish gray, shading nearly to white ventrally, with a large black spot dorsally on caudal peduncle; a blue-edged black spot may be present on snout; blue markings on head as in *puella*, and fin coloration similar. Attains 5 inches. Florida and the West Indies. The most common species of the genus in the Florida Keys but relatively rare in the West Indies.

Slide-Mouth Bass

Schultzea beta (Hildebrand, 1940).

Figure 124

Dorsal rays X, 11 or 12; pectoral rays 15 to 17; lateral-line scales 49

Figure 123. Butter Hamlet (*Hypoplectrus unicolor*), Bonaire.

Figure 124. Slide-Mouth Bass (*Schultzea beta*), 2.3 inches, Curaçao.

to 54; gill rakers 29 to 39; body moderately elongate, the depth 3.9 to 4.5 in standard length; maxilla narrowing posteriorly and not reaching center of eye (reaching or extending beyond center of eye in *Serranus*); upper jaw highly protrusible; orange-brown above, bluish silver below, with two orange stripes and irregular bars which are brownish above and orange below; caudal peduncle and fin largely yellow (the most conspicuous color marking when fish viewed underwater). Reaches 4 inches. Florida Keys and Caribbean Sea in from 80 feet to 350 feet. Occurs in small schools a foot or more above the bottom, but never far from the shelter of rock or coral.

Orangeback Bass

Serranus annularis (Günther, 1880).
Figure 125

Dorsal rays X,10 to 12 (usually 12); pectoral rays 13 or 14 (usually 13); lateral-line scales 46 to 50; fourth or fifth dorsal spines the longest, about 2.5 to 2.9 in head; lower edge of operculum smooth; caudal fin emarginate, the tips of the lobes of adults prolonged as filaments; orange or salmon on back, shading to white on sides, with seven pale orange-yellow bars on lower sides; two squarish blocks of orange or yellow on head behind eye, each outlined in black; a series of dark blotches or a broad blackish area anteriorly on body. Attains about 3.5 inches. Bermuda and the West Indies to Brazil. Common in the depth range of 100 to 200 feet, but rare at lesser depths.

Lantern Bass

Serranus baldwini (Evermann & Marsh, 1900).
Figure 126

Dorsal rays X,11 to 13 (usually 12); pectoral rays 13 to 15; lateral-line scales 42 to 48; third dorsal spine nearly as long as fourth, and

Figure 125. Orangeback Bass (*Serranus annularis*), Puerto Rico.

Figure 126. Lantern Bass (*Serranus baldwini*), Bonaire.

Figure 127. Vieja (*Serranus dewegeri*), 8.5 inches, Isla de Margarita, Venezuela.

fourth to tenth spines subequal, about 2.9 in head; lower edge of operculum smooth; white with lengthwise and vertical bands of red and yellow and rows of blackish spots, the most conspicuous being a row posteriorly on lower sides; in shallow water the species is not as brightly colored. Rarely exceeds 2.5 inches. Southern Florida and the Caribbean Sea from less than 2 to at least 240 feet. Often found in seagrass beds, but may be taken around rocks, coral rubble or old shells.

Vieja

Serranus dewegeri Metzelaar, 1919.
Figure 127
Dorsal rays X,13 or 14; pectoral rays 17; lateral-line scales 55 to 63; third or fourth dorsal spines notably the longest, 2 to 2.4 in head; lower edge of operculum serrate; yellowish gray shading on sides and ventrally to yellow; median fins and upper two-thirds of head and body with brownish orange spots; seven broad bars on body; a large dark spot at pectoral base with a dark band in front and behind. Largest specimen, 12.5 inches. Southern Caribbean. One of the most abundant inshore fishes of rocky bottom around islands off Venezuela.

Two-Spot Bass

Serranus flaviventris (Cuvier, 1829).
Figure 128
Dorsal rays X,12 or 13; pectoral rays 16 or 17; lateral-line scales 39 to 44; body moderately deep, the depth 2.7 to 3 in standard length (2.9 to 3.9 in standard length of other species of *Serranus* discussed herein); fourth or fifth dorsal spines the longest, 2.6 to 2.8 in head; lower edge of operculum smooth; indistinct brown streaks on body following scale rows; seven dark bars on body, the anterior ones broader, some extending into dorsal fin; a large white area on abdomen; two prominent black spots, one above the other, at base of caudal fin; head with small irregular orange-brown

Figure 128. Two-spot Bass (*Serranus flaviventris*), 2.5 inches, Puerto Rico.

markings. A specimen from Brazil is said to have been 7.7 inches long; however none from Puerto Rico have exceeded 3 inches. Caribbean Sea to Uruguay from depths of a few feet to 1320 feet. Not common. Apparently most often found in seagrass beds; has been taken on reefs, but not where the water is very clear.

Tobacco Fish

Serranus tabacarius (Cuvier, 1829).
Figure 129

Dorsal rays X, 12 (rarely 11); pectoral rays 15 (rarely 14); lateral-line scales 50 to 52; fourth or fifth dorsal spines the longest, 2.2 to 2.5 in head; lower edge of operculum finely serrate; light brownish orange with large pale blotches on back; each lobe of caudal fin with a broad lengthwise dark band. Attains 7 inches. Bermuda, southern Florida and throughout the West Indies; although it has been observed in as little as 15 feet, it is not common in less than about 60 feet.

Harlequin Bass

Serranus tigrinus (Bloch, 1790).
Figure 130

Dorsal rays X, 12; pectoral rays 14; lateral-line scales 48 to 51; fourth to tenth dorsal spines subequal, 2.6 to 3 in head; lower edge of operculum smooth; greenish on the back, shading to pale yellow ventrally, with about seven irregular dark brown or black bars on body; superimposed on this pattern are lengthwise rows of small dark blotches which become vertically elongate in adults; lower part of head and chest with dark blotches; median fins with small dark spots, the dorsal with a large black spot between third and fifth spines. Rarely exceeds 4 inches. Bermuda, southern Florida, the Bahamas and throughout the Caribbean. The most common species of the genus on West Indian reefs but nowhere abundant.

Figure 129. Tobacco Fish (*Serranus tabacarius*), Guadeloupe.

Figure 130. Harlequin Bass (*Serranus tigrinus*), Guadeloupe.

Figure 131. Chalk Bass (*Serranus tortugarum*), Bonaire.

Chalk Bass

Serranus tortugarum Longley, 1935.

Figure 131

Dorsal rays X, 12; pectoral rays 14 or 15; lateral-line scales 46 to 50; fourth or fifth dorsal spines the longest, 2.2 to 2.6 in head; lower edge of operculum serrate; orange-brown, shading to white below, with pale blue bars on upper part of body. Underwater the fish appears bright blue with black bars. Rarely exceeds 3 inches. Southern Florida and the West Indies in from 40 to 1300 feet. Lives over sand or silty sand bottoms. Often seen in small groups hovering over a patch of coral rubble or an old conch shell.

BASSLETS
(LIOPROPOMINAE)

Candy Basslet

Liopropoma carmabi (Randall, 1963).

Figure 132

Dorsal rays VI-I-I, 12 or 13; depth of body 2.9 to 3.3 in standard length; snout 4.7 to 5 in head; head, body, and caudal fin alternately striped with yellow-orange and lavender (the lavender becoming blue posteriorly in caudal fin), these stripes separated by red lines; a large blue-edged black spot at each posterior corner of caudal fin; a similar spot in soft dorsal fin, but none in anal fin. Attains 2 inches. Known from reefs of Curaçao, Bonaire, Puerto Rico, Barbados and the Bahamas at depths of 45 to 200 feet.

Figure 132. Candy Basslet (*Liopropoma carmabi*), 1.6 inches, Curaçao.

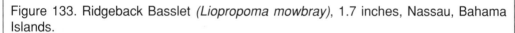

Figure 133. Ridgeback Basslet *(Liopropoma mowbray)*, 1.7 inches, Nassau, Bahama Islands.

Ridgeback Basslet

Liopropoma mowbrayi Woods & Kanazawa, 1951. Figure 133

Dorsal rays VI-I-I,12; depth of body 3.3 to 3.9 in standard length; snout relatively long, as in *rubre;* salmon to deep red or reddish gray; a yellow band from tip of snout and chin to eye; caudal fin with a whitish posterior margin and a broad submarginal zone of black; black spot in soft dorsal fin. Reaches 3.3 inches. Bermuda, Bahamas, Curaçao and Puerto Rico in from 100 to 180 feet where it is a common reef fish.

Swissguard Basslet

Liopropoma rubre Poey, 1861. Figure 134

Dorsal rays VI-I-I,12; seventh dorsal spine the shortest, not linked by a membrane to sixth or eighth; depth of body 3 to 3.7 (usually 3.2 to 3.5) in standard length; snout 3.7 to 4.6 in head; no serrations on preopercle; head, body, and caudal fin alternately striped with dark reddish brown and light pinkish tan, the tan bands bisected by a yellowish green line; black spot on anal fin, and two on caudal fin which are connected medially. Largest specimen, 3.25 inches. Florida, Yucatan, Venezuela and the West Indies; collected by the author in from 10 to 140 feet. Common, but rarely seen underwater; lives deep in the recesses of reefs.

SOAPFISHES
(GRAMMISTINAE)

The soapfishes are named for their ability to secrete copious quantities of mucus, especially under stress.

Figure 134. Swissguard Basslet (*Liopropoma rubre*), 2.9 inches, St. John, Virgin Islands.

This contains a toxic substance, grammistin, which serves to repel predators.

Although some authors have classified these fishes as a separate family, most now regard them as a subfamily of the Serranidae. They are characterized by having a flap of skin connecting the upper end of the operculum to the body, small pelvic fins which are inserted anterior to the pectoral fins, a large mouth with projecting lower jaw, small villiform teeth, two or three spines on opercle and one to four on preopercle, nasal organ vertically elongate (made up of a number of parallel longitudinal lamellae) and caudal fin rounded.

The only New World genus, *Rypticus*, is represented by eight species in the western Atlantic. The largest species and the one most commonly encountered on reefs is discussed below.

Another subfamily, the Pseudogrammatinae, is known in the Caribbean from only a single small cryptic species, *Pseudogramma gregoryi* (*P. bermudensis* is a synonym).

Soapfish

Rypticus saponaceus (Bloch & Schneider, 1801). Figure 135

Dorsal rays III,23 to 25; depth of body 3 to 3.3 in standard length; three well-developed spines on opercle and two on upper margin of preopercle; dorsal and anal fins very fleshy basally, especially in adults; cycloid scales, embedded in adults; anterior nostrils in a short tube; gray or brownish gray, often with a fine dark linear pattern which becomes reticulate on fins; pale spots about the size of the pupil or smaller on body and some on dorsal fin, many of

Figure 135. Soapfish (*Rypticus saponaceus*), Bonaire.

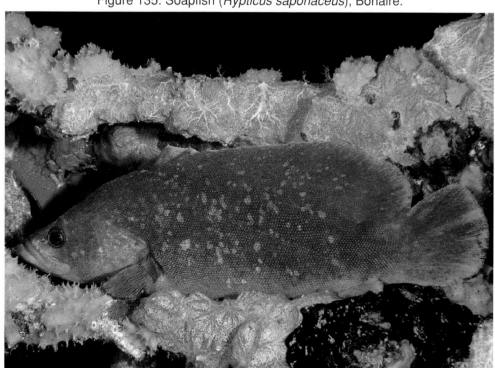

these spots merging; a pale mid-dorsal band often present on head, particularly in young. Largest collected by author, 11 inches, from Venezuela. Recorded to 12 inches from West Africa. Tropical Atlantic. *R. subbifrenatus* and *R. bistrispinus* are smaller species which may be collected from reefs but are rarely observed; the former is olivaceous to brown with scattered black spots smaller than the pupil (smaller and fewer in number on adults); the latter is covered with numerous small close-set spots which are notably darker on the upper half of head and body, and it has three upper preopercular spines.

FAIRY BASSLETS
(GRAMMATIDAE)

The grammatids are small colorful reef fishes which are closely related to the Serranidae. They differ in having an interrupted lateral line (upper anterior part ends beneath soft portion of dorsal fin; posterior part begins below end of upper and runs mid-laterally to caudal base) or none at all. They have a single continuous dorsal fin of XI to XIII spines with no prominent notches in the membranes between the spines. The pelvic fins of I,5 rays are below or slightly anterior to the pectoral fins.

Nine species are known from the tropical western Atlantic, three in the genus *Gramma* and six in *Lipogramma*. Species of the latter genus are distinctive in having no lateral line, no spines on opercle or serrations on preopercle, and long filamentous pelvic fins; they are very small (less than 2 inches) and are known only from the depth range of 60 to 860 feet.

Figure 136. Fairy Basslet (*Gramma loreto*), Bonaire.

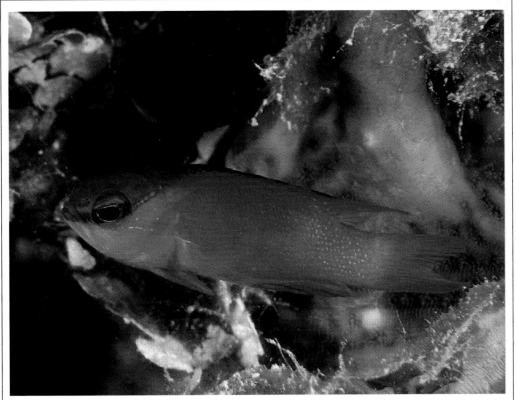

Figure 137. Blackcap Basslet (*Gramma melacara*), Long Island, Bahamas.

Fairy Basslet

Gramma loreto Poey, 1868.   Figure 136

Dorsal rays usually XII,10; pectoral rays 15 or 16; pelvic fins moderate, their length 1.9 to 3.2 in standard length; front half of fish purple or violet, the back half bright yellow; two golden streaks on head; a black spot at front of dorsal fin. Reaches a total length of slightly more than 3 inches. Bermuda, West Indies and western Caribbean. Taken at depths of a few feet to 200 feet. Commonly found in caves or beneath ledges; orients ventrally to the substratum, thus under ledges is seen upside down; hides in small holes when frightened. A lovely fish, highly prized in the aquarium trade. Sometimes called the "Royal Gramma."

Blackcap Basslet

Gramma melacara Böhlke & Randall, 1963.   Figure 137

Dorsal rays usually XIII,9; pectoral rays 17 or 18; pelvic fins short, their length 3.5 to 3.9 in standard length; magenta except upper part of head and nape which are abruptly black, this color continuing onto dorsal fin; a few gold lines on head, and faint gold dots on body. Attains nearly 4 inches in length. Known thus far only from the Bahamas and off British Honduras; occurs at depths of 35 to at least 200 feet, but rare in less than 80 feet; appears to be the most common fish on steeply inclined reef fronts of the Bahamas at depths greater than about 150 feet.

SNOOKS AND THEIR ALLIES
(CENTROPOMIDAE)

The snooks, or robalos, consist of the single genus *Centropomus* which is found only in American waters. They have two dorsal fins, the first of VIII spines. The head is long and pointed, the upper profile straight or concave. The lateral line extends to the end of the caudal fin. There are no spines on the opercle; the preopercle is double-edged, the posterior edge with coarse serrae. The teeth are villiform.

Snooks are most often found in mangrove sloughs and river mouths. Four species are known from the Caribbean, and a fifth was recently described from the southern Gulf of Mexico. The largest and most common species, *C. undecimalis*, is occasionally seen in reef areas near mangroves.

Snook

Centropomus undecimalis (Bloch, 1792).
Figure 138
Dorsal rays VIII-I,10; anal rays III,6; lateral-line scales 69 to 80; lower-limb gill rakers 7 to 9 (excluding rudiments); pelvic fins not reaching anus; lower edge of preorbital bone weakly serrate in young, smooth in adults; silvery on sides and ventrally, the lateral line black. The world record for hook and line is a 53-pound, 10-ounce fish caught at Parismina Ranch, Costa Rica. *C. undecimalis* occurs in the Atlantic from South Carolina to Rio de Janeiro. A question exists as to whether to regard the form in the eastern Pacific as the same or to apply its oldest name there, *C. nigrescens*. In the Pacific the species is reported to have slightly lower scale counts and slightly higher gill-raker counts than in the Atlantic. A very popular game fish.

BIGEYES
(PRIACANTHIDAE)

The bigeyes, also known as catalufas, have large eyes, a very oblique mouth with projecting lower jaw, a single dorsal fin (with X dor-

Figure 138. Snook (*Centropomus undecimalis*), 10.5 inches, Puerto Rico.

sal spines in western Atlantic species), small conical teeth in a narrow band in the jaws, and on vomer and palatines, small rough scales of unusual structure, head entirely scaled (including maxilla) and large pelvic fins of I,5 rays inserted in advance of pectoral fins and broadly joined to the body by a membrane.

Priacanthids are primarily red. Their color and large eyes are suggestive of nocturnal habits, and this has been attributed to these fishes by several authors. These fishes are not entirely nocturnal, however, for their stomachs often contain fresh food items during daylight hours. The bigeyes are carnivorous, feeding primarily on small fishes, various crustaceans and polychaete worms; often their food is from the zooplankton. They are easily approached underwater, hence easily speared.

There are four western Atlantic species. Not discussed below are the Short Bigeye *(Pseudopriacanthus altus)*, which would not be expected to occur in water less than 100 feet, and the bull-eye *(Cookeolus japonicus)* with a depth range that begins at about 600 feet.

Glasseye

Heteropriacanthus cruentatus (Lacepède, 1801).   Figure 139

Dorsal rays X, 13; anal rays III, 14; lateral-line scales 54 to 63; gill rakers 5 + 16 to 19; depth of body 2.3 to 2.6 in standard length; pelvic fins about 1.5 in head; preopercular spine well developed, nearly reaching border of opercle; color varying from deep red to mottled silvery pink and red; small dark spots usually visible on caudal fin and soft portions of dorsal and anal fins. Attains about 1 foot in length. Circumtropical. A common shallow-

Figure 139. Glasseye (*Heteropriacanthus cruentatus*), St. Croix, Virgin Islands.

water reef fish but not often seen because it tends to hide in cracks and caves by day.

Bigeye

Priacanthus arenatus Cuvier, 1829.

Figure 140

Dorsal rays X,13 to 15 (usually 14); anal rays III,14 to 16; lateral-line scales 61 to 73; gill rakers 6 to 8 + 21 to 26; depth of body 2.5 to 3 in standard length; pelvic fins about 1.2 in head; usual color bright red; pelvic membranes dusky, especially outwardly. Reaches about 16 inches. Both sides of the tropical Atlantic. Moderately common in the Caribbean area, but not often observed at depths of less than about 50 feet. Usually encountered in small schools over reefs.

BOGAS
(INERMIDAE)

The bogas are small slender plankton-feeding fishes that are usually seen in schools off the bottom, often over reefs. They have an oblique mouth with the lower jaw longer or equal to the upper; the premaxilla is very protractile (hence the upper jaw very protrusible), the upper median process reaching to or even beyond the orbits. The scales are ctenoid; the head is scaled except for the snout and jaws; there is a scaly sheath along the base of the soft-rayed portions of the dorsal and anal fins which on the two species below, at least, extends out over the last few rays. The spinous dorsal fin is continuous with the

Figure 140. Bigeye (*Priacanthus arenatus*), 10.6 inches, St. John, Virgin Islands.

Figure 141. Boga (*Inermia vittata*), Bonaire.

soft dorsal or separate, the spines ranging in number from VII to XVII; the caudal fin is emarginate to deeply forked. The gill rakers are numerous.

There are two West Indian species of the family. Neither is common in shallow water.

Bogita

Emmelichthyops atlanticus Schultz, 1945.
Figure 142

Dorsal rays X-I, 10 or 11 (the two fins well separated); anal rays II, 10 or 11; pectoral rays 18 or 19; lateral-line scales about 75; slightly more slender on the average than

Figure 142. Bogita (*Emmelichthyops atlanticus*), 3.9 inches, Berry Islands, Bahama Islands.

Inermia vittata; yellowish gray (a little bluish anteriorly), becoming silvery white on sides, with four (juveniles with three) brown stripes on upper half of body (one of which is mid-dorsal) which are more evident anteriorly. Attains 4.5 inches. West Indies. Collected by the author in the Bahamas, Virgin Islands, Barbados and Tobago in from 10 to 140 feet. Also reported from north of Yucatan and east of Honduras at depths to 300 feet. Usually seen in small aggregations above coral heads; not common.

Boga

Inermia vittata Poey, 1861.

Figures 141 & 143

Dorsal rays XIV-I, 10 (the two fins close together); anal rays II,9; pectoral rays 19 or 20; lateral-line scales about 80; body fusiform, the depth about 4.5 to 5 in standard length; blue dorsally, becoming bluish silver on the sides, with three narrow dark stripes on the back (one being the pigmented lateral line) and a fourth, slightly broader stripe mid-laterally on body; snout yellowish; lobes of caudal fin with broad blackish bands, the upper and lower edges whitish. Attains about 9 inches. Bermuda and West Indies. Most commonly found as schools at depths of 50 feet or more in the clear blue water over outer reef areas. Feeds on mid-water zooplankton, for which the highly protrusible mouth is well adapted.

CARDINALFISHES
(APOGONIDAE)

These small fishes have two well-developed dorsal fins, large eyes, a double-edged preopercle, and a moderately large mouth with oblique cleft. They are carnivorous, nocturnal and mostly reef-dwelling. Many are red or bronze in color.

Figure 143. Boga (*Inermia vittata*), 6.1 inches, Curaçao.

Figure 144. Flamefish (*Apogon maculatus*), night photo, St. Croix, Virgin Islands.

Characteristically, the males incubate the eggs in the mouth.

Twenty shallow-water species are known from the western Atlantic, most of which occur in the Caribbean. All share the following counts: dorsal rays VI-I,9; anal rays II,8; lateral-line scales 23 to 25.

Although these fishes may be abundant, they are rarely seen by the average underwater observer. They are small (all less than 4 inches, and most less than 2.5 inches) and are secretive by day, hiding in the interstices of reefs or in burrows or empty shells. Nine of the more common species are discussed in separate accounts below.

Barred Cardinalfish

Apogon binotatus (Poey, 1867). Figure 145

Lower-limb gill rakers 12 to 14; scales around narrowest part of caudal peduncle 15 or 16; posterior

edge of preopercle serrate, without a protruding membranous lower lobe; teeth in villiform bands in jaws, none enlarged; body moderately elongate, the depth 3.0 to 3.3 in standard length; pink to light red, often with a suffusion of yellow on side, with two narrow black bars of about equal width, one posteriorly on caudal peduncle and the other linking rear portions of second dorsal and anal fins. Reaches 4 inches. Bermuda, Bahamas, southern Florida and the Caribbean Sea; collected by the author in the West Indies at depths ranging from 2 to 160 feet. The second bar is always notably broader in other species with two posterior dark bars.

Whitestar Cardinalfish

Apogon lachneri Böhlke, 1959. Figure 146

Lower-limb gill rakers 16 or 17; posterior margin of preopercle ser-

Figure 145. Barred Cardinalfish (*Apogon binotatus*), night photo, Bonaire.

Figure 146. Whitestar Cardinalfish (*Apogon lachneri*), night photo, Belize.

rate, without a lower membranous lobe; villiform teeth in bands in jaws, none enlarged; body depth 2.8 to 3.2 in standard length; eye large, 2.7 to 2.8 in head; first dorsal spine short, 3.5 to 4.0 in length of second spine; red with a short transverse black band dorsally on caudal peduncle behind base of second dorsal fin, followed by a brilliant white spot; first dorsal fin with a large dusky area; second dorsal and anal fins with a distal dusky patch. A small species, rarely exceeding 2.5 inches in length. Known from the Bahamas and southern Florida to Curaçao. The most common cardinalfish at dropoffs on reefs off Belize and Honduras, with its greatest abundance at depths of 80 to 86 feet.

Flamefish

Apogon maculatus (Poey, 1861).
Figures 144 & 147

Lower-limb gill rakers 13 or 14; scales around caudal peduncle 19 or 20; posterior margin of preopercle serrate, without a lower membranous lobe; villiform teeth in bands in jaws, none enlarged; body depth about 2.7 in standard length; red to dusky red with a round black spot beneath rear of second dorsal fin and a broad blackish saddle-like bar on caudal peduncle (may be faint on large individuals); a longitudinal dusky band on head behind eye, ending in a blackish spot on operculum; two horizontal white lines through eye. Attains a maximum length of about 4 inches. Reported from New England south to Brazil and throughout the West Indies; occurs in a variety of inshore habitats. The similar *A. pseudomaculatus* has a black spot on the caudal peduncle instead of a dark bar and 15 or 16 circumpe duncular scales.

Figure 147. Flamefish (*Apogon maculatus*), 2.3 inches, Puerto Rico.

Mimic Cardinalfish

Apogon phenax Böhlke & Randall, 1968.
Figure 148

Lower-limb gill rakers 13 or 14; circumpeduncular scales 12 or 13 (rarely 13); posterior margin of preopercle serrate, without a protruding membranous lower lobe; dorsal profile of head nearly straight; teeth in villiform bands in jaws, none enlarged; body depth 2.8 to 2.9 in standard length; light red with two posterior dark brown bars, the first linking rear base of second dorsal and anal fins, and the broader second posteriorly on caudal peduncle; a narrow light red band at base of dorsal and anal fins. Reaches about 3 inches. Florida Keys, Bahamas and Caribbean Sea. *A. planifrons* is similar in color but has 15 or 16 circumpeduncular scales. Also similar, *A. robinsi* has 16-18 lower-limb gill rakers and more pointed caudal lobes and second dorsal and anal fins.

Sawcheek Cardinalfish

Apogon quadrisquamatus Longley, 1934.
Figure 149

Lower-limb gill rakers 12 to 14 (rarely 12); circumpeduncular scales 16 to 18; median predorsal scales 3 to 5 (usually 4); posterior pre opercular margin coarsely serrate, without a protruding lower membranous lobe; teeth in villiform bands in jaws, none enlarged; body depth about 2.7 in standard length; eye large; pelvic fins joined by membrane to abdomen along less than half of median edge; translucent red, some individuals with dusky stripes following scale rows; a large dusky spot may be present posteriorly on side of caudal peduncle; fins

Figure 148. Mimic Cardinalfish (*Apogon phenax*), Roatan, Honduras.

Figure 149. Sawcheek Cardinalfish (*Apogon quadrisquamatus*), Bonaire.

yellowish. Reaches 2.5 inches. Occurs in Florida, Bahamas and Caribbean Sea. As noted in Figure 149, it may hide among the tentacles of a sea anemone. The related *A. aurolineatus* has 11 or 12 lower-limb gill rakers, 5 or 6 median predorsal scales, and two short dusky lines extending posteriorly from the eye.

Belted Cardinalfish

Apogon townsendi Breder, 1927.
Figure 150
Lower-limb gill rakers 16 to 18; median predorsal scales 6; posterior preopercular margin serrate, without a protruding membraneous lower lobe; teeth in villiform bands in jaws, none enlarged; body depth about 3.0 in standard length; eye large; translucent red, shading to golden over lower head and abdomen, with a narrow black bar link-

ing posterior bases of second dorsal and anal fins, and a broad black-edged dusky bar posteriorly on caudal peduncle. Attains 2.5 inches. Southern Florida and Bahamas to the Caribbean Sea. The most common cardinalfish in the spur and groove habitat (depth about 5 to 10 feet) at reefs of Belize and Honduras.

Conchfish

Astrapogon stellatus (Cope, 1869).
Figure 151
Pectoral rays usually 15 (West Indian species of *Apogon* have 12); lower-limb gill rakers 10 or 12; scales cycloid (ctenoid on *Apogon*); no median predorsal scales; posterior margin of preopercle smooth; pelvic fins long, reaching posterior to mid-base of anal fin; snout 3.8 to 4.8 in head; brown, the edge of the scales pale, with a few small dark spots

Figure 150. Belted Cardinalfish (*Apogon townsendi*), night photo, St. Croix, Virgin Islands.

Figure 151. Conchfish (*Astrapogon stellatus*), 2.1 inches, St. John, Virgin Islands.

Figure 152. Freckled Cardinalfish (*Phaeoptyx conklini*), 2.1 inches, Puerto Rico.

arranged mostly in three rows; anterior part of body and posterior head primarily silvery; three or four dusky bands radiating from posterior half of eye; pelvics blackish. Reaches slightly more than 2 inches. Tropical western Atlantic. Lives as a commensal in the mantle cavity of the Queen Conch (*Strombus gigas*). *A. puncticulatus* is very similar, differing in a shorter snout (4.5 to 6.2 in head), usually 16 pectoral rays, and usually 12 or 13 lower-limb gill rakers. A third species of the genus, *A. alutus*, has shorter pelvic fins (not reaching beyond base of second anal soft ray), and usually 14 pectoral rays.

Freckled Cardinalfish

Phaeoptyx conklini (Silvester, 1915).
Figure 152
Pectoral rays usually 11; lower-limb gill rakers 14 to 16; circumpeduncular scales 12; poste-rior margin of preopercle serrate, the lower part with a membranous lobe which extends distinctly posterior to rest of margin; villiform teeth in bands in jaws, none enlarged; eye large; pelvic fins joined by membrane to abdomen along their entire medial edge; translucent coppery, with iridescence; enlarged dark pigment cells on body produce a freckled effect; a basal blackish band on second dorsal and anal fins separated by a narrow pale zone from fin bases; a vertically elongate blackish blotch at caudal-fin base; often a diagonal dark streak running posteroventrally from eye. Attains slightly more than 2 inches. Occurs throughout the West Indian region; the most common cardinalfish at rocky and patch reef habitats (depths of about 20 to 40 feet) at reefs off Belize and Honduras.

Figure 153. Dusky Cardinalfish (*Phaeoptyx pigmentaria*), night photo, Belize.

Dusky Cardinalfish

Phaeoptyx pigmentaria (Poey, 1860).

Figure 153

Pectoral rays usually 12; lower-limb gill rakers 11 to 13; circumpeduncular scales 16; posterior margin of preopercle serrate, the lower part with a membranous lobe which extends posterior to rest of margin; villiform teeth in bands in jaws, some teeth at front of upper jaw and along the side of lower jaw enlarged; eye of moderate size; pelvic fins joined to abdomen along their entire medial edge; color similar to *P. conklini*, but pigment spots smaller, and no dark band at base of second dorsal and anal fins. Attains nearly 3 inches. Widespread in the Bahamas and throughout the Caribbean. A third species of the genus, *P. xena*, is commensal in sponges; it is intermediate in eye size, gill-raker count (those on lower limb 12 to 15), and in color to *P. conklini* and *P. pigmentaria*.

SAND TILEFISHES
(MALACANTHIDAE)

The Sand Tilefishes may be characterized externally as follows: body elongate, lips moderately fleshy; maxilla exposed on cheek; no teeth on roof of mouth; scales small and ctenoid, none on dorsal and anal fins; dorsal fin long and continuous, not deeply notched, the base of the spinous portion much shorter than the soft; anal fin with I or II spines.

The related family Latilidae (Branchiostegidae), sometimes regarded as a subfamily, is represented in the Caribbean area by two genera, *Caulolatilus* and *Lopholatilus*, the species of which are found in relatively deep water.

Figure 154. Sand Tilefish (*Malacanthus plumieri*), juvenile, Belize.

Figure 155. Sand Tilefish (*Malacanthus plumieri*), St. Croix, Virgin Islands.

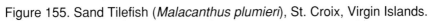

Sand Tilefish

Malacanthus plumieri (Bloch, 1787).
Figures 154 & 155

Dorsal rays IV or V,53 to 57; anal rays I,50 to 52; lateral-line scales 140 to 144; body elongate, the depth 6 to 7 in standard length; snout long, nearly half the length of head; mouth nearly horizontal, the maxilla ending in front of eye; moderately long curved canine teeth at front of upper jaw, side of lower jaw, and one posteriorly on each jaw; a single stout spine on opercle; preopercle smooth; caudal fin lunate; light bluish gray, the dorsal and anal fins yellowish, especially outwardly; lavender and light yellow markings on head; caudal fin with lobes orange, the median part of fin and margins dusky, and a pale crescent posteriorly. Attains about 2 feet. Bermuda and South Caro-

lina to Brazil; also known from Ascension Island. Common in the West Indies. Lives over sand bottoms, but often near reefs, and usually at depths greater than 30 feet. When frightened, it seeks out a burrow of its own construction which it enters head-first. Feeds on many different kinds of invertebrate animals and fishes. Takes a hook readily. Prone to bite when handled.

HAWKFISHES
(CIRRHITIDAE)

Redspotted Hawkfish

Amblycirrhitus pinos (Mowbray, 1927).
Figure 156

Dorsal rays X,11; anal rays III,6; pectoral rays 14, the lower five unbranched and enlarged, the membranes deeply incised; lateral-line scales 41 to 44; a tuft of cirri from

Figure 156. Redspotted Hawkfish (*Amblycirrhitus pinos*), 2.7 inches, St. John, Virgin Islands.

membrane near tip of each dorsal spine; body with five broad dark bars, the first three yellowish brown, the upper rounded part of the fourth black and the fifth (across caudal peduncle) black; white interspaces between first four dark bars bisected by narrow yellowish brown bars; head, anterior part of body and dorsal fin with bright orange-red dots. Reaches 3.3 inches. A single species of the family in the tropical western Atlantic. Bottom-dwelling on hard substratum; not uncommon.

MULLETS
(MUGILIDAE)

The mullets are thick-bodied blunt-snouted fishes which are dark on the back and silvery on the sides. They have two short-based dorsal fins, the first of IV spines; the pelvic fins of I,5 rays are abdominal in position. The mouth is shaped like an inverted "V" when viewed from the front; the teeth are minute.

Most mugilids have a thick-walled gizzard-like stomach and a very long intestine. They feed primarily on fine algal and detrital material from the surface of bottom sediments. Mullets are more characteristic of brackish water than sea water of full salinity; however the young of several species may be found along clear-water sandy shores, and occasional small schools of adults, particularly *Mugil curema*, may also be observed in such an environment.

White Mullet

Mugil curema Valenciennes, 1836.
Figures 157 & 158
Dorsal rays IV-I,8; anal rays III,9; scales 33 to 41; soft dorsal and anal

Figure 157. White Mullet (*Mugil curema*), Bonaire.

Figure 158. White Mullet (*Mugil curema*), 10.3 inches, Puerto Rico.

fins densely scaled; adipose eyelid present; dark greenish or bluish above, silvery on sides, with no dark stripes; axil and upper part of pectoral base deep bluish; opercle brassy; posterior margin of caudal fin often dusky. Attains 15 inches. Known from both coasts of the Americas; in the Atlantic from Massachusetts to Brazil. The most common mullet in the West Indies.

BARRACUDAS
(SPHYRAENIDAE)

The barracudas are elongate with cylindrical bodies, small scales, two

Figure 159. Southern Sennet (*Sphyraena picudilla*), St. Croix, Virgin Islands.

widely separated dorsal fins (the first of V spines and the second with the ray formula I,9), few or no gill rakers, a well-developed lateral line, a pointed head with lower jaw projecting and long sharp-edged teeth.

Once in the same suborder as the mullets, barracudas are now grouped with the scombroid fishes (mackerels and tunas).

All barracudas are classified in the genus *Sphyraena*. Three species are known from the Caribbean; *S. guachancho* is generally found in turbid water along silty shores; it has 7 or 8 anal soft rays, 108 to 122 lateral-line scales, and the last dorsal and anal rays somewhat prolonged.

The Great Barracuda, *S. barracuda*, may be poisonous to eat and has been known to attack man.

Great Barracuda

Sphyraena barracuda (Walbaum, 1792).
Figures 160 & 161

Anal rays II,7 or 8; lateral-line scales 75 to 87; interorbital space flat to slightly concave; dark green to gray on back, silvery on side, with several to many black blotches on lower side, variable in size and position. Probably does not exceed 6 feet, in spite of unauthenticated reports to the contrary. The world's record on hook and line is a 5.5-foot fish taken in the Bahamas that weighed 103 pounds. Occurs in all tropical seas except the eastern Pacific; in the western Atlantic known from Massachusetts to Rio de Janeiro. Large individuals are responsible for more cases of ciguatera in Florida and the Caribbean Sea than any other fish (see Intro-

Figure 160. Juvenile Great Barracuda (*Sphyraena barracuda*), in mangroves, Belize.

Figure 161. Great Barracuda (*Sphyraena barracuda*), Long Island, Bahamas.

duction). Feeds mainly on fishes. When the prey is relatively large, the barracuda may slash it in two pieces and swim back to retrieve them. About 30 cases are known of attacks on humans. Nearly all have occurred in murky water (presumably when a barracuda might have mistaken a bather's limb for a fish) or when the fish was provoked, as by spearing.

Southern Sennet

Sphyraena picudilla Poey, 1860.
Figures 159 & 162
Anal rays II,9; lateral-line scales 113 to 133; interorbital space slightly convex; last rays of soft dorsal and anal fins not notably longer than penultimate rays (in contrast to *S. guachancho* whose last dorsal and anal rays are 1.4 to 2 times longer than penultimate rays); dusky blue on back, shading to silvery white on sides and ventrally, with two lengthwise dusky yellow bands. A small schooling species which probably does not greatly exceed 18 inches. Bermuda, Florida, Gulf of Mexico and West Indies south to Uruguay.

Figure 162. Southern Sennet (*Sphyraena picudilla*), 14.3 inches, St. John, Virgin Islands.

THREADFINS
(POLYNEMIDAE)

Threadfins are adapted for life on mud or sand bottoms. The lower pectoral rays, which are separate and thread-like, can be brought in contact with the bottom and probably serve both tactile and chemoreceptor functions. The mouth is not large and is ventral in position; the teeth are small and occur in many close-set rows; an adipose eyelid is present; the upper margin of the preopercle is serrate. The usual color is dull silvery. Either of the two Caribbean species may be observed on sand flats near reefs.

Smallscale Threadfin

Polydactylus oligodon (Günther, 1860).

Figure 163

Dorsal rays VIII-I,12; anal rays III,14; pectoral rays 16 + 7; lateral-line scales 68 to 74; anal fin base 4.4 to 4.8 in standard length; posterior edge of maxilla rounded. Larg-

Figure 163. Smallscale Threadfin (*Polydactylus oligodon*), 16 inches, 1.5 pounds, Trinidad.

Figure 164. Barbu (*Polydactylus virginicus*), 10 inches, Puerto Rico.

est collected by the author, 16 inches, from Trinidad. Known also from Florida, Bahamas, Jamaica and Brazil.

Barbu

Polydactylus virginicus (Linnaeus, 1758).
Figure 164

Dorsal rays VIII-I,11; anal rays III, 12 to 14; pectoral rays 15 + 7; lateral-line scales 53 to 65; anal fin base 5.2 to 5.8 in standard length; posterior edge of maxilla truncate or slightly indented. Probably does not exceed 1 foot in length. Chesapeake Bay to Brazil; common in the West Indies.

COBIA FAMILY
(RACHYCENTRIDAE)

Cobia

Rachycentron canadum (Linnaeus, 1766).
Figure 165

Dorsal rays VIII or IX-I,27 to 33; anal rays II,23 to 27; dorsal and anal spines very short and not connected by membranes; soft portion of these fins moderately elevated; body elongate and only slightly compressed; head broad; teeth small, in bands on jaws, vomer, palatines and tongue; caudal fin truncate in young, deeply emarginate in adults; dark olive brown on back, abruptly pale brown on sides with a broad dark brown midlateral stripe. The world record on hook and line is a 5-foot 10-inch fish from Virginia that weighed 102 pounds. Found in all warm seas; in the W. Atlantic from Massachusetts to Argentina. Rare in the West Indies. Not uncommon in coastal continental waters, but infrequently seen in clear-water reef areas. One of its common names is "Crab-eater," in reference to heavy feeding on crabs; it also feeds on shrimps, fishes and squids.

REMORAS
(ECHENEIDAE)

The remoras are unmistakable in their possession of a unique sucking disc on the top of the head with which they attach to other fishes,

Figure 165. Cobia (*Rachycentron canadum*), 22.3 inches, 3.8 pounds, Trinidad.

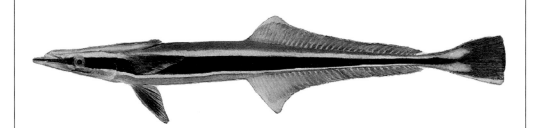

Figure 166. Sharksucker (*Echeneis naucrates*), 12.6 inches, St. John, Virgin Islands.

sea turtles and aquatic mammals. There is no spinous dorsal fin; the disc is believed to be derived from this fin, perhaps from an ancestor similar to the cobia. Eight wideranging species are known in the family, all but one of which have been recorded from the Caribbean region.

The host animals for most of the species are pelagic. *Remora osteochir,* for example, lives primarily on billfishes, *R. australis* on whales and porpoises, and the usual habitat for *Remorina albescens* is the gill chamber or mouth of manta rays. Remoras may feed on zooplankton or the smaller nekton, take scraps from their hosts' meals or remove their hosts' ectoparasites.

Sharksucker

Echeneis naucrates Linnaeus, 1758.

Figure 166

Dorsal rays 33 to 45; anal rays 31 to 41; pectoral rays 20 to 26; lowerlimb gill rakers 10 to 17; disc laminae 21 to 27; body elongate, the depth about 8 to 13 in standard length (larger individuals are more robust); pectoral fins pointed; middle rays of caudal fin of young prolonged; fin of adults deeply emarginate; a black lateral stripe running from tip of the protruding lower jaw through eye to base of caudal fin, this stripe usually bordered below and sometimes above by a narrow pale band. Largest collected by author, 32 inches, 4 pounds, from the Dominican Republic.

Known from all warm oceans except the eastern Pacific. It attaches to a wide variety of hosts such as sharks, rays, sea turtles, and many fishes including the larger reef species; it is also often observed freeliving. Easily caught on hook and line. *E. neucratoides* is closely related, differing in being stouter-bodied at any specific length, having better developed white margins on the dorsal, caudal and anal fins, and lower (but overlapping) counts (the disc laminae, for example, range from 18 to 23).

Remora

Remora remora (Linnaeus, 1758).

Figure 167

Dorsal rays 21 to 27; anal rays 20 to 24; pectoral rays 25 to 30; lowerlimb gill rakers 23 to 30; disc laminae 16 to 20; body not very elongate, the depth about 6 in standard length; pectoral fins rounded; caudal fin moderately to deeply emarginate; color usually uniform, tan to brownish black. Largest specimen, 31 inches, from a whale shark; most

Figure 167. Remora (*Remora remora*), 8 inches, Grand Bahama Island.

are less than 15 inches. The most common species of the genus *Remora;* found in all warm seas. Offshore species of sharks are the usual hosts. Although known to make its way into the gill cavity of the host, it is usually found attached externally.

JACKS
(CARANGIDAE)

The jacks are strong-swimming roving predaceous fishes which are usually silvery in color. They are variable in shape, ranging from the elongate fusiform *Decapterus* to the high-bodied and extremely compressed *Selene.* The caudal peduncle is slender and often reinforced with a series of sharp external bony plates or scutes (thus necessitating the use of fork length for proportional measurements of these fishes). The lateral line is complete, arched anteriorly, the posterior part straight and overlaid by the scutes of those fishes having them. The scales are small and cycloid; on some fishes they become embedded or obsolete. There are two dorsal fins, or the spinous portion is so deeply notched as to seem separated from the soft part; the spinous dorsal is often

poorly developed, and in the large adults of some species it may become embedded. Dorsal and anal fins depressible into grooves; a procumbent spine at front of spinous dorsal fin (usually not visible externally). Probably the most distinctive family character is the pair of stout anal spines that precede the anal fin (these too can be embedded in some large adults); the soft portions of the dorsal and anal fins are usually elevated anteriorly. The caudal fin is deeply forked or lunate; the pectorals are narrow and often falcate. The teeth are small to moderate in size, sometimes absent in large adults. There are no spines on the opercle; the preopercle is smooth or scalloped, not serrate. An adipose eyelid is present, moderately to well-developed.

Many of the carangids, such as the pompanos, are highly esteemed as food fishes. Some, such as the Greater Amberjack *(Seriola dumerili),* the species of *Caranx,* particularly the Horse-eye Trevally *(C. latus)* and Black Jack (C. *lugubris*), and the Yellow Jack *(Carangoides bartholomaei),* have often been implicated in ciguatera. In some West Indian localities where the fish poisoning

Figure 168. Horse-eye Trevally (*Caranx latus*), Belize.

problem is acute, one cannot give away large adults of these species. The jacks are not reef fishes in the sense of being residents of reefs; however they may enter the reef community by feeding on the resident fishes.

The species discussed below are the ones most often encountered over reefs in clear water. Other carangids are common in the Caribbean but occur primarily in brackish environments, relatively deep water, or off-shore. Examples are the Rudderfish *(Seriola zonata)*, the Lesser Amberjack *(S. fasciata)*, the Pilotfish *(Naucrates ductor)*, the Rough Scad *(Trachurus lathami)*, the Bumper *(Chloroscombrus chrysurus)*, the Bluntnose Jack *(Hemicaranx amblyrhynchus)*, the Cottonmouth Jack *(Uraspis secunda)*, the Pompano *(Trachinotus carolinus)*, the Guiana Pompano *(T. cayennensis)*, the Moonfish *(Selene*

setapinnis), the Lookdown *(Selene vomer)* and the Sauteur *(Oligoplites saliens)*.

African Pompano

Alectis ciliaris (Bloch, 1788).   Figure 169
Dorsal rays VII (juveniles only; fin of adults becomes covered by epidermis)-I,18 or 19; anal rays II (also embedded with age)-I,15 or 16; pectoral rays 18 to 20; scales small, about 120 to 140 in lateral line, the last 24 to 41 as scutes; gill rakers 5 or 6 + 14 to 16; body of young very deep and compressed, the depth about 1.5 in fork length; body of adults becoming more elongate, about 2.5 in fork length; upper profile of head steep; upper profile of body with a broad angular prominence, the apex at origin of soft dorsal fin; anterior seven soft rays of dorsal fin and first five rays of anal fin extremely elongate (as much as four times length of body) and

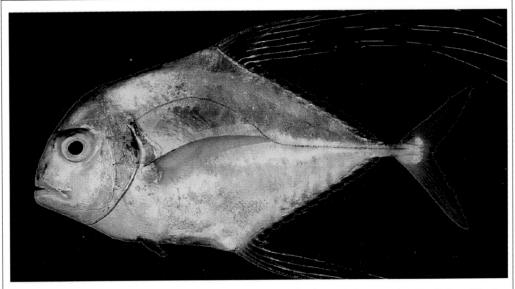

Figure 169. African Pompano (*Alectis ciliaris*), 16 inches, 2.1 pounds, St. John, Virgin Islands.

filiform in the young, these rays progressively shorter with age; silvery, the young with five obscure dark bars on side of body. Attains about 3 feet. The world record for hook and line is a 50-pound, 8-ounce fish from Daytona Beach, Florida. Circumtropical; in the western Atlantic from Massachusetts to Brazil. An open-water fish. The filamentous soft dorsal and anal rays of the young bear resemblance to the tentacles of some jellyfishes; it has been suggested that the fish might gain some protection from predation by mimicking jellyfishes. *A. crinitus* is a synonym.

Yellow Jack

Carangoides bartholomaei (Cuvier, 1833).
Figure 170

Dorsal rays VIII-I,25 to 28; anal rays II-I,22 to 25; pectoral rays 20 to 21; lateral-line scales 91 to 114, the last 25 to 36 as scutes; gill rakers 7 to 9 + 19 to 21. Similar to the bar jack, differing in slightly lower fin-ray counts, lower gill-raker counts, slightly steeper profile and in color. The back is iridescent blue but there is no blackish band; much of the fish is suffused with yellow; the caudal fin is yellow as are the other fins to a lesser extent. Attains about 30 inches. Massachusetts to Brazil. Not common inshore; more often seen ranging over outer reefs. Usually solitary or in very small groups. The young, which have large yellow spots and vivid yellow fins, have a tendency to swim close to a diver.

Blue Runner

Carangoides crysos (Mitchill, 1815).
Figure 171

Dorsal rays VIII-I,23 to 25 (rarely 25); anal rays II-I,19 to 21 (rarely 21); pectoral rays 21 to 23; lateral-line scales 86 to 98, the last 42 to 50 as scutes; gill rakers 12 to 14 + 23 to 28. Similar to *C. bartholomaei* and *C. ruber*; differs primarily in counts, a larger mouth (maxilla extending to below center of eye), larger

Figure 170. Yellow Jack (*Carangoides bartholomaei*), Belize.

teeth, vomerine teeth restricted to an anterior "V"–shaped patch and in color. There is an elongate black spot posteriorly on the gill cover at level of eye, and the tips of the caudal lobes are blackish. Largest collected by author, 23 inches, from the Virgin Islands. Western Atlantic from Nova Scotia and Bermuda to Brazil. Abundant in the Gulf of Mexico. Usually occurs in schools; these visit reefs sporadically from offshore waters but rarely linger. The best-eating of Caribbean jacks. *Carangoides fusus* is a closely related eastern Atlantic species.

Figure 171. Blue Runner (*Carangoides crysos*), Andros, Bahamas.

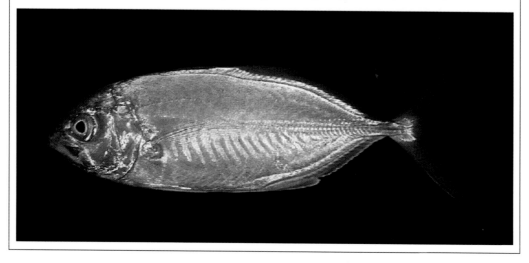

Figure 172. Bar Jack (*Carangoides ruber*), Long Island, Bahamas.

Bar Jack

Carangoides ruber (Bloch, 1793).

Figure 172

Dorsal rays VIII-I,26 to 30; anal rays II-I,23 to 26; pectoral rays 19 to 21; lateral-line scales 97 to 104, the last 27 to 35 as scutes (none on curved anterior portion of lateral line); gill rakers 12 to 15 + 29 to 34; body moderately deep, the depth about 3.2 to 3.5 in standard length, and compressed, the width 1.7 to 2 in depth; small conical teeth in jaws and on vomer, palatines and tongue (those on vomer in a broad kite-shaped patch); pectoral fins very long and falcate, reaching well beyond origin of soft portion of anal fin; upper profile of head not very steep; maxilla usually reaching a vertical at front edge of eye or extending slightly beyond. The most diagnostic color markings are a blackish band on back below soft dorsal fin which runs across top of caudal peduncle, crosses caudal base and extends onto lower lobe of caudal fin, and a brilliant blue band on body below and adjacent to the blackish band and extending anteriorly to it. Largest collected by author, 2 feet. Tropical western Atlantic, extending north as far as New Jersey. The most common jack of West Indian waters and the one most often seen over reefs. Usually encountered in small aggregations. Large individuals have caused ciguatera (fish poisoning) when eaten, as have the other western Atlantic species of the genus.

Crevalle Jack

Caranx hippos (Linnaeus, 1766).

Figure 173

Dorsal rays VIII-I,19 to 21; anal rays II-I,15 to 17; pectoral rays 20 or 21; scutes 25 to 42; no scales on

Figure 173. Crevalle Jack (*Caranx hippos*), 12.8 inches, Miami, Florida.

chest, except a small mid-ventral patch in front of pelvic fins (other species of *Caranx* discussed herein have scales on the chest region); gill rakers 6 to 8 + 14 to 16; body deep, the depth about 2.7 to 3.8 in fork length (large individuals more elongate); upper profile of head steep; maxilla ending approximately below posterior edge of eye (maxilla of juveniles shorter); teeth in jaws well-developed, a few at front in outer row as small canines; teeth on vomer in a small triangular to roundish patch; front of soft dorsal and anal fins of adults notably elevated; olivaceous to bluish green above, silvery to brassy on sides; a prominent black spot posteriorly on gill cover at level of eye, another at upper axil of pectoral fins, and often a third on lower pectoral rays; caudal yellowish. The young have broad dark bars on the body. The world record for angling is a 57-pound, 5-ounce fish from Angola. A 33.7-inch fish from Venezuela weighed 13.7 pounds. Cosmopolitan in tropical and temperate waters; in the western Atlantic from Nova Scotia to Uruguay (higher latitudes during warm months). The young are not uncommon in shallow brackish-water environments where they tend to run in schools. Adults are rare in clearwater reef areas. Relatively more common in the northern part of its range; along the eastern seaboard of the United States it is rivalled in abundance only by the Blue Runner. A hard-fighting fish when hooked. The flesh is said to be coarse and lacking in flavor.

Horse-Eye Trevally

Caranx latus Agassiz, 1829.
Figures 168 & 174

Dorsal rays VIII-I,20 to 22; anal rays II-I,16 or 17; pectoral rays 19 to 21; lateral-line scales 84 to 92, the last 30 to 50 as scutes; gill rakers 6 to 8 + 14 to 18. Similar to *Caranx hippos,* differing in having the chest entirely scaled (at least to

Figure 174. Horse-Eye Trevally (*Caranx latus*), Long Island, Bahamas.

sizes as small as 2 inches), a larger eye, the upper profile of head not as steep, and in color. There are no spots on the pectoral fins, and the spot posteriorly on the gill cover is small or absent; the scutes tend to be dusky or blackish (but not as dark as those of the Black Jack); the caudal fin is yellow. The young have broad blackish bars on the body. Largest collected by author, 30 inches, from Puerto Rico. One of 28.3 inches weighed 8.5 pounds. The world record for angling is a 28-pound, 8-ounce fish from Miami, Florida. Bermuda and New Jersey to Rio de Janeiro. Juveniles are characteristic of shallow brackish regions with mud bottoms and may penetrate fresh water. Small aggregations of fish about a foot in length often take up residence over inshore reefs. Large adults run in small schools more offshore but of-ten range over outer reefs; they are relatively fearless and will approach a swimmer closely. Often with two parasitic isopods in mouth, one very large.

Black Jack

Caranx lugubris Poey, 1860.   Figure 175

Dorsal rays VIII-I,21 or 22 (first dorsal spine may be embedded and hence not visible externally); anal rays II-I,17 to 19; pectoral rays 20 to 22; scutes 26 to 33; gill rakers 6 to 8 + 18 to 20; upper profile of head steep, the anterior part slightly concave; mouth relatively large, the maxilla nearly reaching center of eye; dark olive gray to almost black on the back, shading to bluish gray ventrally; scutes black; a small black spot at upper end of gill opening. Largest collected by author, 30 inches, from Puerto Rico. The world record for hook and line is a 28-

Figure 175. Black Jack (*Caranx lugubris*), 70 foot depth, Rum Cay, Bahamas.

pound, 8-ounce fish from Revillagigedo Islands, Mexico. No young individuals were collected or observed. Circumtropical. Not common, at least in shallow water. Usually seen at depths of 100 feet or more swimming along the edges of drop-offs to deep water. Will approach a diver closely. Three ob-served at 170 feet in the Bahamas displayed different color phases; two of the fish were nearly black and the third was blue with black scutes.

Mackerel Scad

Decapterus macarellus (Cuvier, 1833).
Figure 176
Dorsal rays VIII-I,32 or 33-1; anal

Figure 176. Mackerel Scad (*Decapterus macarellus*), 7 inches, St. John, Virgin Islands.

rays II-I,27 to 29-1 (the last dorsal and anal rays as a well-separated finlet); pectoral rays 22 to 24; lateral-line scales about 122 to 138, the last 24 to 40 as scutes; scutes small, the height of the largest about one-third or less of eye diameter; gill rakers long, 11 or 12 + 35 to 39; body elongate, the depth about 5 to 6.5 in fork length (to end of middle caudal rays), and little compressed, the width about 1.3 to 1.6 in depth; mouth small, the maxilla not reaching front edge of eye; blue-green on back, silvery on sides; a black spot posteriorly on edge of gill cover at level of upper part of eye; no dark dots on lateral line; caudal fin reddish. Reported to attain a length of at least 1 foot; largest collected by author, 11 inches, from Puerto Rico. Circumtropical; in the western Atlantic occasionally straying as far north as Nova Scotia. A fish of open water, occasionally seen as schools over outer reefs.

Round Scad

Decapterus punctatus (Agassiz, 1829).
Figure 177
Dorsal rays VIII-I,28 to 33-1; anal rays II-I,24 to 27-1 (the last dorsal

and anal rays as a well-separated finlet); pectoral rays 19 to 21; lateral-line scales 80 to 93, the last 36 to 44 as scutes; scutes not small, the height of the largest about three-fourths eye diameter; gill rakers long, 12 to 15 + 34 to 40; body elongate, the depth about 5 in fork length, and little compressed; mouth small, the maxilla just reaching front edge of eye; blue-green on back, silvery on sides, with a narrow yellow stripe on side of body at level of upper part of eye; a black spot posteriorly on gill cover just in front of yellow body stripe; about 13 black dots along anterior half of lateral line. Said to reach a length of 1 foot, but most individuals are considerably smaller. Atlantic; on the western side from Nova Scotia to Rio de Janeiro. A pelagic schooling fish which may come close enough to shore to be taken in beach seines. Feeds on zooplankton, especially copepods.

Rainbow Runner

Elagatis bipinnulatus (Quoy & Gaimard, 1824).
Figure 178
Dorsal rays VI-I,24 to 27-2; anal rays II-I,15 to 17-2 (last two dorsal

Figure 177. Round Scad (*Decapterus punctatus*), 6.3 inches, Curaçao.

Figure 178. Rainbow Runner (*Elagatis bipinnulatus*), 16.5 inches, 1 pound, St John, Virgin Islands.

and anal rays as a separate finlet); lateral-line scales about 100; no scutes; lower-limb gill rakers 25 to 28; body moderately elongate and fusiform, the depth 3.5 to 5 in standard length; bluish green on back with two blue stripes on side separated by a broader yellow band; yellow below lower blue stripe and white ventrally; caudal fin yellow. World record for hook and line, 37 pounds 9 ounces, from Revillagigedo Islands, Mexico. Circumtropical, ranging in the western Atlantic to the northern Gulf of Mexico and Massachusetts. Pelagic, but occasionally seen near shore, sometimes in schools. Gamy and excellent eating.

Leatherjacket

Oligoplites saurus (Bloch & Schneider, 1801).
Figure 179

Dorsal rays V-I,19 to 21; anal rays II-I,18 to 21; pectoral rays 15 to 17; scales very elongate, horizontal or slightly oblique, and partially embedded; no scutes; lower-limb gill rakers 13 to 15; body moderately elongate, the depth about 3.6 to 3.9 in standard length, and compressed, the width about 3 in depth; head small; mouth oblique and large, the maxilla nearly reaching poste-

Figure 179. Leatherjacket (*Oligoplites saurus*), 10 inches, Miami, Florida.

rior edge of eye; long posterior portion of dorsal and anal fins low with each ray almost a separate finlet; pectoral fins short, just reaching tips of pelvic fins; greenish silver on back, silvery on sides and ventrally (sometimes golden); caudal fin bright yellow. Attains a length of slightly more than a foot. Eastern Pacific and western Atlantic; in the latter region from the Gulf of Maine to Uruguay. A schooling fish more often occurring in turbid than clear water; tolerates water of low salinity; often swims near the surface and may leap free of the water. *O. palometa* and *O. saliens* of the southern Caribbean have larger mouths and deeper bodies; *saliens* has 16 to 20 lower-limb gill rakers.

Bigeye Scad

Selar crumenophthalmus (Bloch, 1793).
Figures 180 & 181

Dorsal rays VIII-I,23 to 26; anal rays II-I,20 to 23; no finlets; pectoral rays 20 to 22; lateral-line scales 84 to 94, the last 30 to 44 as scutes; scutes moderately large, the height of largest about half eye diameter; gill rakers long, 9 to 11 + 27 to 30; lower shoulder girdle (edge of gill opening beneath lower part of gill cover) with a prominent papilla, below and adjacent to which is a deep groove; body slightly elongate, the depth about 3.7 to 4.4 in fork length, and moderately compressed, the width 1.7 to 2 in depth; maxilla reaching to or slightly beyond a vertical at front of pupil; gray-green on upper third of body, silvery with iridescence on lower two-thirds, the two regions separated by a brassy yellow band one-half pupil or less in width; tips of caudal lobes dusky;

there may be a little dark pigment along upper edge of gill cover, but no definite spot as on *Decapterus* (and usually on *Trachurus*). Attains about 16 inches. Circumtropical, straying as far north in the western Atlantic as Nova Scotia and as far south as Rio de Janeiro. May occur in large schools or small aggregations, often near enough to shore to be captured by beach seines or throw nets. May be seen over shallow reefs, but usually where the water is somewhat turbid. Feeds primarily on the larger elements of the plankton but may ingest benthic animals. The similar *Trachurus lathami* is distinctive in having the anterior lateral-line scales enlarged (about as high as the scutes).

Greater Amberjack

Seriola dumerili (Risso, 1810). Figure 182

Dorsal rays VI or VII-I,29 to 35; lateral-line scales 141 to 163; no scutes; lower-limb gill rakers 10 to 13 (excluding rudiments); depth of body 2.9 to 3.9 in standard length; front of soft dorsal and anal fins not greatly elevated, the height of the dorsal 6.2 to 7.2 in standard length; usually a lengthwise brassy stripe on side of body at level of eye; back above stripe olivaceous to blue, below silvery white; a diagonal dark band running from snout, through eye, to nape. Recorded to a weight of 177 pounds. The record for hook and line is a 155-pound, 10-ounce fish from Bermuda. Known from all tropical and subtropical seas.

The most common species of the genus in the tropical western Atlantic and the one most inclined to range into inshore waters. Like most

Figure 180. Bigeye Scad (*Selar crumenophthalmus*), Bonaire.

Figure 181. Bigeye Scad (*Selar crumenophthalmus*), Bonaire.

Figure 182. Greater Amberjack (*Seriola dumerili*), 3 feet 8 inches, 31 pounds, St. John Virgin Islands.

of the carangids, the amberjack feeds primarily on fishes. It seems to be second only to the barracuda in causing cases of ciguatera in the West Indies when eaten.

Almaco Jack

Seriola rivoliana Valenciennes, 1833.
Figure 183

Dorsal rays VII-I, 28 to 32; lateral-line scales 122 to 143; no scutes; lower-limb gill rakers 16 to 18; depth of body 2.5 to 3.5 in standard length; front of soft dorsal and anal fins very elevated, the height of the dorsal 3.6 to 5 in standard length; silvery, sometimes with brassy or lavender reflections, the back varying from bluish green to olivaceous or brown; front of head brownish; a diagonal dark brown bar on head as in *dumerili* but even more marked. The young of both species are more yellowish and have dark bars on the

Figure 183. Almaco Jack (*Seriola rivoliana*), 2 feet 2 inches, 6.3 pounds, St. John, Virgin Islands.

body; at first the bands are solid; later they become narrower and irregular, and at a length of about 7 inches they disappear; at any one size the bars of *rivoliana* are more prominent than those of *dumerili.* The black bars of *S. zonata,* a species with 33 to 40 soft dorsal rays and a more elongate body as an adult than other *Seriola,* persist to a length of about 10 inches. The Almaco Jack probably attains a weight of at least 50 pounds. Cosmopolitan; ranges in the Atlantic from the Mediterranean to the Cape of Good Hope on the eastern side and North Carolina to Argentina on the western; often seen well offshore; rare in shallow water.

Permit

Trachinotus falcatus (Linnaeus, 1758).
Figures 184 & 185

Dorsal rays VI-I,18 to 21; anal rays II-I,16 to 18; pectoral rays 17 to 20; lateral-line scales about 135; no scutes; gill rakers 3 to 9 + 9 to 15 (fewer countable rakers on adults); body deep, the depth 1.3 to 2.3 in standard length (the large adults more elongate); spinous dorsal fin low; front of soft dorsal and anal fins elongate, but not reaching posterior to middle caudal rays when laid back; snout short and obtuse; teeth similar to those of the Palometa when young (except for a small patch of teeth on tongue), but disappearing with age; iridescent blue or blue-

Figure 184. Permit (*Trachinotus falcatus*), 12.3 inches, 1 pound, Puerto Rico.

Figure 185. Permit (*Trachinotus falcatus*), 3 feet 5 inches, 33.5 pounds, St. John, Virgin Islands.

green on back, silvery on sides, sometimes pale yellow below level of pectoral fins; a broad patch of orange-yellow on abdomen in front of anal fin; pectoral fins blackish. The world record for hook and line is a 51-pound, 8-ounce fish from Lake Worth, Florida. Both sides of the Atlantic; on the western side from Massachusetts to Brazil. Occurs on sand flats and reefs from a few to at least 100 feet; may also be seen over mud bottoms. Feeds primarily on mollusks and to a lesser extent on sea urchins and crustaceans, particularly hermit crabs; it crushes the hard parts of the mollusks and may expel shell fragments from its gill openings. One permit of 33.5 pounds speared by the author contained enough fragments of a Queen Conch (*Strombus gigas*) to determine that the shell measured 70 mm (2 3/4

inches) in length. An exceptionally good-eating fish. The related *T. carolinus* has 23 to 27 dorsal soft rays; it has a similar distribution to *T. falcatus* but seems more characteristic of turbid than clear water. *T. cayennensis* of the southern Caribbean and Guianas has 27 or 28 dorsal soft rays and a short head (about 5 in standard length).

Palometa

Trachinotus goodei Jordan & Evermann, 1896.   Figure 186

Dorsal rays VII-I,19 or 20; anal rays II-I,16 to 18; pectoral rays 16 to 19 (modally 17); lateral-line scales about 107; no scutes; gill rakers 7 to 9 + 9 to 13; body compressed and moderately deep, the depth varying from about 3 in standard length for small juveniles to about 2 in adults; spinous dorsal fin very low; ante-

Figure 186. Palometa (*Trachinotus goodei*), 8.3 inches, St. John, Virgin Islands.

rior part of soft dorsal and anal fins of adults greatly prolonged, the rays reaching well beyond middle caudal rays; snout short and obtuse; small teeth in irregular rows in jaws; a few small teeth on vomer and palatines, none on tongue; bluish silver on back, shading to silver on sides, with four narrow dark bars on upper side of body; lower third of body light golden yellow; elongate lobes of soft dorsal and anal fins blackish. The smallest of the western Atlantic pompanos. Said to approach 20 inches in length; the largest collected by the author, 14.5 inches, from the Virgin Islands. Bermuda and Massachusetts to Argentina; also has been recorded from the eastern Atlantic. Feeds primarily on small fishes and mollusks. Frequently observed in clear water along sandy shores; often comes close to the feet of bathers wading in shallows, perhaps to feed on inverte-

brates exposed by the disturbance to the sand. Often classified under the name *T. glaucus.*

TUNAS AND MACKERELS
(SCOMBRIDAE)

The tunas and their allies are swift-swimming pelagic fishes which often travel in schools. Many are of great commercial importance. They have a streamlined body with a slender caudal peduncle and a broadly lunate caudal fin; the base of the fin is strengthened by two or three keels (two in the true mackerels, represented in the southern Caribbean by *Scomber japonicus;* when there are three keels, the middle is notably the largest). The first dorsal fin consists of slender spines which are depressible in a groove. The second dorsal and anal fins are elevated anteriorly; finlets are present poste-

Figure 187. Cero (*Scomberomorus regalis*), Long Island, Bahamas.

rior to these fins. The pectoral fins, which vary greatly in length with the different species, fit into a depressed area in the side of the body. The scales are cycloid and small; they may be restricted to the pectoral region of the body. The tunas have a well-developed cutaneous vascular system which functions as a counter-current heat exchanger.

The muscle tissue of the body is sharply divisible into an outer lateral deep red portion and a larger inner whitish part. Physiologists have shown recently that the red muscle is responsible for the slow continuous swimming of these fishes; the massive white portion is brought into action when speed is needed.

The tunas and mackerels are excellent eating when very fresh, but the flesh deteriorates rapidly in tropical heat. Cases of food poisoning are common from eating tunas which have spoiled.

The scombrid fishes range in size from the small mackerels to the giant Bluefin Tuna *(Thunnus thynnus)* which is known to a length of 14 feet and a weight of 1800 pounds. Most species occur only in the offshore blue water.

Little Tuna

Euthynnus alletteratus (Rafinesque, 1810).
Figure 188

Dorsal rays XV or XVI, 12 or 13-8; anal rays 14-7 (first two or three dorsal and first two anal rays unbranched and not segmented); pectoral rays 25 to 28; gill rakers 10 + 27 to 29; body naked except for an irregular region of scales anteriorly; dorsal fins not broadly separated (as in *Auxis*); depth of body about 4 in fork length; blue-green dorsally, silvery on sides, with irregular dark

Figure 188. Little Tuna (*Euthynnus alletteratus*), 12.8 inches, 1 pound, St. John, Virgin Islands.

bands on back and several black spots slightly smaller than pupil below pectoral fin; no stripes on lower sides of body (as in *Katsuwonus pelamis)*. The world record for angling is 35 pounds, 2 ounces, from Algeria. Tropical and subtropical Atlantic; in the western Atlantic from Bermuda and Maine to Brazil. Characteristic of the inshore water of continental and insular shelves; swims in fast-moving compact schools; the presence of flocks of active diving birds over green water is often indicative of the feeding by schools of Little Tuna on

small surface-dwelling fishes. The Indo-Pacific *E. affinis* is very closely related to *E. alletteratus.*

Serra Spanish Mackerel

Scomberomorus brasiliensis Collette, Russo & Zavala-Camin, 1978.   Figure 189
Similar in counts, body proportions and shape of lateral line to the Cero; differs in lacking scales on the pectoral fins, having shorter pelvic fins (3.6 to 5.7% fork length), having a smaller keel on caudal peduncle and in color; there is no broken line of yellow on the side of the body; there are numerous yel-

Figure 189. Serra Spanish Mackerel (*Scomberomorus brasiliensis*), 21 inches, 1.9 pounds, Trinidad.

low to bronze spots which are larger in average size and rounder than those of the Cero (the number of spots increases with age); there is a large black area at the front of the dorsal fin (as in the Cero but absent in the King Mackerel). Only recently has this species been distinguished from the Spanish Mackerel (S. maculatus) which is colored almost the same. The two species differ notably in the number of vertebrae (47 to 49 for S. brasiliensis compared to 50 to 53 for S. maculatus); also brasiliensis has more pectoral rays on the average (21 to 24, usually 22 to 23, compared to 20 to 22 for maculatus). The largest specimen of the type series measures 630 mm in fork length (hence about 28 inches total length), but the species undoubtedly attains larger size. Known from waters of the continental shelf of Central and South America from Belize to Rio Grande do Sul, Brazil; apparently does not occur in the West Indies except at Trinidad. S. maculatus ranges from the Gulf of Mexico north to Maine. S. brasiliensis is more closely related to S. sierra of the eastern Pacific than to other Atlantic Scomberomorus.

King Mackerel

Scomberomorus cavalla (Cuvier, 1829).

Figure 190

Similar to the preceding species of Scomberomorus; differs principally in the abrupt downward curve of the lateral line below the front of the second dorsal fin, fewer gill rakers (1 or 2 + 7 to 9), no scales on pectoral fins (like brasiliensis in this respect), in color and in attaining larger size. There is no black area in the first dorsal fin; the side of adults is plain silvery; the young have spots like the Spanish Mackerel; the upper three-fifths of the body of a 15-inch one had numerous bronze spots smaller than the pupil of the eye in about five or six irregular rows. The world record fish for hook and line weighed 90 pounds; it was caught at Key West. Maine to Rio de Janeiro. Always on the move like other scombrids; occurs singly or in small groups; often seen over outer reef

Figure 190. King Mackerel (*Scomberomorus cavalla*), 3 feet 7.6 inches, 23.5 pounds, St. John, Virgin Islands.

Figure 191. Cero (*Scomberomorus regalis*), 16.3 inches, 1 pound, St. John, Virgin Islands.

areas. Highly prized as a food and game fish, but it has been known to cause ciguatera when eaten. Sometimes called "Kingfish." The Wahoo (*Acanthocybium solanderi*), which is also an elongate fish, has at times been confused with the King Mackerel; it differs in its more fusiform body, longer snout (longer than postorbital part of head), the maxilla slipping under the suborbital region (exposed on the cheek in *Scomberomorus*), no gill rakers and a long first dorsal fin of XXI to XXVII spines, the front not notably elevated as in *Scomberomorus*. The King Mackerel feeds primarily on fishes, occasionally on squids; among the fishes identified from the stomachs of Caribbean specimens are the herrings *Harengula humeralis* and *Opisthonema oglinum*, the flyingfish *Parexocoetus brachypterus*, the jack *Carangoides ruber*, and the snapper *Ocyurus chrysurus*.

Cero

Scomberomorus regalis (Bloch, 1793).
Figures 187 & 191
Dorsal rays XVI to XVIII-I, 15 or 16-8 or 9; anal rays II, 15 or 16-7 to 9 (first two or three dorsal and one or two anal soft rays not branched and difficult to distinguish from preceding spines); pectoral rays 20 to 23 (usually 21 or 22); lateral line descending gradually in region of body below front of second dorsal fin; gill rakers 2 to 4 + 10 to 14 (usually 3 + 12 or 13); body elongate, the depth about 5 in fork length; base of caudal fin with three keels, the large middle one extending forward onto caudal peduncle; teeth broad-based, triangular and compressed with sharp edges, about 30 to 34 in each jaw; small scales on body, none on head except nape; pectoral fins scaled; pelvic fins 4.4 to 6.3% of fork length; bluish green on back, silvery on sides, with a mid-lateral row of yellow streaks of variable length; small yellow spots above and below this row; a large black area at front of first dorsal fin. Said to attain a length of 4 feet and a weight of 26 pounds. The world angling record is 17 pounds, 2 ounces. Largest of many collected by the author, 32 inches. Massachusetts to Rio de Janeiro. The most common member of the genus *Scomberomorus* in the West Indies;

often seen swimming over reefs and may come very close to shore in its pursuit of small schooling clupeid, engraulid and atherinid fishes. Typically solitary but may travel in very small groups. May jump free of the surface in a long graceful arc. A fine-eating fish when fresh. Sometimes called the "Painted Mackerel."

SNAPPERS
(LUTJANIDAE)

The snappers represent one of the most important fish families of tropical seas. In addition to the general characters of perciforms (see Serranidae), those of the western Atlantic share the following characteristics: dorsal rays X to XII,9 to 15; anal rays III,7 to 10; dorsal spines heteracanthous (alternating slightly in size and position, the stronger of successive spines displaced slightly to the right); caudal fin emarginate or forked, the principal rays 17; jaws equal or the lower slightly projecting; maxilla for most of its length slipping under edge of preorbital when mouth is closed; fixed canine teeth in jaws; teeth on vomer and palatines; no spines on opercle; edge of preopercle usually finely serrate; scales ctenoid.

The lutjanids are carnivorous, usually benthic, and many are primarily nocturnal in habits. Not included herein are the deeper-water species such as the Silk Snapper *(L. vivanus),* Caribbean Red Snapper *(L. purpureus),* and the genera *Apsilus, Rhomboplites, Etelis* and *Pristipomoides,* all of which are taken commercially when deep fishing with hook and line. Rarely are individuals of any of these species observed at normal diving depths, and then nearly always as juveniles.

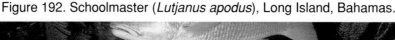

Figure 192. Schoolmaster (*Lutjanus apodus*), Long Island, Bahamas.

Figure 193. Mutton Snapper (*Lutjanus analis*), St. Croix, Virgin Islands.

Snappers, in general, feed heavily on crustaceans; the larger species eat mostly fishes. The large fish-eating species such as the Dog Snapper and Cubera Snapper are often implicated in ciguatera (fish poisoning) if taken from toxic sectors of reefs.

Mutton Snapper

Lutjanus analis (Cuvier, 1828). Figure 193
Dorsal rays IX to XI,13 or 14 (usually X,14); anal rays III,7 or 8 (rarely 7); pectoral rays 15 to 17; lateral-line scales 47 to 51; lower-limb gill rakers 7 to 9 (excluding rudiments); depth of body about 2.5 to 3.2 in standard length; canine teeth relatively small, those at front of upper jaw much smaller than more posterior large teeth; teeth on vomer in a crescent-shaped patch; caudal fin deeply emarginate; margin of soft portion of anal fin angulate, the longest middle ray contained 2 or less in head; pectoral fins relatively long, considerably greater than distance from snout to preopercular margin, about 3.2 to 3.8 in standard length; a black spot smaller than eye just above lateral line below front of soft portion of dorsal fin; an irregular narrow blue band from above middle of maxilla to lower edge of eye; another diagonal blue line on snout, continuing in back of eye; fins reddish, particularly the anal, pelvics and lower part of caudal; posterior edge of caudal fin dusky. The world record for hook and line, 27 pounds, 6 ounces, from Johns Pass, Florida. One of 27.5 inches weighed 10 pounds. Tropical western Atlantic, north to Massachusetts. Introduced to Bermuda. Although this species may be seen over reefs, it is usually encountered

in more open water over sand bottom. An exceptionally good-eating fish.

Schoolmaster

Lutjanus apodus (Walbaum, 1792).

Figures 192 & 194

Dorsal rays X,14; anal rays III,8; pectoral rays 16 to 18 (rarely 18); lateral-line scales 40 to 45; lower-limb gill rakers 7 to 9 (excluding rudiments). Similar in body form to the Dog Snapper. Lacks the pale bar below the eye, but has a series of narrow pale bars on body (which may be faint or absent on large adults); the body, and particularly the fins, are more yellow; a solid or broken blue line under eye. Largest collected by the author, 22 inches; another of 21 inches weighed 5.5 pounds. Weights to 8 pounds have been recorded. Littoral in the tropical Atlantic, including the northern and eastern Gulf of Mexico, the young straying as far north as Massachusetts. The most common snapper on West Indian coral reefs, particularly among stands of Elkhorn Coral.

Blackfin Snapper

Lutjanus buccanella (Cuvier, 1828).

Figure 195

Dorsal rays X,14; anal rays III,8; pectoral rays 16 to 18; lateral-line scales 47 to 50; lower-limb gill rakers 15 to 18 (including rudiments); body depth 2.5 to 2.9 in standard length; caudal fin moderately forked; margin of anal fin rounded, the rays not long (longest 2.45 to 3.0 in head); maxilla reaching front edge of eye; vomerine teeth in an arrow-shaped patch; a single patch of teeth on tongue (double on other red snappers); adults red with a jet black spot at axil and base of pectoral fins;

Figure 194. Schoolmaster (*Lutjanus apodus*), Grand Bahama Island.

Figure 195. Blackfin Snapper (*Lutjanus buccanella*), St. Croix, Virgin Islands.

no black spot on side. Young with a broad yellow region on upper part of caudal peduncle. Largest specimen reported, 20.5 inches. Juveniles may occur in as little as 20 feet, but they are rare in less than 100 feet. Adults generally found in 100 fathoms or more. Florida Keys, West Indies, and Gulf of Mexico to Brazil. One of the common names for this fish in Martinique is Boucanelle, hence the origin of the scientific name.

Cubera Snapper

Lutjanus cyanopterus (Cuvier, 1828).
Figure 196
Dorsal rays X, 14; anal rays III, 7 or 8; pectoral rays 16 to 18; lateral-line scales 45 to 47; lower-limb gill rakers 6 to 8 (excluding rudiments). Similar to the Gray Snapper, differing in having a crescentic patch of villiform teeth on the vomer (without a median

backward projection), less body depth on the average (depth 3.1 to 3.4 in standard length in the size range of 10 inches to 2 feet) and longer canine teeth in the jaws. The world record for angling is a 121-pound, 8-ounce fish caught off Cameron, Louisiana. Tropical western Atlantic; rare north of Florida but recorded to North Carolina; ranges south to Brazil. Not common. A wary fish, it is not easily approached underwater. Feeds mainly on fishes; among those found in its stomachs are herrings, grunts, parrotfishes, and porcupinefishes.

Gray Snapper

Lutjanus griseus (Linnaeus, 1758).
Figures 197 & 198
Dorsal rays X, 14; anal rays III, 7 or 8; pectoral rays 15 to 17 (rarely 15); lateral-line scales 43 to 47; lower-limb gill rakers 7 to 9 (exclud-

Figure 196. Cubera Snapper (*Lutjanus cyanopterus*), Belize.

Figure 197. Gray Snapper (*Lutjanus griseus*), 40 feet deep, Long Island, Bahamas.

Figure 198. Gray Snapper (*Lutjanus griseus*), juvenile, Andros, Bahamas.

ing rudiments); depth of body 2.6 to 3.2 in standard length; villiform teeth in an arrow-shaped patch on vomer; pectoral fins about equal to distance from snout to upper preopercular margin, 3.7 to 4.2 in standard length; no black spot on side. The world record for hook and line, 17 pounds, from off Port Canaveral, Florida. Littoral in the tropical Atlantic, including the Gulf of Mexico, the young straying north to Massachusetts. A common inshore fish found in various habitats such as rocky areas, coral reefs, around docks, mangrove sloughs (hence sometimes called the "Mangrove Snapper"), and even into fresh water. Very good eating.

Dog Snapper

Lutjanus jocu (Bloch & Schneider, 1801).
Figure 199
Dorsal rays X,13 or 14 (usually

14); anal rays III,8; pectoral rays 16 or 17; lateral-line scales 45 to 49; lower-limb gill rakers 8 to 11 (excluding rudiments); body relatively deep, the depth 2.3 to 2.8 in standard length; teeth on vomer in an arrow-shaped patch; pectoral fins usually greater than the distance from snout to preopercular margin, 2.9 to 3.8 in standard length; a pair of teeth at front of upper jaw notably enlarged; the most characteristic color marking a pale bar below eye which broadens as it passes ventrally on head (this marking obscure or absent on young); no black spot on side of body; young with a lengthwise blue line beneath eye (which breaks up into a row of spots on adults). Largest collected by the author, 31 inches. The angling world record, 20 pounds, from San Salvador, Bahamas. Tropical western Atlantic, with a few records of indi-

Figure 199. Dog Snapper (*Lutjanus jocu*), Bonaire.

viduals as far north as Massachusetts. Introduced to Bermuda. The young occur inshore and may be found in brackish or even fresh water. Adults are characteristic of coral reefs.

Mahogany Snapper

Lutjanus mahogoni (Cuvier, 1828).

Figure 200

Dorsal rays X, 11 or 12 (rarely 11); anal rays III,8; pectoral rays 14 to 16; lateral-line scales 47 to 50; lower-limb gill rakers 11 to 13 (excluding 3 to 6 rudiments). Similar to the Lane Snapper (these two species are the only ones of the genus *Lutjanus* with 12 soft rays in the dorsal fin). The Mahogany Snapper differs in having the angle of the preopercle projecting to or beyond a line following the upper margin of the preopercle (not extending posterior to line on *synagris*), coarser serrations at the angle of the preopercle, a more projecting lower jaw, anal base shorter than maxilla (equal to or longer than maxilla on *synagris*) and in color. There is a black spot about as large as eye beneath the front of the soft portion of the dorsal fin, but about one-fourth to one-half lies below the lateral line; no broad yellow stripes on the side, but there may be yellow lines following scale rows on lower half of body; posterior dark margin on caudal fin more marked than on *synagris*. Largest collected by author, 15 inches. Caribbean Sea north to the Carolinas. A coral reef species.

Lane Snapper

Lutjanus synagris (Linnaeus, 1758).

Figure 201

Dorsal rays X, 12 or 13 (rarely 13); anal rays III,8 or 9 (rarely 9); pecto-

Figure 200. Mahogany Snapper (*Lutjanus mahogoni*), Grand Bahama Island.

Figure 201. Lane Snapper (*Lutjanus synagris*), St. Croix, Virgin Islands.

ral rays 15 or 16 (usually 16); lateral-line scales 47 to 52; lower-limb gill rakers 8 to 11 (excluding about 4 rudiments which may be coalesced in adults); depth of body about 2.4 to 2.9 in standard length; anterior upper canine teeth about equal to or slightly smaller than other canines; teeth on vomer in an arrow-shaped patch; caudal fin moderately emarginate; margin of anal fin not angulate, the longest middle ray about 2.3 to 2.6 in head; pectoral fins 3.3 to 3.8 in standard length; a diffuse black spot about as large as eye below soft portion of anal fin, the lateral line running along its lower edge or passing through its lowermost portion; silvery pink to red with about eight yellow stripes; upper part of body with diagonal yellow lines; caudal fin light red, the posterior edges a little dusky; outer part of dorsal fin and most of anal and pelvic fins yellow. The world angling record, 7 pounds, from Perdido Pass, Alabama. North Carolina and Bermuda south to Brazil, including the Gulf of Mexico, from shallow water to depths of 1300 feet. Although often occurring in clear water on coral reefs, it may also be found over mud bottom in turbid water. Often occurs in schools.

Yellowtail Snapper

Ocyurus chrysurus (Bloch, 1791).

Figure 202

Dorsal rays X,12 to 14 (usually 13); anal rays III,8 or 9 (rarely 8); pectoral rays 15 or 16 (usually 16); lateral-line scales 46 to 49; lower-limb gill rakers 21 or 22 (including rudiments); depth of body 2.9 to 3.3 in standard length; canine teeth in

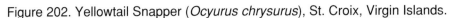

Figure 202. Yellowtail Snapper (*Ocyurus chrysurus*), St. Croix, Virgin Islands.

jaws not large; teeth on vomer in an arrow-shaped patch; caudal fin deeply forked; a narrow band of scales basally and posteriorly on membranes of dorsal and anal fins aligned with the rays; a prominent mid-lateral yellow stripe beginning on snout, broadening as it passes posteriorly on body, the color continuous with the all-yellow caudal fin; yellow spots on back above yellow band and narrow yellow stripes below. World record for hook and line, 8 pounds, 8 ounces, from Ft. Myers, Florida. One of 28 inches from Puerto Rico weighed 5 pounds. Bermuda and Massachusetts to Brazil; also recorded from the Cape Verde Islands. One of the most common and active of shallow-water reef fishes of the Caribbean area. Frequently seen well above the bottom where it feeds on planktonic organisms, especially when young, but it also eats benthic crustaceans and small fishes. Highly esteemed as food.

GRUNTS
(HAEMULIDAE)

Most of the general characteristics given for the snapper family apply also for the Haemulidae (Pomadasyidae of some authors). The grunts differ primarily in dentition. The mouth is low on the head, and the upper jaw usually projects slightly in front of the lower; all the teeth are pointed but none are developed as prominent canines; there are no teeth on the vomer of western Atlantic species of the family. These fishes are named for the sounds they produce by grinding their well-developed upper and lower pharyngeal teeth together. The inside of the mouth of many grunts is bright orange red. Two individuals of some

Figure 203. French Grunt (*Haemulon flavolineatum*), St. Croix, Virgin Islands.

species have been observed to approach one another with mouths open and then press them together.

The family is well represented on Caribbean reefs, both in number of species and in number of individuals. Dense aggregations of these fishes are often seen on small isolated reefs by day. At night they disperse to feed individually over adjacent sand and grass flats.

The young of the species of *Haemulon* except *plumieri* have a black lateral stripe and a black spot at the base of the caudal fin; these markings are lost on the adults of the majority of these fishes. Young grunts (which are often found in seagrass beds) feed primarily on the animals of the plankton within a few feet of the bottom. These food habits are retained to a large degree by the adults of *Haemulon striatum, H. boschmae*, and to a lesser extent *H. aurolineatum* and *H. chrysargyreum*. Most other species feed as adults mainly on a wide variety of benthic invertebrates. Large *Haemulon macrostomum* and *Anisotremus surinamensis* ingest primarily sea urchins, particularly the long-spined dark-colored *Diadema antillarum*.

Not included among the haemulid accounts below are *Pomadasys crocro, P. corvinaeformis, Genyatremus luteus* and *Conodon nobilis*. Although abundant in the Caribbean, these species are characteristic of mud bottoms and turbid, often brackish water.

Black Margate

Anisotremus surinamensis (Bloch, 1791).
Figure 204

Dorsal rays XII,16 to 18; anal rays III,8 to 10 (usually 9); pectoral rays 18 or 19; lateral-line scales 50 to 53; 6 or 7 scales between lateral line and origin of dorsal fin; gill rakers 30 to 36; depth of body 2.2 to 2.6 in standard length; width of body 2.2 to 2.4 in depth; mouth low on head, nearly horizontal and small, the maxilla reaching to or slightly beyond a vertical at front edge of eye; lips very fleshy; a median groove on chin; a row of close-set conical teeth in jaws, with smaller teeth inside; caudal fin forked; dorsal fin deeply notched between spinous and soft portions; fins scaled except spinous portion of dorsal fin; silvery gray, the scales of the back with a dark central spot, thus tending to form diagonal dotted bands; anterior half of body more darkly pigmented than remaining portion; fins dusky, the anal and pelvics darkest; peritoneum not black (darkly pigmented on *Haemulon*); young with two black stripes and a black spot at base of caudal fin. Largest specimen, 23.5 inches, 9 pounds, from the Virgin Islands. Florida to Brazil, including the Gulf of Mexico. A common inshore fish of rocky bottom; often found in caves by day. Edible, not but highly esteemed.

Porkfish

Anisotremus virginicus (Linnaeus, 1758).
Figures 205 & 206

Dorsal rays XII,16 or 17; anal rays III,9 to 11; pectoral rays 17 or 18; lateral-line scales 51 to 53; 10 or 11 rows of scales between lateral line and origin of dorsal fin; gill

Figure 204. Black Margate (*Anisotremus surinamensis*), Bonaire.

Figure 205. Porkfish (*Anisotremus virginicus*), Roatan, Honduras.

Figure 206. Porkfish (*Anisotremus virginicus*), juvenile, 2.5 inches, Puerto Rico.

rakers 27 to 29; depth of body 2 to 2.4 in standard length; width of body 2.7 to 2.9 in depth; mouth similar to *A. surinamensis*, but more diagonal and lips not so fleshy; a diagonal black band from corner of mouth through eye to nape; a black bar anteriorly on body; body posterior to bar with alternating stripes of silvery blue and yellow; fins yellow; young with whitish body bearing two black stripes and a black spot at base of caudal fin; head and fins yellow. Attains about 1 foot in length. Tropical western Atlantic; introduced to Bermuda. A common reef fish sometimes seen in sizeable schools. The young, and occasionally the adults pick ectoparasites from the bodies of other fishes; the adults feed upon a wide variety of small invertebrate animals.

Margate

Haemulon album Cuvier, 1830. Figure 207

Dorsal rays XII,15 to 17; anal rays III,7 or 8; pectoral rays 18 or 19; lateral-line scales 49 to 52; scales around caudal peduncle 25 to 27; gill rakers 21 to 24; scale rows just below lateral line oblique; eye small; usual color phase dull silvery, the fins largely gray; no black pigment below upper margin of preopercle; a second phase has a mid-lateral dark stripe and two narrower ones on the back; the dorsal and caudal fins of subadults and the back above a line from dorsal base to lower margin of caudal fin are often blackish. The largest species of the genus; largest individual taken by the author, 25.6 inches, from the Virgin Islands. Bermuda, Florida Keys, and West Indies to Brazil; not yet recorded from continental shores of the Caribbean Sea. A clear-water species that may be seen over reefs but is more often encountered over nearby sand flats and seagrass beds. Although active at night like most grunts, it also feeds heavily by day. Has been observed to nose into the sand to eat such subsurface invertebrates as peanut worms and heart urchins. Highly regarded as a food fish.

Tomtate

Haemulon aurolineatum Cuvier, 1830.
Figure 208

Dorsal rays XII to XIV,14 or 15

Figure 207. Margate (*Haemulon album*), Long Island, Bahamas.

Figure 208. Tomtate (*Haemulon aurolineatum*), St. Croix, Virgin Islands.

(usually XIII,15); anal rays III,9; pectoral rays 17 or 18 (usually 17); lateral-line scales 49 to 52; scales around caudal peduncle 22; gill rakers 24 to 28; depth of body 2.7 to 3.7 in standard length; scale rows below lateral line parallel to long axis of body; silvery white with a mid-lateral yellow stripe running from eye to a large round black spot at base of caudal fin; a second narrower yellow stripe on back above lateral line. Only this species, *striatum*, and *boschmae* of the genus *Haemulon* have XIII dorsal spines. Maximum length slightly less than 10 inches. Cape Cod to Brazil. Common. Classified at times in the genus *Bathystoma*.

Black Grunt

Haemulon bonariense Cuvier, 1830.

Figure 209

Dorsal rays XII,15 or 16; anal rays III,8 or 9 (usually 8); pectoral rays 16 or 17; lateral-line scales 45 to 48; scales around caudal peduncle 21 or 22; gill rakers 19 to 23; scale rows below lateral line oblique; bluish silver with about 18 blackish yellow oblique stripes on body; a small amount of black pigment under upper margin of preopercle. Reaches a length of about 11 inches. Southern Gulf of Mexico and Cuba to Brazil. Rare in the West Indies, but abundant along the southern shore of the Caribbean. Found in a variety of habitats such as coral reefs, beds of algae or seagrass, and mud.

Bronzestriped Grunt

Haemulon boschmae (Metzelaar, 1919).

Figure 210

Dorsal rays XIII (rarely XIV),13 or 14; anal rays III,7 to 9 (usually 8); pectoral rays 17 to 19; lateral-line scales 49 to 54; scales around caudal peduncle usually 26; gill rakers

Figure 209. Black Grunt (*Haemulon bonariense*), 7.3 inches, Puerto Rico.

Figure 210. Bronzestriped Grunt (*Haemulon boschmae*), 4.5 inches, Isla Cubagua, Venezuela.

29 to 36; body relatively slender, the depth 2.9 to 4.2 in standard length; scale rows below lateral line mostly horizontal; head scaled except for tip of snout and chin; mouth small and oblique; yellowish to greenish silver on back, silvery on sides, with four brown to bronze stripes on upper half of body and a large black spot at caudal base. The smallest species of *Haemulon;* attains about 7.5 inches. Colombia to French Guiana, including islands on the continental shelf.

Caesar Grunt

Haemulon carbonarium Poey, 1860.
Figure 211

Dorsal rays XII,15 to 16 (usually 15); anal rays III,8; pectoral rays 16 or 17 (usually 17); lateral-line scales 47 to 50; scales around caudal peduncle 22; gill rakers 23 to 26; scale rows below lateral line approximately parallel to long axis of body; bluish silver on back, silver on sides, the edges of the scales narrowly grayish brown; narrow yellow to bronze stripes on body; snout and fins primarily brownish. Largest collected by author, 14.2 inches.

Tropical western Atlantic. Not uncommon.

Smallmouth Grunt

Haemulon chrysargyreum Günther, 1859.
Figure 212

Dorsal rays XII,13; anal rays III,9 or 10 (usually 9); pectoral rays 15 to 17; lateral-line scales 49 to 51; scales around caudal peduncle 21 or 22; gill rakers 30 to 33; depth of body 2.9 to 3.7 in standard length; scale rows below lateral line parallel to long axis of body; scales on top of head extending forward to anterior nostrils and on side of head to corner of mouth; snout short, its length about 8 to 10 in standard length; mouth nearly horizontal and small, the maxilla usually not reaching a vertical at front edge of pupil; color pattern of alternating broad stripes of silver and yellow; fins largely yellow. Largest collected by author, 9.2 inches. Tropical western Atlantic, but not Bermuda. Often seen in small schools by day in the shelter of reefs. Some authors have placed this species by itself in the genus *Brachygenys*.

Figure 211. Caesar Grunt (*Haemulon carbonarium*), Roatan, Honduras.

Figure 212. Smallmouth Grunt (*Haemulon chrysargyreum*), Bonaire.

Figure 213. French Grunt (*Haemulon flavolineatum*), Puerto Rico.

French Grunt

Haemulon flavolineatum (Desmarest, 1823).

Figures 203 & 213

Dorsal rays XII,14 or 15; anal rays III,7 or 8 (usually 8); pectoral rays 16 or 17; lateral-line scales 47 to 50; scales around caudal peduncle 22; gill rakers 22 to 24; scales below lateral line larger than above; scale rows beneath lateral line oblique; bluish silver with yellow stripes, those above lateral line horizontal and those below decidedly oblique; fins yellow; a black region beneath upper free margin of preopercle. A relatively small species, it reaches a length of only about 1 foot. Tropical western Atlantic. Generally the most common grunt on reefs of southern Florida and the West Indies.

Spanish Grunt

Haemulon macrostomum Günther, 1859.

Figure 214

Dorsal rays XII,15 to 17; anal rays III,9; pectoral rays 17 or 18 (rarely 17); lateral-line scales 50 to 52; scales around caudal peduncle 22; gill rakers 26 to 28; body relatively deep, the depth 2.4 to 3.2 in standard length; scale rows just below lateral line oblique; snout long, 5.3 to 7.7 in standard length, and mouth large, the maxilla reaching to below center of eye; soft portion of dorsal fin relatively high; silvery gray with dark stripes on upper half of body, the region between the uppermost stripe and the dorsal fin yellow; a light yellow area dorsally on caudal peduncle. Largest collected by the author, 17 inches. Tropical western Atlantic. Moderately common.

Figure 214. Spanish Grunt (*Haemulon macrostomum*), Belize.

Figure 215. Cottonwick (*Haemulon melanurum*), 7 inches, St. John, Virgin Islands.

Figure 216. Sailor's Choice (*Haemulon parra*), Bonaire.

Cottonwick

Haemulon melanurum (Linnaeus, 1758).
Figure 215

Dorsal rays XII,15 to 17; anal rays III,8 or 9 (usually 8); pectoral rays 16 to 18; lateral-line scales 49 to 52; scales around caudal peduncle 23 to 25; gill rakers 20 to 23; scale rows beneath lateral line slightly oblique; silvery white with narrow yellow stripes, the broadest mid-lateral; body black above a sharp demarcation from front of dorsal fin to lower center of caudal base, this color continuous with black at base of dorsal fin and broad black bands in lobes of caudal fin. Reaches 13 inches. Tropical western Atlantic. Prefers clear water. Not very common.

Sailor's Choice

Haemulon parra (Desmarest, 1823).
Figure 216

Dorsal rays XII,16 to 18; anal rays III,8; pectoral rays 17; lateral-line scales 51 or 52; scales around caudal peduncle 21 or 22; gill rakers 21 to 26; scale rows below lateral line oblique; predominately silvery, the edges of the scales narrowly brown, the centers on about upper half of body with a spot which may vary in color from yellow through bronze to dark brown (thus forming oblique dotted lines following scale rows); eye yellow; usually black under upper margin of preopercle. Attains 16 inches. Tropical western Atlantic, but not Bermuda. May be common in continental waters, but relatively rare at most islands of the West Indies.

Figure 217. White Grunt (*Haemulon plumieri*), Long Island, Bahamas.

White Grunt

Haemulon plumieri (Lacepède, 1802).
Figure 217

Dorsal rays XII,15 to 17; anal rays III,8 or 9 (usually 9), pectoral rays 16 or 17; lateral-line scales 48 to 52; scales around caudal peduncle 22; gill rakers 21 to 27; similar to *macrostomum* in body depth and large size of mouth; scales above lateral line larger than those below; scale rows just below lateral line oblique; color variable but usually light yellowish, the head with narrow light blue stripes; scales of body with a bluish silver spot, the spots tending to merge in middle of body to form wavy lines. Reaches a length of about 16 inches. A common species ranging from Chesapeake Bay to Brazil. Introduced to Bermuda.

Bluestriped Grunt

Haemulon sciurus (Shaw, 1803).
Figure 218

Dorsal rays XII,16 or 17 (usually 16); anal rays III,8 or 9 (usually 9); pectoral rays 16 or 17; lateral-line scales 48 to 51; scales around caudal peduncle 22; gill rakers 27 to 32; scale rows below lateral line slightly oblique; yellow with blue stripes. Largest collected by author, 15.5 inches; recorded to 18 inches. Tropical western Atlantic, with stragglers ranging north to South Carolina. One of the most colorful and most common of the grunts of West Indian reefs.

Latin Grunt

Haemulon steindachneri (Jordan & Gilbert, 1882).
Figure 219

Dorsal rays XII,15 to 17 (rarely 17); anal rays III,8 to 10; pectoral

Figure 218. Bluestriped Grunt (*Haemulon sciurus*), Long Island, Bahamas.

rays 17 or 18; lateral-line scales 51 or 52; scales around caudal peduncle usually 26; gill rakers 22 to 25; body not elongate, the depth 2.5 to 2.8 in standard length (in contrast to *H. boschmae* which is more slender; depth of remaining species of *Haemulon* 2.3 to 3 in standard length); scales below lateral line oblique; anal fin more heavily scaled than other species; silvery gray or brown on back, silvery on sides, with dark lines following oblique scale rows; a large black spot at caudal base; black under upper margin of preopercle; a dark mid-lateral stripe may be present on head and body. Reaches about 10.5

Figure 219. Latin Grunt (*Haemulon steindachneri*), 5.5 inches, Trinidad.

Figure 220. Striped Grunt (*Haemulon striatum*), 7.1 inches, Venezuela.

inches. Both sides of tropical America; in the Atlantic from Panama to Rio de Janeiro; common in the southern Caribbean; collected by the author only at Isla de Margarita, Trinidad and Tobago.

Striped Grunt

Haemulon striatum (Linnaeus, 1758).

Figure 220

Dorsal rays XIII,13 or 14; anal rays III,7 to 9 (usually 8); pectoral rays 17 to 19; lateral-line scales 51 to 53; scales around caudal peduncle 25 to 27; gill rakers 28 to 34; depth of body 3.1 to 3.8 in standard length; body less compressed than other species of the genus; scale rows below lateral line oblique; head entirely scaled except for front of snout near upper lip and front of chin (scales on top of head of other

Figure 221. Corocoro (*Orthopristis rubra*), 10 inches, Trinidad.

species of *Haemulon* except *boschmae* end at about level of nostrils); snout very short, the length 9 to 12 in standard length; mouth small, the maxilla not reaching a vertical through center of eye, and relatively protractile; silvery gray with five dusky yellow stripes, the two lowermost the broadest. Attains 11 inches. Gulf of Mexico to Brazil. Rare inshore; appears to prefer water of moderate depth.

Corocoro

Orthopristis rubra (Cuvier, 1830).

Figure 221

Dorsal rays XII,14 or 15; anal rays III,10 or 11 (usually 10); pectoral rays 18; lateral-line scales 53 or 54; gill rakers 20 to 23; body moderately deep, the depth 2.4 to 2.7 in standard length, and somewhat compressed, the width about 2.3 to 2.4 in depth; mouth small and moderately oblique, the maxilla not reaching posterior to front edge of eye; caudal fin slightly forked; grayish brown with violet hues on the back, silvery on the sides, with many small brown-orange spots on head, upper half of body and dorsal fin. Reaches 13 inches. Southern Caribbean to Brazil on rock, sand, or mud bottoms from the shore to at least 200 feet.

PORGIES
(SPARIDAE)

The porgies are similar in a number of respects to the grunts. Typically they are deep-bodied and compressed. The mouth is small, low on the head and horizontal; the maxilla slips under the edge of the suborbital region for most of its length;

the distal end of the premaxilla overlaps the maxilla externally; the premaxilla is only slightly protractile. The teeth are stout, those of the sides of the jaws broad and blunt; there are no teeth on the roof of the mouth. The posterior nostrils are usually large and elongate. There are no spines on the opercle. There is a single continuous dorsal fin.

Four genera are known from the Caribbean Sea: *Calamus, Archosargus, Diplodus* and *Pagrus. Calamus,* with 11 western Atlantic species, is represented by only five in the Caribbean; one of these, *C. cervigoni,* which has a large black area in the dorsal fin, is a mud-bottom form of the southern part of the sea. The remaining four are discussed below. Three others, C. *leucosteus, C. proridens* and *C. nodosus,* appear to have the Campeche Bank in the southeastern Gulf of Mexico as the southern limit of their range, and *C. campechanus,* a close relative of the Grass Porgy *(C. arctifrons)* from the northeastern Gulf, is thus far known only from the bank. *Archosargus* has two western Atlantic species, the well-known Black-barred Sheepshead *(A. probatocephalus),* with a southern subspecies *(aries)* that occurs in brackish water areas from Belize to Brazil, and *A. rhomboidalis.* Of the three western Atlantic species of *Diplodus,* only *D. argenteus* is known from the Caribbean Sea. *Pagrus* is represented in the western Atlantic only by *P. sedecim.*

Porgies are bottom-dwelling, and although they are often seen over rocky areas or reefs, they also occur on flat bottoms. They do not seek shelter in reefs but rely on keeping

Figure 222. Jolthead Porgy (*Calamus bajonado*), night photo, Long Island, Bahamas.

a considerable distance between themselves and a potential source of danger. Species of *Calamus* are carnivorous, feeding mainly on invertebrates with hard parts such as sea urchins, crabs and mollusks which they crush with their molariform teeth. *A. rhomboidalis* and *D. argenteus* are omnivorous, but feed more on plant material than animal. Porgies, in general, are good food fishes.

At night porgies may assume a disruptive color pattern of irregular dark bars (Figure 222).

Sea Bream

Archosargus rhomboidalis (Linnaeus, 1758).
Figure 223

Dorsal rays XIII, 10 or 11 (usually 11); anal rays III, 10 or 11 (usually 10); lateral-line scales 46 to 49; dorsal fin preceded by a small forward-directed spine (not obvious due to covering by epidermis); teeth incisiform at front of jaws and molariform on the sides, the latter in three rows above and two below; body deep, the depth 1.8 to 2.2 in standard length, and compressed, the width 3 to 3.4 in depth; silvery with yellow stripes and a blackish spot about as large as eye just below front part of lateral line. Maximum length about 13 inches. New Jersey to Brazil, including the eastern Gulf of Mexico and the West Indies. A shallow-water species most commonly found in mangrove sloughs and seagrass beds; occasionally seen on *Porites* reefs near such habitats. Omnivorous but feeds mainly on seagrasses and algae; those animals in its diet are mainly small benthic crustaceans and mollusks. *Archosargus unimaculatus* is a synonym.

Figure 223. Sea Bream (*Archosargus rhomboidalis*), 6.6 inches, Puerto Rico.

Figure 224. Jolthead Porgy (*Calamus bajonado*), Long Island, Bahamas.

Jolthead Porgy

Calamus bajonado (Bloch & Schneider, 1801).   Figures 222 & 224

Dorsal rays XII,12; anal rays III,10; pectoral rays 15 (rarely 14 or 16); lateral-line scales 50 to 57; third canine tooth from center of upper jaw enlarged (in individuals greater than about 7 inches) but not outcurved; an irregular row of small molariform teeth inside and toward the front of the three usual rows of molars at side of upper jaw; dorsal profile of head evenly convex and not very steep; eye large; prefrontal tubercle above posterior nostril poorly developed; silvery, the scales with a faint iridescence of blue-green and lavender in the centers and brassy on the edges; cheeks brassy, with or without blue markings; a blue line under eye; no blue spot at upper end of gill opening; a small blue spot at upper pectoral base; lips and throat purplish; corner of mouth orange. Underwater the most characteristic markings are two horizontal white bands on the cheek. The largest species of the genus, it reaches at least 22 inches in length. Bermuda and Rhode Island to Belize and throughout the West Indies, from shallow water to 150 feet. Usually seen in clear-water areas over or near reefs. Adults feed heavily on sea urchins, including *Diadema*, when available.

Saucereye Porgy

Calamus calamus (Valenciennes, 1830).   Figure 225

Very similar to *Calamus pennatula*. Differs in having 11 (rarely 10) anal soft rays, the prefrontal tubercle moderately developed; the fleshy width of the maxil-

Figure 225. Saucereye Porgy (*Calamus calamus*), Andros, Bahamas.

Figure 226. Sheepshead Porgy (*Calamus penna*), Puerto Rico.

lary tubercle smaller than the largest molariform tooth (usually larger on *pennatula)* and in color. The cheek area is usually blue with yellow spots; the blue markings on the scales are more linear (usually a vertical line or vertical row of spots); there is no horizontal blue band above the gill opening, but a dark bluish smudge may often be seen behind the upper end of the opening. Largest, 14.5 inches, from Bermuda. Known from Bermuda, Florida Keys, West Indies and reefs off Belize.

Sheepshead Porgy

Calamus penna (Valenciennes, 1830).
Figure 226

Dorsal rays XII,12; anal rays III,10; pectoral rays 15 (rarely 14 or 16); lateral-line scales 45 to 49; canine teeth at front of jaws about equal in size; no small teeth medial to three rows at side of upper jaw; eye relatively small; suborbital depth the least, on the average, of any species of *Calamus;* usually no free margin on lower edge of maxillary tubercle (above upper lip); prefrontal tubercle poorly developed; silvery, the scales with iridescent reflections; usually a faint longitudinal banding on body; a blue-gray line under eye present or absent; no other blue markings; no orange or yellow at corner of mouth; a small black spot at upper base of pectoral fins. Attains a length of at least 16 inches. Tropical western Atlantic from 10 to 270 feet. When close to the bottom this species may display dark bars on the body (barred color phases are known for other porgies as well).

Pluma

Calamus pennatula Guichenot, 1868.

Figure 227

Dorsal rays XII, 12; anal rays III, 10 (rarely 9 or 11); pectoral rays 14 (rarely 13 or 15); lateral-line scales 51 to 56; fourth canine tooth from front of upper jaw enlarged and strongly outcurved in adults (enlargement begins at a length of about 5 inches, and the outcurving at about 8.5 inches); a partial row of small molariform teeth inside and toward the front of the three usual rows of molars at side of upper jaw; dorsal profile of head moderately steep; prefrontal tubercle not well developed; silvery with a lavender iridescence, the edges of the scales brownish yellow and the centers with a vertically elongate iridescent blue-green or blue spot (posteriorly the spots more round); nape and a broad anterior region of back with a wash of yellow; a broad pale blue band approximately centered above upper end of gill opening; a horizontal blue line under eye; three blue lines extending anteriorly from eye; unscaled portion of cheek with alternate irregular lines of brassy yellow and purplish blue; a bright iridescent blue area and a small orange-red spot at upper base of pectoral fins; corner of mouth pale yellow. Largest specimen collected by author, 14.6 inches, from the Bahamas. Caribbean Sea, south to Brazil, from the shore to 280 feet. The most common porgy of the genus in the West Indies.

Silver Porgy

Diplodus argenteus (Valenciennes, 1830).

Figure 228

Dorsal rays XII, 13 or 14 (usually 13); anal rays III, 12 to 14; pectoral rays 15 or 16; lateral-line scales 58

Figure 227. Pluma (*Calamus pennatula*), Andros, Bahamas.

Figure 228. Silver Porgy (*Diplodus argenteus*), 10.8 inches, St. John, Virgin Islands.

to 62; dorsal fin not preceded by a forward-directed spine; well-developed incisiform teeth at front of jaws, and molariform teeth in three rows on sides of jaws (two rows posteriorly in lower jaw); depth of body 1.7 to 2 in standard length; width of body 2.9 to 3.4 in depth; suborbital depth about 5 to 6 in head; silvery with a black spot larger than eye on upper anterior part of caudal peduncle; about nine faint narrow dark bars may be visible on upper two-thirds of body. Reaches a length of about 1 foot. Southern Florida and Caribbean Sea to Argentina; not common in the West Indies. An inshore fish most often seen in clear-water areas with rocky bottom. *Diplodus caudimacula* is a synonym.

Red Porgy

Pagrus sedecim Ginsburg, 1952.

Figure 229

Dorsal rays XII,9 to 11 (usually

Figure 229. Red Porgy (*Pagrus sedecim*), 11 inches, Punto Fijo, Venezuela.

10); anal rays III,8; pectoral rays 15 or 16; lateral-line scales 54 to 57; dorsal fin not preceded by a forward-projecting spine (present in *Calamus*, but largely hidden by skin and scales); teeth at front of jaws conical; sides of jaws with two rows of molariform teeth except those at front of outer row which are subconical; a cleft in side of snout above upper lip; posterior nostrils diagonal and elongate (but not as long and slit-like as in *Calamus*); depth of body 2.4 to 2.8 in standard length (1.9 to 2.6 in above species of *Calamus*); eye large; suborbital depth moderate, 3.7 to 5 in head length; pinkish silver with an indistinct yellow spot on each scale on about upper half of body, these spots giving a yellow-striped effect; a wedge of yellow across interorbital and some yellow on snout and upper lip; dorsal, caudal and pectoral fins pink. Reaches a length of at least 20 inches. New York to Argentina, but not the West Indies. Closely related to *P. pagrus* of the eastern Atlantic and Mediterranean. A fish of moderate depths (30 to at least 270 feet).

CROAKERS AND DRUMS
(SCIAENIDAE)

The sciaenids are carnivorous bottom-dwelling fishes of shallow tropic and temperate seas. Most are characteristic of open sedimentary bottoms, and many occur only in turbid brackish environments. They are usually more-or-less elongate in general body form and silvery in color. Most have inferior mouths with the maxilla slipping under the free edge of the suborbital region, and the teeth very small, but others such as the Weakfishes or Seatrouts *(Cynoscion)* have serranid-like heads with projecting lower jaw and canine teeth. Typically the chin of

Figure 230. Reef Croaker (*Odontoscion dentex*), night photo at a depth of 60 feet, Belize.

croakers has large pores, and there may be barbels. There are no incisiform or molariform teeth, and no teeth in the roof of the mouth. The bones of the skull are cavernous; the opercle usually ends in two flat points. The dorsal fin is deeply notched or divided into two fins; the anal fin has only I or II spines; the caudal fin is usually not forked.

The common names "Drum" and "Croaker" are derived from the noise–making capacity of these fishes. The well-developed swimbladder serves as a resonance chamber for sounds produced by the vibration of special muscles which are attached to the air bladder walls. The structure of the swimbladder is important in the generic classification. The otoliths (ear bones) are large and often of characteristic shape.

Many of the sciaenids are valuable food fishes. Seventeen genera occur in the Caribbean Sea. Only four species of two of these genera are reef fishes, all of which are primarily nocturnal. A few others such as the two Caribbean species of *Umbrina* (characterized by a serrate preopercle, a single short barbel at the tip of the chin and dark bars on the body) can be taken along sandy shores not too distant from reefs. Adults of the Blue Croaker *(Bairdiella batabana)* have on a few occasions been observed in the shelter of reefs of moderate depth. This species lacks barbels on the chin; it has narrow dark stripes below the lateral line and a few small dark spots above, some arranged in short rows; there are usually 20 or 21 gill rakers.

Jackknife Fish

Equetus lanceolatus (Linnaeus, 1758).
Figure 231
Dorsal rays XIII or XIV, 49 to 55; pectoral rays 15 or 16; lateral-line

Figure 231. Jackknife Fish (*Equetus lanceolatus*), Bonaire.

Figure 232. Spotted Drum (*Equetus punctatus*), Bonaire.

scales 48 to 55; teeth in jaws in a villiform band, the outer row not enlarged; first dorsal fin very elevated, its height in adults 2.7 to 3.1 in standard length; pelvic fins of adults not reaching anus; gray with three white-edged dark brown to black bands, the first running vertically through eye, the second from nape across operculum and chest to front of pelvic fins, and the last beginning on first dorsal fin and running to end of caudal fin. The young are similar to the juveniles of *Equetus punctatus*, but they lack a black spot on the snout. Attains about 9 inches. Bermuda and South Carolina to Brazil. Not common in the West Indies; usually found in deeper water, on the average, than *E. punctatus* and *Pareques acuminatus*. Feeds mainly on small shrimps and crabs, but also on polychaete worms and gastropod mollusks.

Spotted Drum

Equetus punctatus (Bloch & Schneider, 1801). Figures 232 & 233

Dorsal rays XI or XII-I,45 to 47; pectoral rays 17 or 18; lateral-line scales 52 to 56; teeth similar to *Pareques acuminatus;* first dorsal fin very elevated, its height in adults 2.4 to 3.4 in standard length (extremely high in juveniles); pelvic fins of adults reaching posterior to anus; head white with two dark brown bars, one through eye, the other more posterior and more diagonal, extending across chest to pelvics; body white with a broad dark brown band beginning on front of first dorsal fin, curving across nape, above pectoral fin, and running to mid-base of caudal fin; two narrower dark stripes above and below this band; second dorsal, caudal and anal fins dark brown with white spots; paired fins dark brown; juveniles with a black spot at front

Figure 233. Spotted Drum (*Equetus punctatus*), juvenile, St. Croix, Virgin Islands.

of snout. Largest specimen, 10.6 inches, from the Virgin Islands. Southern Florida and the West Indies. Secretive by day in reefs and usually solitary.

Reef Croaker

Odontoscion dentex (Cuvier, 1830).
Figures 230 & 234

Dorsal rays XI or XII-I or II,22 to 25; lateral-line scales 48 to 51; gill rakers 25 or 26; no barbels; preopercular margin weakly serrate; mouth terminal; jaws with widely spaced canine teeth of moderate size as well as smaller conical teeth; caudal fin truncate. Brownish silver with dark dots on scales;

Figure 234. Reef Croaker (*Odontoscion dentex*), 5.6 inches, Puerto Rico.

Figure 235. High Hat (*Pareques acuminatus*), Puerto Rico.

Figure 236. High Hat (*Pareques acuminatus*), juvenile, Belize.

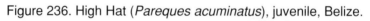

a large black spot at base and axil of pectoral fins. Although said to reach 1 foot, none of many collected by the author in West Indian localities have exceeded 7 inches. Tropical western Atlantic. Forms aggregations in small caves in reefs by day; feeds at night, primarily on small fishes and shrimps, and their larvae.

High Hat

Pareques acuminatus (Bloch & Schneider, 1801).   Figures 235 & 236

Dorsal rays IX or X-I,37 to 40; pectoral rays 16 or 17; lateral-line scales 45 to 50; teeth in jaws in a villiform band, the outer row of upper jaw enlarged; first dorsal fin elevated, its height in adults 5.3 to 7.5 in standard length; pelvic fins of adults usually just reaching anus (fins of juveniles greatly prolonged, the first dorsal of a 1-inch fish is half the standard length, and the

pelvic fins reach beyond the spinous portion of the anal fin); color pattern of dark brown and white stripes, the dark stripes alternating in width from narrow to broad. Probably does not exceed 9 inches. Bermuda and South Carolina to Rio de Janeiro. Typically found as small groups hiding beneath rock ledges by day.

GOATFISHES
(MULLIDAE)

The goatfishes, sometimes called the surmullets, are distinctive among inshore fishes in their possession of a pair of long barbels on the chin. Their bodies are elongate and only slightly compressed. There are two widely separated dorsal fins, the first of VI to VIII spines. The mouth is small and ventral in position, the upper jaw slightly protruding; the teeth are small and conical.

Figure 237. Yellow Goatfish (*Mulloidichthys martinicus*), Bonaire.

Goatfishes live in close association with sand or mud bottoms. During feeding the barbels, which are supplied with chemosensory organs, are moved rapidly over the substratum or thrust deeply into the sediment. When not in use they can be carried in a median groove in the throat region. The food consists primarily of a great variety of small invertebrate animals, many of which normally live beneath the surface of the sand or mud.

Four species, each in a different genus, are known from the western Atlantic. The two discussed below are often seen as adults in reef-sand areas, and the young are common in seagrass beds. The other two species, *Mullus auratus* and *Upeneus parvus*, are found in deeper water and are characteristic of mud or silty sand bottoms. Both have teeth on the roof of the mouth which are lacking on *Mulloidichthys* and *Pseudupeneus*. *U. parvus* has blackish bands on the lobes of the caudal fin and VII dorsal spines.

Yellow Goatfish

Mulloidichthys martinicus (Cuvier, 1829).

Figures 237 & 238

Dorsal rays VIII-I,8 (first dorsal spine minute, often embedded); pectoral rays 15 to 17; lateral-line scales 34 to 39; teeth in jaws in two irregular rows at front and a single row at sides; light olivaceous on back, whitish on sides, with a lateral yellow stripe on body; median fins yellow. Recorded to 15.5 inches off Venezuela. Tropical western Atlantic. Often observed in aggregations. Very closely related to *Mulloidichthys dentatus* of the eastern Pacific and *M. vanicolensis* of the Indo-Pacific region.

Figure 238. Yellow Goatfish (*Mulloidichthys martinicus*), St. Croix, Virgin Islands.

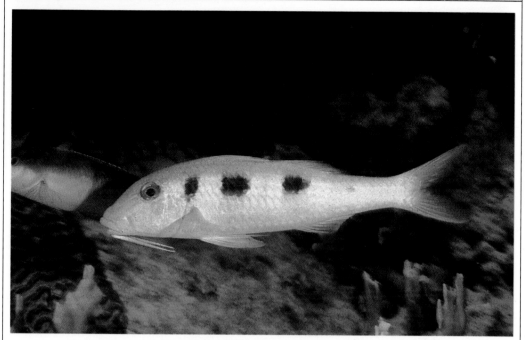

Figure 239. Spotted Goatfish (*Pseudupeneus maculatus*), Bonaire.

Spotted Goatfish

Pseudupeneus maculatus (Bloch, 1793).
Figure 239

Dorsal rays VIII-I,8 (first dorsal spine minute); pectoral rays 13 to 16; lateral-line scales 27 to 31; a series of three large blackish blotches on upper side of body beneath dorsal fins; color otherwise variable but usually pale, the scales of the back with reddish or yellowish brown edges and a central pale blue spot; diagonal light blue lines on head. Capable of displaying a pattern of large red blotches on head and body in less than a minute. Reaches a maximum length of about 11 inches. Bermuda and New Jersey to Rio de Janeiro.

SWEEPERS
(PEMPHERIDAE)

The sweepers are a small tropical family of two genera; only *Pempheris*

is here considered. The body is compressed and moderately deep anteriorly, tapering markedly toward the tail. There is a single short dorsal fin, higher than its base, all of which is anterior to the center of the body; the anal fin is very long, scaled and not elevated; the caudal fin is emarginate or forked. There are no spines on the opercle. The scales are both cycloid and ctenoid; the head is nearly fully scaled. The lateral line is highly arched anteriorly, thence follows the contour of the back to the end of the middle caudal rays. The eye is large. The mouth is moderately large and very oblique, the upper jaw somewhat protrusible; the maxilla, which is broad posteriorly, is exposed on the cheek. There are small incurved teeth in narrow bands in the jaws and on the palatines and vomer, those on the vomer in a "V"-shaped patch.

The two West Indian species are

Figure 240. Copper Sweeper (*Pempheris schomburgki*), Grand Bahama Island.

usually found in caves by day, sometimes in large aggregations; they are nocturnal and feed on zooplankton.

Shortfin Sweeper

Pempheris poeyi Bean, 1885.   Figure 241

Dorsal rays IV or V,8 or 9 (usually IV,9); anal rays III,22 to 24; pectoral rays 15 or 16; lateral-line scales 49 to 51; gill rakers 5 or 6 + 19 or 20; depth of body about 2.4 in standard length; width about 2.7 in depth; ctenoid scales along back beginning at nape, on side of body posterior to pectoral fins, and ventrally on head and body; color varies from light yellowish brown, only slightly dusky on back, to blackish on entire upper sides and caudal fin. Attains about 4 inches. Caribbean Sea.

Copper Sweeper

Pempheris schomburgki Müller & Troschel, 1848.   Figures 240 & 242

Dorsal rays V,8 or 9; anal rays III,32 to 35; pectoral rays 17 or 18; lateral-line scales 52 to 60; gill rakers 6 or 7 + 18 to 20; depth of body about 2.2 in standard length; width about 3.2 in depth; scales ctenoid along the back posterior to dorsal fin and ventrally on head and body, otherwise cycloid; coppery with a dark band at base of anal fin; young nearly transparent, silvery over abdomen (a color pattern that has given rise to another common name, "Glassy Sweeper"). Attains 6 inches. Tropical western Atlantic. Feeds at night on zooplankton, particularly the larger larval stages of invertebrates.

Figure 241. Shortfin Sweeper (*Pempheris poeyi*), 2.9 inches, Tobago.

Figure 242. Copper Sweeper (*Pempheris schomburgki*), 4.5 inches, St. John, Virgin Islands.

MOJARRAS
(GERREIDAE)

The mojarras are silvery fishes which are usually found on sand or mud bottoms in shallow water. They are characterized by moderately compressed bodies that range from slightly elongate to elevated in shape; the snout is pointed; the upper jaw is very protractile, angling downward when protruded; the posterior part of the maxilla is exposed on the cheek; the teeth in the jaws are small, slender, numerous and close-set; there are no teeth on the roof of the mouth; there is a single dorsal fin, usually with IX dorsal spines and 10 soft rays; the dorsal and anal fins fold into a scaly sheath at their base; the caudal fin is deeply forked and covered with small scales.

Only the three species discussed below may be found on or near Caribbean coral reefs. Other species of *Eucinostomus* and the high-bodied genus *Diapterus* with serrate preopercle are confined to brackish or fresh water regions—usually with mud bottoms.

The gerreids feed on small benthic invertebrates such as polychaete worms, peanut worms, mollusks, crabs, shrimps, amphipods, and other crustaceans.

Unfortunately, the common name "Shad" is applied to these fishes in Bermuda and some English-speaking islands of the West Indies. Mojarras are not related to the true shads.

Spotfin Mojarra

Eucinostomus argenteus Baird & Girard, 1854. Figure 244

Anal rays III,7; lateral-line scales

Figure 243. Yellowfin Mojarra (*Gerres cinereus*), Bonaire.

Figure 244. Spotfin Mojarra (*Eucinostomus argenteus*), 4.6 inches, Curaçao.

44 to 48; depth of body 2.8 to 3.3 in standard length; posterior part of premaxillary groove (in interorbital space) narrow, the scales to the side extending anterior to front edge of eye, almost to nostrils; silvery, the upper anterior part of the dorsal fin dusky. Largest collected by author, 7.5 inches, from Puerto Rico. Eastern Pacific and western Atlantic, the range in the Atlantic from New Jersey to Rio de Janeiro. Most often observed just above the bottom on shallow sand flats.

Mottled Mojarra

Eucinostomus lefroyi (Goode, 1874).

Figure 245

Anal rays II,8; lateral-line scales 44 to 47; depth of body 3.1 to 3.6 in standard length; premaxillary groove similar to that of *argenteus*; silvery, the back broadly mottled. Recorded to 8 inches, but adults are

Figure 245. Mottled Mojarra (*Eucinostomus lefroyi*), 4.8 inches, Culebra, Puerto Rico.

usually much smaller. North Carolina to Brazil. Less common than the preceding species. The character of two anal spines readily separates this species from other western Atlantic species of *Eucinostomus*. Sometimes classified in the genus *Ulaema*.

Yellowfin Mojarra

Gerres cinereus (Walbaum, 1792).

Figures 243 & 246

Anal rays III,7; lateral-line scales 39 to 44; depth of body 2.3 to 2.7 in standard length; premaxillary groove (an unscaled median depressed region which runs on top of snout into interorbital space) broad, the scales to the side not extending to a vertical at front edge of eye; silvery with about seven faint pinkish bars on side of body; pelvic fins yellow. Largest collected by author, 15.3 inches, from the Virgin Islands. Tropical eastern Pacific and western Atlantic, including the Gulf of Mexico. Occurs in brackish environments as well as clear reef areas. Often seen feeding in sand patches among reefs by thrusting its mouth into the sediment and expelling sand from the gill openings.

SEA CHUBS
(KYPHOSIDAE)

The sea chubs, sometimes called the rudderfishes, are plant-feeding fishes usually found near shore over rocky bottoms or coral reefs. They may, however, rise to the surface from moderate depths to feed on floating *Sargassum*. They are relatively deep-bodied, with a small head, and a moderately forked to lunate caudal fin. The mouth is small, and the maxilla slips under the edge of the preorbital. Incisiform teeth are present in one row at the front and sides of the jaws, the horizontal roots visible inside mouth; there are no molariform teeth. The scales are usually ctenoid; the head is scaled except snout (in one eastern Pacific genus, the

Figure 246. Yellowfin Mojarra (*Gerres cinereus*), 14.5 inches, 1.2 pounds, St. John, Virgin Islands.

Figure 247. Bermuda Chub (*Kyphosus sectatrix*), Long Island, Bahamas.

interorbital is also naked). The digestive tract is very long, as is typical of herbivorous fishes. Most are drab-colored.

Chubs may be caught on hook and line with animal material as bait; they are powerful fish and fight vigorously when hooked. The related family Girellidae from the Pacific is now regarded by most recent authors as a subfamily of the Kyphosidae.

Yellow Chub

Kyphosus incisor (Cuvier, 1831).
Figure 248

Dorsal rays XI,13 to 15 (usually 14); anal rays III,12 or 13 (usually 13); pectoral rays 18 to 20 (usually 19); lateral-line scales 54 to 62; gill rakers 6 to 8 + 19 to 22; similar in morphology and color to *sectatrix*; best differentiated by counts. The yellow stripes in *incisor* are brighter,

however, as are the two slightly oblique horizontal bands on the head; the opercular membrane does not seem as darkly pigmented. Has essentially the same distribution as *sectatrix* and apparently attains a comparable size; one collected by the author in the Bahamas measured 26.5 inches in total length and weighed 12 pounds.

Bermuda Chub

Kyphosus sectatrix (Linnaeus, 1758).
Figures 247 & 249

Dorsal rays XI,12 (rarely 11 or 13); anal rays III,11 (rarely 10 or 12); pectoral rays 17 to 19 (usually 18); lateral-line scales 51 to 58; gill rakers 6 to 8 + 16 to 18; depth of body 1.9 to 2.3 in standard length; caudal fin moderately forked; all fins scaled except spinous portion of dorsal; mouth horizontal; a band of small villiform teeth in jaws be-

Figure 248. Yellow Chub (*Kyphosus incisor*), 10 inches, Florida Keys.

hind front row of incisors; villiform teeth on vomer, palatines and tongue; dark gray with dull yellowish stripes on body; two dull yellow horizontal bands on head, both beginning on snout where confluent, the lowermost running under eye to edge of preopercle; upper part of opercular membrane blackish. The young may display pale spots nearly as large as eye on the head, body and fins. Largest collected by author, 30 inches, from Puerto Rico. Atlantic; on the western side from Massachusetts to Brazil.

Figure 249. Bermuda Chub (*Kyphosus sectatrix*), 12.5 inches, Florida Keys.

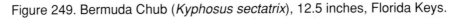

SPADEFISHES
(EPHIPPIDAE)

Spadefish

Chaetodipterus faber (Broussonet, 1782).
Figures 250 & 251

Dorsal rays IX,21 to 23; anal rays III,18 or 19; pectoral rays 17 or 18; lateral-line scales 46 to 49; lower-limb gill rakers 10 to 12; body nearly orbicular, the depth at anus 1.2 to 1.5 in standard length, and compressed, the width 3.7 to 5.3 in depth; mouth small, the maxilla of adults ending beneath nostrils; a band of brush-like teeth in jaws, the outer row the largest (teeth slightly flattened but tips pointed); no teeth on roof of mouth; scales ctenoid; head and fins scaled; opercle ends in an obtuse point; preopercular margin finely and irregularly serrate; anterior parts of dorsal and anal fins of adults prolonged to long lobes; third dorsal spine of young prolonged; pectoral fins short, 1.5 to 1.7 in head; pelvic fins long, nearly reaching origin of anal fin (beyond origin in young); caudal fin emarginate; dull silvery gray with dark bars; the young are more melanistic, the very small juveniles solid black; they resemble dark-colored bits of plant debris. Said to reach a length of 3 feet and a weight of 20 pounds, but any individual over 18 inches is exceptional. Massachusetts to Brazil, in a variety of habitats. Introduced to Bermuda. Adults are often encountered in small schools, swimming well above the bottom; they will circle a diver closely. The diet is exceedingly diverse; feeds on sessile organisms such as sponges, zoantharians,

Figure 250. Spadefish (*Chaetodipterus faber*), Belize.

Figure 251. Spadefish (*Chaetodipterus faber*), 13.8 inches, 3 pounds, St. John, Virgin Islands.

polychaete worms, gorgonians and algae, and on planktonic animals such as pelagic tunicates. The flesh is good to eat.

LEFT-EYE FLOUNDERS
(BOTHIDAE)

The Bothidae is one of seven families of flatfishes (order Pleuronectiformes). They are distinctive in having both eyes on one side. Also the dorsal fin is usually very long, extending forward onto the head. These fishes begin their life as symmetrical larvae; within a few days, one of the eyes migrates to the opposite side of the head. When the little fishes settle out of the plankton and

take up life on the sea bottom, they lie upon their blind side which is usually white.

Most of the flatfishes have a remarkable ability to alter their color to match that of the adjacent bottom. Many partially bury themselves in the bottom sediment and are then even better camouflaged. They are carnivorous; typically they dart out from hiding to feed on small fishes or crustaceans. Many are important food fishes.

The most primitive family, the Psettodidae (no western Atlantic representatives), has spines in the dorsal and pelvic fins, and the dorsal fin does not extend forward on

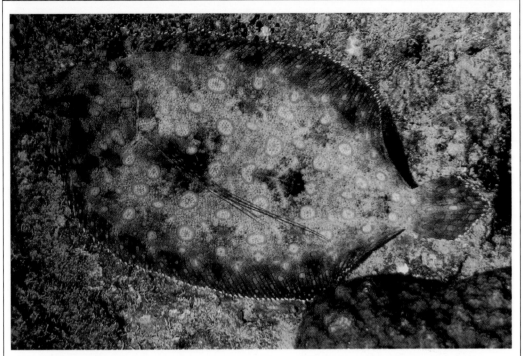

Figure 252. Peacock Flounder (*Bothus lunatus*), St. Croix, Virgin Islands.

the head. The other families are all without spines.

The Bothidae is characterized by normally having both eyes on the left side. The pelvic fin on the blind side is short-based, its first ray distinctly posterior to the first ray of the fin on the ocular side. The lateral line is usually very highly arched at the front. Some authors prefer to classify the bothids as a subfamily of the Pleuronectidae.

A number of species of the family occur in the Caribbean Sea such as members of the genera *Citharichthys*, *Etropus* and *Syacium*, but only the two species of *Bothus* discussed below are commonly encountered on sand in and about shallow reefs. Also not considered here are representatives of the sole family (Soleidae), such as species of *Achirus*, *Trinectes* and *Gymnachirus*, which are usually confined to turbid water.

Peacock Flounder

Bothus lunatus (Linnaeus, 1758).

Figures 252 & 253

Dorsal rays 92 to 99; anal rays 71 to 76; pectoral rays (ocular side) 11 or 12, the upper rays very elongate in large males; lateral-line scales 84 to 95; lower-limb gill rakers 8 to 10; depth of body 1.7 to 2 in standard length; dorsal profile of head of adults notched in front of eyes; eye 5 to 6 in head length; lower eye nearly an eye's length in front of upper; eyes of adult males farther apart than those of females; gray to brown with numerous circles, curved spots, and dots of light blue on head and body; fins with small light blue spots; two or three large diffuse blackish spots on straight portion of lateral line. Reaches a length of about 18 inches. Tropical western Atlantic. The related *B. maculiferus* lacks the notched pro-

Figure 253. Peacock Flounder (*Bothus lunatus*), 11 inches, St. John, Virgin Islands.

Figure 254. Eyed Flounder (*Bothus ocellatus*), female, 2.9 inches, St. John, Virgin Islands.

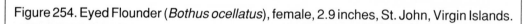

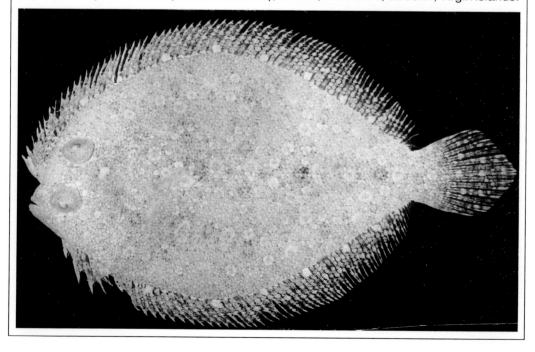

file of the head and has 6 or 7 lower-limb gill rakers.

Eyed Flounder

Bothus ocellatus (Agassiz, 1831).

Figures 254 & 255

Dorsal rays 79 to 91; anal rays 59 to 69; pectoral rays (ocular side) 10, the upper ray or rays somewhat prolonged in males; lateral-line scales 72 to 78; lower-limb gill rakers 8 or 9; depth of body 1.5 to 1.7 in standard length; dorsal profile of head straight to slightly concave before eyes; eye 3.2 to 4.5 in head length; lower eye about a half an eye's length in front of upper in females and a full eye's length in front in males; eyes of adult males much farther apart than females; males with a small spine on snout and generally one or two in front of each eye; light tan to light gray with irregular pale rings or rosettes, some of which are dark-edged; scattered small dark spots and three large blackish spots along straight portion of lateral line, the middle one the best defined. Reaches 7 inches. Bermuda and New York to Rio de Janeiro. The related *B. robinsi* has two obvious black spots in a horizontal row on the caudal fin (on fin of *ocellatus* there are two obscure dark spots in a transverse row). About one-third of the diet of *B. ocellatus* consists of fishes; the rest of its food is crustacean: crabs, shrimps, amphipods, and mantis shrimps.

Tropical Flounder

Paralichthys tropicus Ginsburg, 1933.

Figure 256

Dorsal rays 69 to 80; anal rays 55 to 64; pectoral rays 10 to 12 (usu-

Figure 255. Eyed Flounder (*Bothus ocellatus*), male, 3.9 inches, Curaçao.

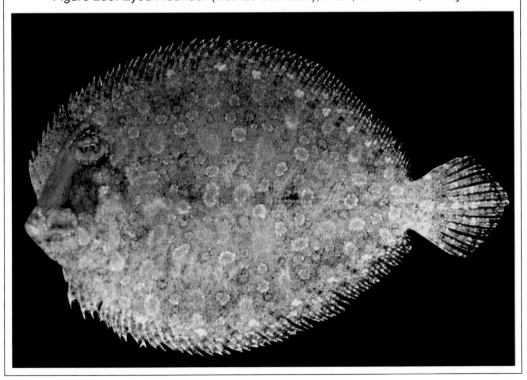

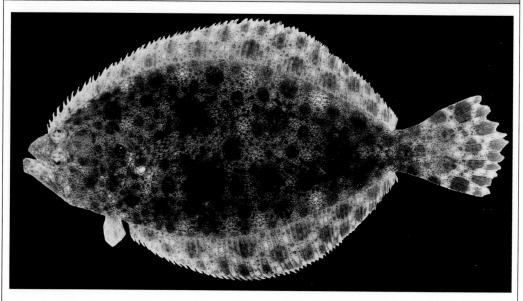

Figure 256. Tropical Flounder (*Paralichthys tropicus*), 9.3 inches, Isla de Margarita, Venezuela.

ally 11); lower-limb gill rakers 10 to 12; lateral line well developed on both sides, the pored scales on ocular side 95 to 98; scales cycloid (ctenoid on ocular side of the two species of *Bothus*); depth of body 2.1 to 2.3 in standard length; head moderately pointed, the head length 3.4 to 3.8 in standard length; lower eye directly below upper or slightly posterior to it; maxilla reaching or nearly reaching a vertical at posterior edge of eyes; teeth uniserial, the anterior ones enlarged; origin of dorsal fin above or slightly anterior to the front edge of eyes; caudal fin biconcave; pelvic fins short-based, symmetrically placed, and subequal; brown with numerous roundish dark spots on head, body and fins, many as large or larger than eyes; also numerous small dark and small pale spots. Attains a length of at least 20 inches. Known from the southern Caribbean Sea from Colombia to Venezuela and Trinidad.

Not uncommon on sand or mud bottoms in shallow water, but recorded to depths as great as 600 feet. The type specimen was collected with a trawl in 186 feet off Trinidad. In spite of its apparent abundance, this species has not been fully exploited commercially. Although it does not preserve well salted, the flesh is of good quality. *P. tropicus* is one of five species of the genus *Paralichthys* in the western North Atlantic, but it is apparently the only one recorded from the Caribbean (however, *P. albigutta*, a distinctive species with three dark ocellated spots forming a triangle on the body, is reported from the Bahamas).

TONGUEFISHES
(CYNOGLOSSIDAE)

The tonguefishes are easily differentiated from other flatfishes by their lanceolate body, confluent median fins, no pectoral fins, a single pelvic fin, small close-set eyes, small curved asymmetrical mouth, and eyes on the left side of the head. They are often called "Tongue Soles," some authors have classified them in the related family Soleidae.

All western Atlantic cynoglossids belong to the genus *Symphurus*; 17 species are known from the region, but others remain in museum collections to be described. A few of the small species are not infrequently collected on sand bottoms near coral reefs with the use of rotenone. Because of their small size and protective coloration they are very difficult to detect alive. One species is discussed below as a representative of the family.

Caribbean Tonguefish

Symphurus arawak Robins & Randall, 1965.
Figure 257

Dorsal rays 69 to 75; anal rays 56 to 61; caudal rays 11 to 14; lateral scale rows 55 to 67: body moderately deep for a tonguefish, the depth 2.8 to 3.6 in standard length; body pale with six to ten large dark blotches which are variously positioned in different individuals but frequently at the periphery of the body; upper and lower blotches are generally in vertical alignment, the last pair often confluent; scattered small dark spots on head and body, including one at upper end of gill opening; caudal fin and adjacent posterior parts of dorsal and anal fins blackish. Largest specimen, 1.8 inches. Known thus far only from the Caribbean Sea in the depth range of 10 to 60 feet.

BUTTERFLYFISHES
(CHAETODONTIDAE)

The chaetodontids are deep-bodied highly compressed fishes which live on coral reefs. They are usually seen as solitary individuals or in pairs. As a group they are among the most colorful of the marine fishes. They have small protractile mouths with slender brush-like teeth in a narrow band in the jaws; there are no teeth on the roof of the mouth. The scales, which are ctenoid, cover the head, body, me-

Figure 257. Caribbean Tonguefish (*Symphurus arawak*), 1.1 inches, St. John, Virgin Islands.

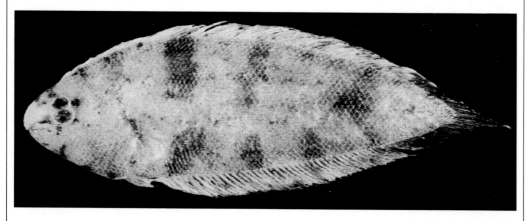

Figure 258. Foureye Butterflyfish (*Chaetodon capistratus*), night photo, Belize.

dian fins, and at least the bases of the paired fins. There is a single continuous dorsal fin with no definite notch between spinous and soft portions. The caudal fin varies in shape from emarginate to rounded; there are 17 principal caudal rays (15 branched).

Most chaetodontids are diurnal; at night they are inactive though generally alert; often they exhibit a nocturnal color pattern which is somewhat different from that of the day (Figure 258). The three shallow-water species of *Chaetodon* from the Caribbean feed principally on tentacles of polychaete tubeworms, coral polyps, and zoantharians (colonial sea anemones).

One other butterflyfish, *Chaetodon guyanensis*, is known from the Caribbean area in addition to the five discussed below. It is a deep-dwelling species (occurs in about 350 to 700 feet), and very few specimens are known. It has two posterior diagonal pale-edged black bands which lie nearly at a right angle to the diagonal black band from the eye to the origin of the dorsal fin. It is a very close relative of *C. aya*, a continental shelf species that ranges from Yucatan to North Carolina.

Foureye Butterflyfish

Chaetodon capistratus Linnaeus, 1758.
Figures 258 to 260

Dorsal rays XIII,19 or 20; anal rays III,16 or 17; lateral-line scales 31 to 35; depth of body 1.3 to 1.6 in standard length; width of body about 4.5 in depth; upper profile of head steep and slightly concave due to protruding snout; light gray, shading to pale yellowish on sides, with two sets of diagonal dark lines on the body, one dorsal and one ven-

Figure 259. Foureye Butterflyfish (*Chaetodon capistratus*), Andros, Bahamas.

Figure 260. Foureye Butterflyfish (*Chaetodon capistratus*), juvenile, Belize.

tral, which meet approximately mid-laterally; a black bar on head; a large white-edged black spot on upper posterior part of body; pelvic fins yellow; a color phase displays two broad dusky bars on the side of the body. Although reported to reach a length of 6 inches, it rarely exceeds 4. Massachusetts to the Caribbean Sea. The most common butterflyfish in the West Indies. It has been presumed that the large ocellated black spot is a false eye; this, plus the obliterative black bar through the eye, supposedly results in a predator confusing the back end of the fish for the front.

Spotfin Butterflyfish

Chaetodon ocellatus Bloch, 1787.

Figures 261 & 262

Dorsal rays XII,19 to 21; anal rays III,16 to 18; lateral-line scales 33 or 34; depth of body 1.25 to 1.6 in standard length; white, the median fins, pelvic fins and caudal peduncle largely bright yellow; a black bar on head through eye; a large blackish spot basally in soft portion of dorsal fin and a small jet black spot distally in fin; a narrow yellow bar from gill opening to pectoral base. Reaches 7 to 8 inches. Massachusetts to Brazil.

Reef Butterflyfish

Chaetodon sedentarius Poey, 1860.

Figure 263

Dorsal rays XIII (rarely XIV),21 to 23; anal rays III,18 or 19; lateral-line scales 36 to 39; depth of body 1.4 to 1.7 in standard length; dorsal and anal fins rounded posteriorly (more angular on preceding species, especially *ocellatus*); white, the edges of the scales yellowish on

Figure 261. Spotfin Butterflyfish (*Chaetodon ocellatus*), Long Island, Bahamas.

Figure 262. Spotfin Butterflyfish (*Chaetodon ocellatus*), juvenile, Belize.

Figure 263. Reef Butterflyfish (*Chaetodon sedentarius*), Bonaire.

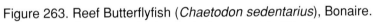

back; a black bar on head through eye; a broad blackish bar across caudal peduncle which extends into soft portions of dorsal fin above and anal fin below; caudal fin light yellow, white at base. Largest collected by author, 5.5 inches, from Puerto Rico. North Carolina to southern Florida, eastern Gulf of Mexico and the Caribbean Sea. Found in deeper water, on the average, than the other species of *Chaetodon*.

Banded Butterflyfish

Chaetodon striatus Linnaeus, 1758.
Figure 264
Dorsal rays XII,21 or 22 (usually 21); anal rays III,16 to 18; lateral-line scales 35 or 36; similar in body form to *C. capistratus*; white with a similar pattern of lines on the body and a black bar through the eye as in *capistratus*, but with two broad black bars on side of body and a

third bar basally in soft portion of dorsal fin which extends onto caudal peduncle; in addition broad black submarginal bands in the median fins; pelvic fins black except for the spine. Attains 6 inches. Both sides of the Atlantic; on the western side from New Jersey to Brazil.

Longsnout Butterflyfish

Prognathodes aculeatus (Poey, 1860).
Figure 265
Dorsal rays XIII,18 or 19; anal rays III,14 to 16; pectoral rays 13 to 15 (15 or 16 for the preceding species of *Chaetodon*); lateral-line scales 22 to 28; depth of body 1.6 to 1.8 in standard length; snout prolonged, the length 2.15 to 2.35 in head; upper half of body yellow-orange, shading into blackish basally in dorsal fin; lower half of body white; orange bands on head and a narrow orange bar on caudal peduncle.

Figure 264. Banded Butterflyfish (*Chaetodon striatus*), Roatan, Honduras.

Figure 265. Longsnout Butterflyfish (*Prognathodes aculeatus*), St. Croix, Virgin Islands.

Largest specimen, 3.5 inches. Southern Florida and the West Indies. Although observed on reefs in as little as 15 feet, this species is rare in less than about 100 feet; beyond this depth (it is known to about 300 feet and probably occurs in even deeper water), it becomes the most common butterflyfish.

ANGELFISHES
(POMACANTHIDAE)

Formerly grouped as a subfamily of the Chaetodontidae, the colorful angelfishes are now considered as a separate family. Although they share a number of general characters with the butterflyfishes, there are significant differences. They have a prominent spine on the cheek at the corner of the preopercle which is lacking in butterflyfishes, but they lack a scaly axillary process at the base of the pelvic fins.

Seven angelfishes occur in the Caribbean Sea. Omitted below is *Centropyge aurantonotus*, recently described from the southern part of the sea and recorded soon after from Brazil.

The juveniles of the species of *Pomacanthus* and *Holacanthus* are colored differently from adults. Although they feed mainly on algae and detritus, they occasionally remove ectoparasites from other fishes. Adults feed primarily on sponges but also ingest tunicates, zoantharians, and algae.

Cherubfish

Centropyge argi Woods & Kanazawa, 1951.
Figure 266

Dorsal rays XIV or XV,15 or 16 (usually XIV,16); anal rays III,17; pectoral rays 15 or 16; lateral-line scales 32 to 34 (lateral line ends beneath rear portion of dorsal fin); gill rakers 22 to 24 (16 to 19 for

Figure 266. Cherubfish (*Centropyge argi*), Bonaire.

other pomacanthid fishes discussed herein); depth of body 1.8 to 2 in standard length (2.3 in the one Bermuda type specimen); a large spine at corner of preopercle and a moderate one on lower margin; upper margin coarsely serrate; three spines on preorbital, the posterior two enlarged and recurved; scales coarsely ctenoid and ridged; caudal fin rounded; deep blue, the head and chest orange-yellow; a narrow blue ring around eye; a small dark blue smudge just behind corner of mouth; spines and spinules of preopercular margin faintly blue; pectoral fins pale yellowish; other fins deep blue with pale blue margins. Largest specimen, 2.7 inches. Bermuda, West Indies and the southern Gulf of Mexico. Although observed in as little as 15 feet of water, it is not common in less than about 100 feet. Also known as the "Pygmy Angelfish."

Blue Angelfish

Holacanthus bermudensis Goode, 1876.

Figure 267

Similar in counts and morphology to the Queen Angelfish; the chief distinction is in color; the scales of the body are yellowish brown to purplish brown with pale edges; the chest and nape are deep purplish blue; there is no large spot on the nape or pectoral base; the blue area posteriorly on gill cover is small; the median fins are purplish, the dorsal and caudal fins with small obscure brownish yellow spots, the dorsal and anal fins with blue margins except for the attenuate posterior part which is yellow; caudal fin with a yellow posterior border (instead of being entirely yellow as in *ciliaris*); the pectorals are blue basally, clear distally, with a broad yellow band separating the two colors; the pelvics are light yellow; the large

Figure 267. Blue Angelfish (*Holacanthus bermudensis*), 9 inches, Grand Bahama Island.

Figure 268. Queen Angelfish (*Holacanthus ciliaris*), St. Croix, Virgin Islands.

spine at the angle of the preopercle is blue, as are the small spines on the margin above it. The caudal fin of the young is entirely yellow, and there are blue bars as in *ciliaris;* the second bar on the body of the Blue Angelfish is straight whereas it is curved on the Queen Angelfish. Reaches 18 inches. Bermuda, southern Florida, Gulf of Mexico and the Bahamas. Observed by the author in the West Indies only off the west end of Grand Bahama Island where it is rare; on the other hand the species is more common in the Florida Keys than the Queen Angelfish. *Holacanthus isabelita* is a synonym. The description of *H. townsendi* was based on hybrid specimens of the Queen and Blue Angelfishes.

Figure 269. Queen Angelfish (*Holacanthus ciliaris*), juvenile, Bonaire.

Queen Angelfish

Holacanthus ciliaris (Linnaeus, 1758).

Figures 268 & 269

Dorsal rays XIV,19 to 21; anal rays III,20 or 21; pectoral rays 19; lateral-line scales 45 to 49; gill rakers 18 to 21; morphology similar to the Rock Beauty, but with no filamentous lobes in the caudal fin; on the other hand the posterior part of the dorsal and anal fins are more prolonged (reaching 1 inch beyond caudal fin of a 15-inch specimen); the spine at the angle of the preopercle is a little shorter; subadults with short spinules on preopercular margin; adults develop short spines on the margin. The color of large adults is purplish blue with yellow-orange rims to the scales; head above eye dark blue, below greenish yellow; mouth, chin, throat, chest and abdomen purplish blue; nape with a large blue-

Figure 270. Rock Beauty (*Holacanthus tricolor*), Bonaire.

edged black spot containing blue flecks; a bright blue blotch posteriorly on gill cover; a blue and black spot at pectoral base; preopercular spines blue; orange anteriorly at base of dorsal fin; paired fins yellow; caudal fin orange-yellow; dorsal and anal fins mostly orange with blue margins. The young have three light blue bars on the body and two on the head bordering a dark bar through the eye. Reported to reach 18 inches; the largest collected by author, 16.8 inches, 3.5 pounds, from the Dominican Republic. Tropical western Atlantic, including the southern Gulf of Mexico and Gulf coast of Florida.

Rock Beauty

Holacanthus tricolor (Bloch, 1795).
Figure 270

Dorsal rays XIV, 17 to 19; anal rays III, 18 to 20; pectoral rays 17 or 18; lateral-line scales about 43 to 46; gill rakers 17 to 20; depth of body 1.5 to 1.9 in standard length; width of body 2.8 to 3 in depth; upper preopercular margin with short spinules; enlarged spine at preopercular angle very long, its length about 2 to 3 in head; lower margin of preopercle with two short spines; a blunt spine on preorbital; caudal fin rounded, the upper and lower rays prolonged in adults (the upper longer); posterior part of dorsal and anal fins prolonged as filaments in adults; most of body of adults black; head, nape, chest, abdomen, front of dorsal fin, hind margin of dorsal and anal fins, and all of paired fins and caudal fin bright yellow; front margin of anal fin and edge of gill cover orange; bright blue on upper and lower part of iris. The young of about an inch in length are entirely yellow except for a blue-edged black spot on the upper side of the body posterior to the midpoint; with growth the black spot soon expands to become the large black area covering most of the body and dorsal and anal fins. Attains a length of about 1 foot; largest collected by author, 10 inches. Tropical western Atlantic, ranging north to Georgia and Bermuda. Appears to be the most common species of the genus on West Indian reefs.

Gray Angelfish

Pomacanthus arcuatus (Linnaeus, 1758).
Figures 271 & 272

Dorsal rays IX,31 to 33; anal rays III,23 to 25; pectoral rays 19 or 20; gill rakers 17 to 19; depth of body about 1.3 to 1.4 in standard length; width about 4.3 in depth; lower jaw extending anterior to upper; a large stout spine at corner of preopercle, the margin above irregularly serrate in young, smooth in adults; anterior soft rays of dorsal and anal fins of subadults and adults prolonged as a filament; caudal fin rounded in young, nearly truncate in adults; pelvic fins long, reaching beyond base of spinous portion of anal fin; scales edged in light brown, the larger scales with a large dark brownish gray spot in center and the smaller ones with brown; head, chest and paired fins dark brown; median fins lighter brown (by virtue of pale rims on scales), shading to dark brown outwardly, the caudal with a whitish terminal border; inside of pectoral fins yellow. Juveniles are black with two light yellow bars on body and three on head (a median one on forehead which crosses mouth and

Figure 271. Gray Angelfish (*Pomacanthus arcuatus*), St. Croix, Virgin Islands.

Figure 272. Gray Angelfish (*Pomacanthus arcuatus*), juvenile, St. Croix, Virgin Islands.

ends on chin, a short one running ventrally from corner of mouth, and one behind eye which continues onto chest); caudal fin yellow with a vertically elongate, nearly rectangular or hemispherical black spot in middle. The pale bars persist on the larger young after the spotted brown adult ground color is assumed; the bar that is retained the longest is the one that passes under the pectoral fin; it is usually still visible on individuals as large as 10 inches. The Gray Angelfish is reported to reach a length of 2 feet; however the largest of many collected by the author measured 17 inches. New York to Rio de Janeiro. This and the French and Queen Angelfishes are not uncommon in the West Indies. Both the Gray and the French Angelfishes have been introduced to Bermuda. They are among the least wary of the reef fishes.

French Angelfish

Pomacanthus paru (Bloch, 1787).

Figures 273 & 274

Dorsal rays X,29 to 31; anal rays III,22 to 24; pectoral rays 19 or 20; gill rakers 17 to 19; similar in morphology to the Gray Angelfish; differs notably in having one more dorsal spine and in color. Black, the scales of the body, except those at front from nape to abdomen, rimmed with golden yellow; a broad orange-yellow bar at pectoral base; dorsal filament yellow; chin whitish; outer part of iris yellow; eye narrowly rimmed below with blue. Young colored much like the juvenile Gray Angelfishes, but the median yellow band on the forehead stops at the base of the upper lip, and the black spot in the center of the caudal fin is large and nearly round. Largest collected by author, 16 inches, from St. Croix. Tropical Atlantic.

Figure 273. French Angelfish (*Pomacanthus paru*), St. Croix, Virgin Islands.

Figure 274. French Angelfish (*Pomacanthus paru*), subadult, Bonaire.

DAMSELFISHES
(POMACENTRIDAE)

The damselfishes (or demoiselles) are small reef fishes which are often very colorful. Their most distinctive family characteristic is a single nostril on each side of the snout (instead of the usual two). They are high-bodied and laterally compressed. The mouth is small; the teeth are conical or incisiform (none as canines or molars); there are no teeth on the roof of the mouth. The lateral line is not fully developed all the way to the base of the caudal fin. The scales are ctenoid; the head is largely scaled, as are the basal portions of the median fins. There is a single continuous dorsal fin; the base of the spinous portion is longer than the soft; there are X to XIV dorsal spines and II anal spines. The caudal fin is usually forked.

Many of the damselfishes are highly territorial and pugnacious; they are therefore not ideal aquarium fishes. Those for which reproductive habits are known lay elliptical eggs which are attached to a hard surface; these are guarded by the male parent.

The food habits are variable, with some species, such as *Abudefduf taurus,* primarily herbivorous and others, like the four *Chromis* discussed below, zooplankton-feeders; most, however, such as the species of *Stegastes (Pomacentrus* or *Eupomacentrus* of some authors, in reference to Atlantic species) are omnivorous, browsing freely on plant and detrital material and on animals such as colonial anemones, worm tentacles and crustaceans.

The western Atlantic species of *Stegastes* are more colorful when

Figure 275. Yellow-edge Chromis (*Chromis multilineata*) spawning at a depth of 80 feet, St. Croix, Virgin Islands.

young; they tend to become dark brown or yellowish brown when large.

Sergeant Major

Abudefduf saxatilis (Linnaeus, 1758).

Figure 276

Dorsal rays XIII,12 or 13 (rarely 12); anal rays II,10 to 12 (rarely 10); pectoral rays 18 or 19; lateral-line scales 21; gill rakers 7 or 8 + 17 to 19; depth of body 1.6 to 1.9 in standard length; mouth terminal, oblique, the opening at about level of lower edge of eye; teeth in one row in jaws, close-set, rigid and incisiform with a prominent notch at tips; lower margin of suborbital free; preorbital not deep; bluish white, the upper part of the body yellow, with five blackish bars on body (fifth bar at front of caudal peduncle), narrower than inter-spaces and nearly uniform in width; a faint sixth bar may be present posteriorly on caudal peduncle; a black spot at upper base of pectoral fin. Reaches a maximum length of slightly more than 7 inches. Formerly believed to be circumtropical, but a recent study restricts the name *saxatilis* to the Atlantic. On the western side from Rhode Island to Uruguay. Abundant on Caribbean reefs. One of the most diversified of fishes in its food habits; feeds on colonial anemones *(Zoanthus)*, benthic algae, copepods, pelagic tunicates, small fishes, larvae of various invertebrates and even adult nudibranchs. Often observed in aggregations well above the bottom when feeding on zooplankton; quickly retires to the shelter of reefs with the approach of danger. When guarding the eggs (visible as a deep

Figure 276. Sergeant Major (*Abudefduf saxatilis*), 25 feet deep, Long Island, Bahamas.

Figure 277. Night Sergeant (*Abudefduf taurus*), Andros, Bahamas.

red or purple patch of several inches in diameter on the sides of the rocks or pilings), the adult male becomes dark bluish, the black bars thus less conspicuous on the body.

Night Sergeant

Abudefduf taurus (Müller & Troschel, 1848). Figure 277

Dorsal rays XIII, 11 or 12 (usually 12); anal rays II, 10; pectoral rays 18 or 19; lateral-line scales 19 or 20; gill rakers 6 to 8 + 11 or 12; depth of body about 1.8 to 2 in standard length; mouth nearly horizontal, slightly ventral (upper lip precedes lower), the opening and upper lip entirely below eye; dentition similar to *A. saxatilis*, but teeth usually more deeply notched; lower margin of suborbital not free; preorbital moderately deep; light brown or yellowish brown with five dark brown bars on body broader than pale interspaces, the anterior bars often wider dorsally; a sixth faint bar or dark saddle-like mark may be present on upper part of caudal peduncle; a prominent black spot at upper base of pectoral fin. Attains about 8 inches. Southern Florida and Caribbean Sea. Characteristic of inshore, somewhat turbulent water and rocky bottom. Feeds primarily on a wide variety of benthic algae.

Blue Chromis

Chromis cyanea (Poey, 1860). Figure 278

Dorsal rays XII, 12; anal rays II, 12; pectoral rays 16 to 18; lateral-line scales 16 to 18; gill rakers 7 or 8 + 21 or 22; similar in morphology to *C. multilineata*; differs in fewer pectoral ray and gill-raker counts, no exposed maxillary tubercle, longer filamentous tips on the caudal lobes and pelvic fins, higher soft dorsal

Figure 278. Blue Chromis (*Chromis cyanea*), 25 feet deep, Long Island, Bahamas.

and anal fins (longest dorsal spine about 1.7 in longest dorsal ray; comparable measurement on *multilineata*, about 1.3) and color. Brilliant blue with a broad black margin on spinous dorsal fin, upper and lower lobes of caudal fin and front of anal fin; no black spot at pectoral base. Attains 5 inches. Bermuda, southern Florida and Caribbean Sea. Common in the blue water above deep outer reefs. Feeds in aggregations on the smaller zooplankton; picks individual copepods, etc. one by one from the passing water mass.

Sunshine Chromis

Chromis insolata (Cuvier, 1830).
Figures 279 & 280
Dorsal rays XIII,11 to 12 (rarely 11); anal rays II,11; lateral-line scales 15 to 17; lower-limb gill rakers 19 to 22; body moderately deep, the depth about 2.0 in standard length; eye large; mouth oblique, the maxilla ending slightly anterior to front edge of eye; teeth small, conical; last dorsal spine 6.3 to 8.3 in standard length; caudal fin moderately forked; adults dark olive brown dorsally, abruptly white ventral to lower edge of eye and pectoral base; dorsal and caudal fins yellowish posteriorly; a black spot at upper base of pectoral fins; juveniles bright yellow to yellow-green on upper third, abruptly violet on side, shading to whitish ventrally; a bright blue line from front of snout to upper edge of eye. Maximum length about 4 inches. Bermuda, Bahamas, southern Florida, Texas, and the Caribbean Sea; also recorded

Figure 279. Sunshine Chromis (*Chromis insolata*), 100 feet deep, Roatan, Honduras.

Figure 280. Sunshine Chromis (*Chromis insolata*), juvenile, Bonaire.

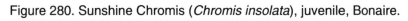

from St. Helena; although known from as little as 35 feet, most individuals will be found below 100 feet, some to at least 300 feet.

Yellow-Edge Chromis

Chromis multilineata (Guichenot, 1853).
Figures 275 & 281

Dorsal rays XII, 12; anal rays II, 11 to 13; pectoral rays 18 to 20; lateral-line scales 19 or 20; gill rakers 8 or 9 + 22 to 25; body moderately elongate, the depth 2.3 to 3 in standard length; mouth oblique, the front of upper lip directly before eye; a bony tubercle projecting from near front of maxilla above upper lip; teeth small, conical, in two or three rows at front of jaws (the outer largest) and a single row posteriorly; preopercular margin finely and irregularly serrate; caudal deeply forked; grayish brown on back, shading to silvery gray on sides; a black spot in axil and upper part of pectoral base; dorsal fin broadly edged with bright yellow; upper and lower edges of caudal fin narrowly yellow with a submarginal dark band. Largest specimen, 6.2 inches, from Isla Cubagua, Venezuela. Tropical western Atlantic. Forms aggregations above reefs while feeding on zooplankton (primarily copepods). *Chromis marginatus* appears to be a synonym.

Purple Chromis

Chromis scotti Emery, 1968.   Figure 282

Dorsal rays XIII, 11 to 12 (rarely 11); anal rays II, 11 to 12 (usually 12); lateral-line scales 15 to 18 (modally 16); lower-limb gill rakers 18 to 20; body deep, 1.8 to 1.95 in standard length; eye large; mouth oblique, the maxilla extending slightly posterior to front edge of eye; teeth small, conical; last dorsal spine 5.3

Figure 281. Yellow-edge Chromis (*Chromis multilineata*), 5 inches, Grand Bahama Island.

Figure 282. Purple Chromis (*Chromis scotti*), Bonaire.

to 6.7 in standard length; caudal fin moderately forked; adults gray-brown dorsally, often shading to white ventrally, with purple-blue markings, many as vertical lines, one per scale; upper edge of eye bright purple-blue; juveniles blue. Described from southern Florida; later recorded from Bermuda, North Carolina, Bahamas, Jamaica, Belize, Columbia, and Curaçao; depth range 50 to 350 feet.

Yellowtail Damselfish

Microspathodon chrysurus (Cuvier, 1830).
Figures 283 & 284

Dorsal rays XII,14 or 15 (usually 15); anal rays II,12 or 13 (usually 13); pectoral rays 20 to 22; lateral-line scales 20 to 22; lower-limb gill rakers 15 to 20 (about 10 for the species of *Stegastes*); depth of body 1.7 to 2 in standard length; preopercle not serrate; preorbital very deep; a prominent groove at anterior lower corner of preorbital between nostril and upper lip; teeth close-set and incisiform, the uppers narrow and movable, the lowers broad and more rigid; adults dark yellowish brown, the edges of the scales darker, with scattered small iridescent blue spots (mostly on upper part of head and body and on dorsal fin); caudal fin abruptly bright yellow (yellowish brown on occasional large individuals). The young are dark blue or bluish brown with brilliant metallic blue spots, relatively larger than those on adults—a color pattern that has led to another common name, "Jewelfish." Second in size among the western Atlantic damselfishes only to *Abudefduf taurus;* attains about 7.5 inches. Tropical Atlantic; on the western side: Bermuda, southern Florida and the Caribbean Sea.

Figure 283. Yellowtail Damselfish (*Microspathodon chrysurus*), St. Croix, Virgin Islands.

Figure 284. Yellowtail Damselfish (*Microspathodon chrysurus*), juvenile, Long Island, Bahamas.

A very common species on coral reefs; the young are usually seen among the branches of yellow stinging coral *(Millepora).* Feeds mainly on fine algae and organic detritus, but also eats coral polyps and other invertebrate animal material; the young occasionally pick at the bodies of larger fishes, apparently in search of parasites.

Longfin Damselfish

Stegastes diencaeus (Jordan & Rutter, 1897).   Figures 285 & 286

Dorsal rays XII-XIII, 14 to 16 (usually XII, 15); anal rays II, 12 to 14; pectoral rays 18 to 21; lateral-line scales 18 to 20; lower-limb gill rakers 11 to 13; teeth in one row in jaws, close-set and rigid, with truncate tips (true of other *Stegastes*); margin of preopercle serrate (also applies to other species of the genus); body depth 1.8 to 2.05 in standard length; anal fin reaching well beyond caudal-fin base; lobes of caudal fin broadly rounded; adults dark gray-brown, the edges of scales blackish, thus giving a pattern of dark vertical lines; a wash of yellowish often present dorsally on head, nape, and on back below spinous portion of dorsal fin; a small black spot at upper base of pectoral fins; pectoral axil black; leading edge of anal fin and pelvic spine blue; juveniles bright yellow with two bright blue lines dorsally on head, extending to beneath middle of dorsal fin where they break into spots; first blue line forming a V on tip of snout with line of other side; second blue line commencing at upper edge of

Figure 285. Longfin Damselfish (*Stegastes diencaeus*), Andros, Bahamas.

Figure 286. Longfin Damselfish (*Stegastes diencaeus*), juvenile 30 feet deep, Long Island, Bahamas.

eye; scattered small blue spots on body and fins, tending to form longitudinal rows, the greatest concentration on spinous portion of dorsal fin; a large blue-edged black spot basally on dorsal fin centered on last spine. Reaches 5 inches. South Florida, Bahamas, and Caribbean. Generally found on reefs in areas protected from heavy surge. The juvenile is known as the Honey Gregory; *Eupomacentrus mellis* is a synonym based on this stage.

Dusky Damselfish

Stegastes dorsopunicans (Poey, 1867).
Figures 287 & 288

Dorsal rays XII,14 to 17; anal rays II,13 to 15; pectoral rays 20 to 22 (modally 21); lateral-line scales 18 to 21 (modally 20); lower-limb gill rakers 9 or 10; anal fin extending to or slightly beyond a vertical at base of caudal fin; adults dark gray to blackish with vertical black lines on body following scale edges; a black spot, sometimes diffuse, at upper base of pectoral fins which are pale; other fins dark; faint blue spots may be present on head, chest, and abdomen; juveniles of about an inch in length are lighter in hue with the spinous portion of the dorsal fin, adjacent region of back, and nape orange-red; a large blue-edged black spot at base of dorsal fin at junction of spinous and soft portions; a smaller blue-edged black spot on upper edge of caudal peduncle. Reported to reach a length of 6 inches; largest collected by author, 5.2 inches, from Puerto Rico. Tropical western Atlantic. One of the most abundant inshore reef fishes of the Caribbean; occurs on rocky shores exposed to wave action. Very catholic in its diet, but feeds more on algae and detritus than animal material.

Figure 287. Dusky Damselfish (*Stegastes dorsopunicans*), Conception Island, Bahamas.

Figure 288. Dusky Damselfish (*Stegastes dorsopunicans*), juvenile, Conception Island, Bahamas.

Beau Gregory

Stegastes leucostictus (Müller & Troschel, 1848). Figures 289 & 290

Dorsal rays XII,13 to 16; anal rays II,12 to 14; pectoral rays 17 to 19 (usually 18); body not very deep, the depth 2.1 to 2.4 in standard length; blue on upper head and most of back and dorsal fin; bright yellow elsewhere; a black spot posteriorly in blue portion of dorsal fin; a small black spot at upper base of pectoral fin; no vertical dark lines on body as in some species. Large males dark gray, the centers of the scales on the nape, anteriorly on the body, and along the back yellowish; scattered blue dots and short lines on head, body and basal part of fins. Reaches a maximum of 4 inches. Maine to Brazil; also recorded from St. Helena and São Tomé in the Gulf of Guinea. Abundant in calm shallow coral and sand areas.

Bicolor Damselfish

Stegastes partitus (Poey, 1867). Figure 291

Dorsal rays XII,14 to 17; anal rays II,13 to 15; pectoral rays 18 to 20; lateral-line scales 18 to 21; cheek scales in three rows (four on preceding *Stegastes)*; depth of body 1.9 to 2.2 in standard length; most common color phase dark brown on head and about anterior two-fifths of body, then abruptly orange (the demarcation vertical) shading posteriorly to white including caudal fin; pectoral fins yellow with a wedge-shaped dark bar at base (upper end of bar broadest); a second phase usually seen in slightly deeper water is blackish anteriorly, light gray posteriorly, the demarcation oblique and not as sharp; caudal fin, most of anal fin, margin of dorsal fin and pelvic fins blackish; pectoral fin coloration as above. Attains about 4 inches. Caribbean Sea. Not as com-

Figure 289. Beau Gregory (*Stegastes leucostictus*), harbor area of Bonaire.

Figure 290. Beau Gregory (*Stegastes leucostictus*), juvenile, Long Island, Bahamas.

Figure 291. Bicolor Damselfish (*Stegastes partitus*), St. Croix, Virgin Islands.

Figure 292. Yellow Damselfish (*Stegastes planifrons*), Long Island, Bahamas.

Figure 293. Yellow Damselfish (*Stegastes planifrons*), juvenile, Belize.

mon in shallow water as most other damselfishes. The related *Stegastes pictus* occurs in Brazil.

Yellow Damselfish

Stegastes planifrons (Cuvier, 1830).
Figures 292 & 293

Dorsal rays XII,15 to 17; anal rays II,13 or 14; pectoral rays 18 to 20; lateral-line scales 18 to 20; body deep, the depth 1.7 to 2.1 in standard length; upper profile of head of adults steep (about 45°) and straight; adults brownish gray with a yellowish cast; vertical dark lines following scale rows; a large blackish spot covering most of pectoral base, darkest near upper part; median fins colored like body; pectorals slightly dusky; pelvics brownish yellow. The young are bright yellow with a large black spot, faintly edged in blue, at base of dorsal fin at junction of spinous and soft portions, a large black spot dorsally on caudal peduncle and a small one at upper pectoral base. Reaches about 5 inches. Southern Florida and the Caribbean Sea. A common fish.

Cocoa Damselfish

Stegastes variabilis (Castlenau, 1855).
Figure 294

Dorsal rays XII,14 to 17; anal rays II,12 to 15; pectoral rays 18 to 21 (rarely 18 or 21, usually 20); depth of body 2 to 2.2 in standard length; large adults similar in color to *S. planifrons*, but the ventral half of the body more yellowish and more sharply demarcated from the dark brown or bluish upper part of the body; pectoral fins yellow with a small blackish spot at upper base; smaller individuals blue on the back and yellow ventrally; all fins yellow except the dorsal which is blue with a small posterior yellow portion; a

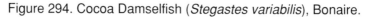

Figure 294. Cocoa Damselfish (*Stegastes variabilis*), Bonaire.

black spot posteriorly in spinous portion of dorsal fin, the lower third or fourth of which extends onto back; a small dark spot often present dorsally on caudal peduncle, this spot sometimes persisting on adults. Reaches slightly more than 4 inches. Gulf of Mexico and Caribbean Sea. The young of *S. diencaeus,* often called the "Honey Gregory," has been confused with juvenile *S. variabilis.* It is yellow with violet streaks on the head which continue onto the back; it has two major scales between the opercular spine and preopercle instead of three as in *variabilis.*

WRASSES
(LABRIDAE)

The Labridae is one of the largest families of fishes of tropical and temperate seas. Some of the species are among the most numerous on coral reefs. The family is perhaps the most diversified of all fish families in body form and size. The wrasses have a terminal mouth varying from small to moderate in size; the maxilla is not exposed on the cheek; the lips are thick. The teeth at the front of the jaws are usually stout curved canines which are often projecting, thus giving a characteristic "bucktoothed" appearance; there are no teeth on the roof of the mouth of Atlantic species; the pharyngeal teeth are conical or tubercular, the lowers on a single "T" or "Y"-shaped pharyngeal plate (formed by the fusion of the pharyngeal bones). The scales are cycloid. The lateral line may be interrupted or continuous; when continuous, it often has a section beneath the soft portion of the dorsal fin which is abruptly bent downward. There is a single dorsal fin, the spines usually slender.

The wrasses are carnivorous. They tend to feed on invertebrates with hard parts which they crush with their well-developed pharyngeal teeth. They are diurnal and swim actively most of the time during the day. Like the related parrotfishes, most use their pectoral fins for "cruising" speed and bring the body and tail musculature into play only when greater speed is needed. At night nearly all of the smaller species bury in the sand.

They are usually brightly, and often gaudily and complexly colored. Generally the juveniles are colored differently from the adults, and the adults frequently display two distinctive color phases. The largest is usually more colorful and male in sex. The other phase may be either male or female. For those species that have been studied, it has been determined that the colorful terminal male phase is the result of sex reversal (a fish originally female changes its sex to male and assumes a different color pattern). This phenomenon is widespread in the family and in the related Scaridae as well. Fishes with two color patterns as adults may have two modes of reproduction (see discussion under *Thalassoma bifasciatum* and Scaridae).

In spite of their attractive colors, the labrid fishes in general are not good aquarium fishes for they often attack other fishes, including those of their own species, and may inflict damage to the fins and eyes. Some of the wrasses, especially the razorfishes, are prone to bite when handled.

Figure 295. Creole Wrasse (*Clepticus parrae*) and Bluehead (*Thalassoma bifasciatum*), Roatan, Honduras.

Three other wrasses in addition to those discussed below are known from the tropical western Atlantic, but all are confined to relatively deep water. One is *Decodon puellaris* which has XI dorsal spines and is red on the back and whitish on the sides with yellow spots. The other two are species of *Halichoeres*: *H. caudalis* (see remarks under *H. poeyi)* and *H. bathyphilus* which has a dark spot on the side between the lateral line and the pectoral fin.

Spotfin Hogfish

Bodianus pulchellus (Poey, 1860.
Figure 296

Similar to the Spanish Hogfish; differs primarily in having 15 or 16 gill rakers and in color. Adults are red with a broad whitish stripe on lower side of head and body and a large area of bright yellow on upper posterior part of body and caudal fin and posterior section of dorsal fin; a prominent black spot anteriorly in dorsal fin (larger than that of *rufus)* and a black area on upper outer part of pectoral fins. The young to nearly 2 inches in length are yellow. Attains about 9 inches. South Carolina to southern Florida and the West Indies, extending to Brazil at 24 °S. Rare in less than about 80 feet of water. The young of *pulchellus* appear to be "cleaners" like the young of *rufus*. Sometimes called the "Cuban Hogfish."

Spanish Hogfish

Bodianus rufus (Linnaeus, 1758).
Figure 297

Dorsal rays XI or XII,9 to 11 (usually XII,10); anal rays III,11 to 13 (usually 12); pectoral rays 15 or 16 (rarely 15); lateral-line scales 29 to 31; gill rakers 17 to 19; lateral line continuous without an abrupt curve;

Figure 296. Spotfin Hogfish (*Bodianus pulchellus*), 5.3 inches, Florida Keys.

Figure 297. Spanish Hogfish (*Bodianus rufus*), Bonaire.

depth of body 2.7 to 3.4 in standard length (juveniles more elongate than adults); four strong canine teeth at the front of each jaw and one small canine posteriorly on upper jaw near corner of mouth; upper preopercular margin serrate; head scaled except snout, chin and interorbital; membranes of spinous portion of dorsal fin deeply incised; posterior tips of dorsal and anal fins reaching beyond caudal base; caudal fin truncate to slightly rounded in young, the lobes prolonged in adults; upper part of head and about anterior two-thirds of body and most of dorsal fin blue (red in specimens from deep water); lower head and rest of body yellow; a black spot at front of dorsal fin. An occasional adult is dark brown with a purplish cast. Said to reach a length of 2 feet, but the largest of which there is record from the Caribbean is 15.5 inches;

it was taken off Venezuela. Bermuda, southern Florida, Gulf of Mexico, Caribbean Sea and south to Brazil. Not uncommon on reefs in the depth range of about 10 to 100 feet. The adults feed on crabs, sea urchins, brittle stars and mollusks. The young are active in the removal of crustacean parasites of other fishes.

Creole Wrasse

Clepticus parrae (Bloch & Schneider, 1801).
Figures 295 & 298

Dorsal rays XII, 10; anal rays III, 12 or 13 (rarely 13); pectoral rays 17 or 18 (rarely 18); lateral line continuous, the pored scales 32; gill rakers 26 to 28; depth of body 2.7 to 3.3 in standard length; head with small scales except snout and front of interorbital space; preopercular margin serrate; mouth very small, highly oblique, the opening directly

Figure 298. Creole Wrasse (*Clepticus parrae*), Puerto Rico.

in front of eye, the upper jaw extremely protractile; teeth small, the upper jaw with two pairs of canines at front and the lower jaw with one pair; dorsal and anal fins with a broad basal scaly sheath; large adults with fifth to seventh dorsal soft rays prolonged; comparable rays of anal fin also prolonged, but to a lesser degree; caudal fin emarginate in young, lunate in adults; color primarily violet or purple; teeth and bones pale blue; large individuals with a wash of yellow on lower two-thirds of body, this most evident on caudal peduncle and basal part of anal fin; prolonged portions of dorsal and anal fins and tips of pelvic fins blackish. The young of about 2 inches have about six short bars on the back above the lateral line which are blackish, mottled with pale. Reported to reach 12 inches in Bermuda; largest collected by author,

10 inches, from 70 feet off Puerto Rico. Bermuda and North Carolina to the Caribbean Sea. Common on outer reef areas; occurs in feeding aggregations well above the bottom (when not molested). Feeds on pelagic copepods, small jellyfishes, pteropods, pelagic tunicates and various invertebrate larvae.

Dwarf Wrasse

Doratonotus megalepis Günther, 1862.
Figure 299

Dorsal rays IX, 10; anal rays III, 9; pectoral rays 11 or 12; lateral line interrupted, with 17 pored scales in upper anterior portion and 4 on caudal peduncular portion to base of caudal fin; gill rakers 15 or 16; body relatively deep, the depth 2.5 to 3.1 in standard length, and compressed, the width 2.2 to 2.7 in depth; head small, the snout pointed; large scales on head except

Figure 299. Dwarf Wrasse (*Doratonotus megalepis*), 2.1 inches, St. John, Virgin Islands.

for the top and region before eye; preopercular margin smooth; teeth progressively longer toward front of jaws where moderate canines are present; a few small teeth at front of jaws inside enlarged outer row; a canine tooth posteriorly on upper jaw near corner of mouth; margin of spinous portion of dorsal fin markedly concave as a result of first three and last three spines being longer than the three in middle; caudal fin rounded; color primarily grass green; an oblique white band on cheek; usually some scattered small white or pale blue spots on head and body; a few scattered small markings of yellowish to reddish brown usually present to a variable degree; often a small reddish brown spot near upper edge of caudal fin and another near lower edge. The smallest Atlantic wrasse; probably does not exceed 3 inches. Bermuda, Florida Keys and Caribbean Sea; recently recorded from the tropical eastern Atlantic. Occurs in shallow seagrass beds; although it may be common, it is very difficult to detect among the blades of turtle grass.

Slippery Dick

Halichoeres bivittatus (Bloch, 1791).

Figures 300 & 301

Dorsal rays IX, 11; anal rays III, 12; pectoral rays 13; lateral line continuous, with an abruptly bent section beneath soft portion of dorsal fin, and 27 scales (true of other western Atlantic *Halichoeres*); anterior lateral-line scales with more than one pore per scale; gill rakers 16 to 19; head without scales (true of other species of the genus); preopercular margin smooth (also applies to other species); one pair of enlarged canine teeth at front of upper jaw and a small canine poste-

Figure 300. Slippery Dick (*Halichoeres bivittatus*), male, 5.6 inches, St. John, Virgin Islands.

Figure 301. Slippery Dick (*Halichoeres bivittatus*), initial phase, Bonaire.

riorly near corner of mouth (other Atlantic species also); two pairs of enlarged canine teeth anteriorly in lower jaw (true of other species except *maculipinna);* caudal fin slightly rounded; the dominant color markings are two dark stripes, one running from snout through eye to caudal base and the other, less pronounced, on lower side of body; a bicolored spot at edge of gill cover within upper dark stripe; a small black spot at rear base of dorsal fin; large adult males green on back, shading to light greenish yellow on sides, the two stripes usually purplish; corners of caudal fin blackish; irregular light red bands on head and on caudal fin. Largest specimen, 8.5 inches, from Bermuda. Bermuda and the Carolinas south to Brazil. The most abundant species of the genus in shallow reef and reef-sand areas of the Carib-

bean. Feeds mainly on crabs, sea urchins, polychaete worms, mollusks and brittle stars.

Yellowcheek Wrasse

Halichoeres cyanocephalus (Bloch, 1791).
Figures 302 & 303

Dorsal rays IX, 12; anal rays III, 12; pectoral rays 13; gill rakers 18 to 21; anterior lateral-line scales with more than one pore (usually 3); two pairs of enlarged canine teeth anteriorly in lower jaw; caudal fin slightly rounded; adults with a broad black stripe on upper half of body; narrowing as it passes posteriorly to end in middle of caudal fin; back yellow-green above stripe posteriorly on body; a row of yellow spots, one per scale, along irregular lower margin of dark stripe; lower half of body light blue-green; head below level of mouth blue-green, above yellow; a diagonal blackish band

Figure 302. Yellowcheek Wrasse (*Halichoeres cyanocephalus*), 9.5 inches, St. Thomas, Virgin Islands.

Figure 303. Yellowcheek Wrasse (*Halichoeres cyanocephalus*), juvenile, 20 feet deep, Belize.

from eye to nape where it broadens; a diagonal dusky band on snout, and a dusky area dorsally on opercle; juveniles blue, abruptly yellow above a demarcation from mouth to midbase of dorsal fin. Reaches 12 inches. Florida, Cuba, Lesser Antilles and Brazil. Juveniles occasionaly seen in shallow water, but adults are rare in less than 100 feet and occur to at least 300 feet.

Yellowhead Wrasse

Halichoeres garnoti (Valenciennes, 1839).
Figures 304 to 306

Dorsal rays IX, 11; anal rays III, 12; pectoral rays 13; anterior lateral-line scales with more than one pore per scale; gill rakers 15 to 19; caudal fin slightly rounded. There are three distinct color phases. Juveniles to about 2.5 inches are bright yellow with a lateral dark-edged pale blue stripe. Intermediate-sized fish are yellowish brown, shading to white ventrally, with two dark lines running diagonally upward from upper posterior part of eye; the median fins are orange or orange-red with blue margins, the dorsal and caudal with blue lines; a dark spot at upper base of pectoral fins. Large adult males develop a vertical black bar on the side which is continuous with a black stripe along base of soft portion of dorsal fin and upper caudal peduncle; upper part of head and body in front of black bar bright yellow; body posterior to bar principally green; tips of pectorals blackish. Reaches 7.5 inches. Tropical western Atlantic.

Clown Wrasse

Halichoeres maculipinna (Müller & Troschel, 1848).
Figures 307 & 308

Dorsal rays IX, 11; anal rays III, 11; pectoral rays 14; a single pore on

Figure 304. Yellowhead Wrasse (*Halichoeres garnoti*), male, Long Island, Bahamas.

Figure 305. Yellowhead Wrasse (*Halichoeres garnoti*), initial phase, Bonaire.

Figure 306. Yellowhead Wrasse (*Halichoeres garnoti*), juvenile, Bahamas.

Figure 307. Clown Wrasse (*Halichoeres maculipinna*), male, 5.2 inches, St. John, Virgin Islands.

Figure 308. Clown Wrasse (*Halichoeres maculipinna*), initial phase, Bahamas.

each lateral-line scale; gill rakers 13 to 15; one pair of enlarged canine teeth anteriorly in lower jaw (other Atlantic *Halichoeres* with two pairs); anterior canine teeth notably outcurved, particularly the uppers; caudal fin slightly rounded; a broad black band on upper side of body; back above this band yellow; sides below white; three transverse red bands on top of head; a dark spot may be present on fifth to seventh interspinous membranes of dorsal fin; a small black spot at posterior end of dorsal fin base and a fainter one at upper pectoral base. Large adult males become primarily rose and green, lose the dark lateral stripe, gain a prominent black spot on mid-side, and have a larger black spot in the spinous portion of the dorsal fin. A small species; attains a maximum of about 5.5 inches in length. Tropical western Atlantic.

Painted Wrasse

Halichoeres pictus (Poey, 1860).

Figures 309 & 310

Dorsal rays IX, 11; anal rays III, 12; pectoral rays 13; a single pore on each lateral-line scale; gill rakers 17 or 18; the pair of canine teeth at front of upper jaw moderately outcurved; eight to ten teeth on side of upper jaw of adults; caudal fin of adults double emarginate; the common color phase is white or yellow with two yellowish brown stripes, one along back next to base of dorsal fin and one on upper side which extends through eye to end of snout. Large adult males are blue–green to yellowish green on the upper half of the body and pale blue on lower half; upper half of head and nape rose; blue stripes on head; a large black spot at caudal base; a broad median triangular orange region in caudal fin containing two blue bands

Figure 309. Painted Wrasse (*Halichoeres pictus*), male, Bonaire.

Figure 310. Painted Wrasse (*Halichoeres pictus*), female, Bonaire.

which converge as they pass posteriorly. Juveniles are pale with a lateral dark stripe that is better defined anteriorly. Largest specimen, 4.4 inches. West Indies. Usually swims well off the bottom; not common.

Black-Ear Wrasse

Halichoeres poeyi (Steindachner, 1867).
Figures 311 & 312

Dorsal rays IX,11; anal rays III,12; pectoral rays 13; anterior lateral-line scales with more than one pore per scale (usually three or more); gill rakers 17 to 20; caudal fin slightly rounded but with upper and lower halves of posterior margin tending to be straight; large adults may have a slightly double emarginate fin; small individuals yellowish green with a black spot, edged in light red, behind eye; a small black spot at rear base of dorsal fin; a dark line at pectoral base, broader dorsally. Large adult males are dull green, the centers of the scales with a dull orangish red spot; anteriorly on body the red is broader on some scales, narrower on others, resulting in indistinct pink bars; caudal fin with a median longitudinal and upper and lower diagonal converging blue-edged rose bands. Largest specimen, 8 inches, from Rio de Janeiro. Tropical western Atlantic. Most commonly seen in seagrass beds, for which the green color is appropriate; occasionally encountered on shallow reefs. The deep-dwelling *Halichoeres caudalis* also has a small dark spot immediately behind the eye; it differs from *poeyi* in having a single pore in each lateral-line scale, no black spot at rear base of dorsal fin, and no dark line at pectoral base.

Figure 311. Black-ear Wrasse (*Halichoeres poeyi*), male, Long Island, Bahamas.

Figure 312. Black-ear Wrasse (*Halichoeres poeyi*), female, Long Island, Bahamas.

Pudding Wife

Halichoeres radiatus (Linnaeus, 1758).
Figures 313 & 314

Dorsal rays IX,11; anal rays III,12; pectoral rays 13; gill rakers 21 to 23, anterior lateral-line scales with three or more pores per scale; gill rakers 21 to 23; depth of body 2.7 to 3.6 in standard length (other Atlantic species of the genus not so deep-bodied, their depth about 3.3 to 4.6 in standard length); caudal fin truncate or with corners only slightly rounded; yellowish olive on back, shading to orange yellow on sides; body with rows of blue spots, and head with diagonal narrow blue bands; five pale blue bars on back, more evident in young; a small black spot at upper base of pectoral fin. Juveniles have two broad yellow stripes on body, a large black spot at front of soft portion of dorsal fin (this spot extending onto back) and a black spot at upper base of caudal fin. Very large males are more greenish and have a dark-edged pale blue bar in the middle of the body. The largest Atlantic species of the genus; attains 18 inches. Bermuda and North Carolina to Brazil, including the southern Gulf of Mexico. Feeds mainly on mollusks, but also eats sea urchins, crabs and brittle stars.

Hogfish

Lachnolaimus maximus (Walbaum, 1792).
Figure 315

Dorsal rays XIV,11; anal rays III,10; pectoral rays 15 or 16; lateral-line scales 32 to 34; gill rakers 15 to 17; body deep and compressed, the depth about 2 to 2.3 in standard length; preopercular margin smooth; first three dorsal spines greatly prolonged (these spines of a 2-inch juvenile longer than other

Figure 313. Pudding Wife (*Halichoeres radiatus*), female, 9.3 inches, St. John, Virgin Islands.

Figure 314. Pudding Wife (*Halichoeres radiatus*), juvenile, Belize.

Figure 315. Hogfish (*Lachnolaimus maximus*), night photo, Grand Bahama Island.

spines but not yet prolonged); interspinous membranes of fin deeply incised; caudal fin emarginate in young, lunate in adults; color variable but generally mottled brownish red with a black spot at rear base of dorsal fin; large males are abruptly dark maroon on head and nape above lower edge of eye and the median fins are blackish basally, the black continuing into the lobes of the caudal fin. Males also have larger snouts, the upper profile of the head concave instead of straight, and larger mouths. Largest collected by author, 32 inches, 14.4 pounds, from Puerto Rico. Fishermen report weights to 25 pounds. Gulf of Mexico and Caribbean Sea north to the Carolinas. Although this species occurs on reefs, it is more often encountered over open bottoms, especially where gorgonians are abundant. It feeds prima-rily on mollusks (about equally on gastropods and pelecypods), but also ingests crabs, hermit crabs, sea urchins and barnacles. Easily speared. Highly esteemed as a food fish.

Bluehead

Thalassoma bifasciatum (Bloch, 1791).

Figures 316 & 317

Dorsal rays VIII,12 or 13 (rarely 12); anal rays III,10 or 11 (rarely 10); pectoral rays 14 or 15; lateral-line continuous, with an angular section beneath posterior part of dorsal fin, the pored scales 26; gill rakers 17 to 21; body elongate, the depth 3.5 to 4.3 in standard length; head without scales; preopercular margin smooth; teeth in jaws progressively longer toward the front where moderate canines are present; no canine tooth at end of upper jaw near corner of mouth; caudal fin of

Figure 316. Bluehead (*Thalassoma bifasciatum*), terminal phase male, Belize.

Figure 317. Bluehead (*Thalassoma bifasciatum*), initial phase, St. Croix, Virgin Islands.

young truncate to slightly rounded, becoming lunate in large adult males. There are three primary color phases, the smallest with a black mid-lateral stripe which continues as pale red blotches on head; back above stripe yellow on reef fish and whitish on fish from inshore non-reef areas, and body below white; a black spot at front of dorsal fin and one at upper pectoral base; on larger fish the black stripe breaks up into a series of squarish dark blotches. The dark stripe or blotches may be so faint that the fish seem almost entirely yellow. The largest phase is the one from which the common name is derived. It has a bright blue head and a green body with two broad vertical black bars anteriorly which are separated by a light blue interspace; the lobes of the caudal fin are black, and the pectorals are tipped with black. This phase is always male. The small yellow phase with the black stripe may be either male or female. Fish in this phase only 1.5 inches long may be fully mature. Spawning by such fish occurs in aggregations; spawning in which the large bluehead fish take place involves only the single male and one female. Largest yellow-phase fish, 5.2 inches, from Curaçao; bluehead-phase individuals are reported to reach 6 inches. Bermuda, southern Florida, southern Gulf of Mexico and Caribbean Sea. One of the most abundant of West Indian reef fishes. It feeds on a great variety of small benthic animals, on zooplankton, and on the ectoparasites of other fishes.

Straight-Tail Razorfish

Xyrichtys martinicensis Valenciennes, 1839.
Figures 318 & 319
Similar to the following species;

Figure 318. Straight-tail Razorfish (*Xyrichtys martinicensis*), male, Bonaire.

Figure 319. Straight-tail Razorfish (*Xyrichtys martinicensis*), female, St. Croix, Virgin Islands.

differs in having 21 to 25 gill rakers, a more elongate body (depth 3.2 to 3.8 in standard length), last dorsal ray of adults not long (2.2 to 3.5 in head length; adults of other two species of *Xyrichtys* have longer dorsal rays, the length of the last ray 1.5 to 2.4 in head), a truncate or slightly rounded caudal fin, the first two dorsal spines of juveniles not elongate, and in color. Females light greenish gray, becoming pinkish ventrally, with a diffuse orange-red stripe from behind eye to base of caudal fin; a broad white area over abdomen, the lower part with vertical lines of red; most of head and chest white with a blackish area on opercle, and centers of scales on chest blackish; there may be faint red bars on the body. Large adult males lose the distinctive red, white and black markings; they develop a vertically elongate blue spot on each body scale, a yellow head with near-vertical pale blue bands, and a large dark spot in axil of pectoral fins. Largest female, 4.5 inches; largest male nearly 6 inches. Yucatan and West Indies, on sand bottom. Not uncommon at depths of about 20 to 70 feet.

Pearly Razorfish

Xyrichtys novacula (Linnaeus, 1758).

Figure 320

Dorsal rays IX, 12; anal rays III, 12; pectoral rays 12; lateral line interrupted, with 5 or 6 (usually 6) pored scales in the posterior section; 5 scales above first scale of lateral line to origin of dorsal fin; head largely naked; a diagonal row of small scales behind and below eye reaching a vertical through center of eye; gill rakers 18 to 21; body compressed and moderately deep, the depth 2.8 to 3.3 in standard length; upper

Figure 320. Pearly Razorfish (*Xyrichtys novacula*), 7 inches, St. John, Virgin Islands.

profile of head of adults steep, the front edge sharp; suborbital deep; pelvic fins not elongate, the tips usually not reaching posterior to anus; first two dorsal spines flexible (elevated in young), the remaining spines stiff; a pair of long canine teeth anteriorly in jaws, but none posteriorly at corner of mouth; caudal fin rounded; dull green on back shading to pale orangish on sides, each scale of body with a blue vertical line or elongate spot; a red bar on body just posterior to pectoral fins; head with alternating vertical lines of light blue and light yellow-orange; median fins rose with blue markings; adult females with a pearly white area on upper abdomen. The young have four vertical dark bars on the body and one on nape at origin of dorsal fin, and they may have two diffuse dark stripes. Largest specimen examined, 8.5 inches, from South Carolina. Both sides of the Atlantic; on the western side from the Carolinas to Brazil. Like other razorfishes this species can dive headfirst into the sand with the approach of danger. Feeds mainly on small mollusks. *Xyrichtys psittacus* is a synonym.

Green Razorfish

Xyrichtys splendens Castelnau, 1855.
Figures 321 & 322

Similar to the pearly razorfish; differs in having 5 pored scales in the posterior section of the lateral line, 4 scales above first scale of lateral line to origin of dorsal fin, diagonal row of small scales behind and below eye not reaching a vertical at center of eye, gill rakers 17 to 22; profile of head not very steep, suborbital not deep; pelvic fins of adult males very long, reaching posterior to origin of anal fin, and in

Figure 321. Green Razorfish (*Xyrichtys splendens*), male, at a depth of 15 feet, Bonaire.

Figure 322. Green Razorfish (*Xyrichtys splendens*), female, St. Croix, Virgin Islands.

color. Adults have a vertically elongate blue spot on each scale, the edges orangish brown; the head has alternating vertical lines of pale blue and brownish orange, but these are broader than on *novacula* (only three of each color between corner of mouth and upper margin of preopercle); adult males are more green in overall color and have a blue-edged inky black spot on midside of body within a pale region of pink or yellow. Reaches a length of 5.5 inches. Southern Florida and Yucatan to Brazil. Occurs in seagrass beds and over sand bottoms. Although individual fish readily dive into sand when harassed, they may first hide among fronds of algae or seagrass, at which time they assume a barred color pattern and hold their bodies in a slight "S" curve. *Xyrichtys ventralis* is a synonym.

PARROTFISHES
(SCARIDAE)

The parrotfishes are colorful herbivorous fishes which abound on reefs of shallow tropical seas. They are distinctive in having their teeth fused to form a pair of beak-like dental plates in each jaw; these are joined at the front of the jaws, a median groove indicative of the suture (except primitive genera such as *Cryptotomus* and *Nicholsina*). Algae often grow on the base of the dental plates of the larger parrotfishes (Figure 323). The pharyngeal dentition is also unique. The upper pharyngeal bones (above the gills) are paired, each side with one to three rows of molariform teeth; there is a single median bone on which the lower pharyngeal teeth, also molar-like, occur in rows; the upper pharyngeal bones are inter-

Figure 323. Rainbow Parrotfish (*Scarus guacamaia*), St. Croix, Virgin Islands.

locking and form a convex surface which bears against the concave surface of the lower pharyngeal bone. Collectively the upper and lower pharyngeal bones and associated teeth are often called the pharyngeal mill. This is used to grind up the algal food with the soft coral rock or sediment that is often ingested with the algae.

The general body form of scarids is oblong and moderately compressed, and the head is usually bluntly rounded at the front. All members of the family have a continuous dorsal fin with IX, 10 dorsal rays, the spines slender and often flexible; the anal rays III, 9. The scales are large and cycloid, usually 22 to 24 in the lateral line; the lateral line follows the contour of the back to below the rear portion of the dorsal fin, then drops down one or two scale rows and continues along the midaxis of the caudal peduncle. The fins have no scales except for a basal row which may be present on the median fins.

The family is divisible into two subfamilies, the Scarinae, represented in the Atlantic only by the genus *Scarus*, and the Sparisomatinae, with the genera *Cryptotomus*, *Nicholsina* and *Sparisoma*. The Scarinae is differentiated as follows: front edge of lower dental plate included within upper when mouth closed, each upper pharyngeal bone with one or two rows of teeth, and cheek below eye with two to four rows of scales. The upper dental plate of the Sparisomatinae is included within the lower when the mouth is closed *(Sparisoma)* or neither plate overlapping *(Cryptotomus* and *Nicholsina)*, each upper pharyngeal bone has three rows of teeth, and the cheek below the eye has a single row of scales.

In contrast to the diverse Labridae, from whence the Scaridae has surely evolved (or at least from common stock), the family is remarkably homogeneous in external morphology. This has resulted in much emphasis being placed on color pattern to differentiate the species. Early naturalists were not aware of the differences in color which the young may exhibit from adults and of the highly contrasting color phases often displayed by the two sexes; consequently many species received multiple scientific names based on the different color forms.

As in many of the wrasses, the terminal male phase of sexually dichromatic parrotfishes generally has the brightest colors, frequently with green or blue-green the dominant hue. The less colorful phase, often brown or red and frequently striped, may be either male or female. The author has observed several of the biphase scarids spawn and noted that they have two modes of reproduction. The colorful terminal-phase male is territorial and spawns with an individual female. The less colorful phase spawns in aggregations, typically with several males fertilizing the eggs of a single female at the peak of the upward spawning rushes. There is reason to believe that the terminal-phase males are the result of sex reversal from fish that were originally female.

The parrotfishes are often the dominant fishes on West Indian reefs on a weight basis and thus important in reef productivity. With their strong dental plates they can scrape even a low stubble of algae from the bottom, and their ability to grind up

Figure 324. Queen Parrotfish (*Scarus vetula*), male, night photo, St. Croix, Virgin Islands.

the plant food in their pharyngeal mill makes them efficient in the utilization of the available nutriment. Thus they are superior competitors among the plant-feeding reef animals.

Because the parrotfishes scrape a good deal of coral rock during feeding (one can see where these fishes have been feeding by the deep scrape marks their dental plates make on the reef) and grind this into fine sand, they are responsible for the production of an enormous amount of sediment over the years. In calm areas where surf action is limited, they may be the most important factor in reef attrition and sand production.

At night parrotfishes sleep on the bottom. Some species of *Scarus* secrete around themselves a veil-like cocoon of mucus (also termed mucous envelope); it is transparent and generally visible only when particulate matter in the water is trapped within. An attempt to demonstrate that the mucous cocoon is a deterrent to a nocturnal moray eel was not conclusive. It is possible that the cocoon is the result of mucus accumulation when the fish is quiescent at night in an area of little or no current (during the nearly constant swimming by day, the mucus is sloughed away).

SPARISOMATINAE

Slender Parrotfish

Cryptotomus roseus Cope, 1871. Figure 325

Pectoral rays 13; median predorsal scales 4; gill rakers 10 or 11; body elongate (the most slender of the parrotfishes), the depth 4 to 4.6 in standard length; snout pointed; teeth not completely coa-

Figure 325. Slender Parrotfish (*Cryptotomus roseus*), Bonaire.

lesced to form dental plates in jaws (teeth at front of upper jaw and most of lower jaw flattened with pointed tips, those at the front overlapping); gill membranes broadly joined to isthmus with a small free fold across; dorsal spines flexible; caudal fin truncate to slightly rounded; color variable, but generally yellowish brown to green. Color of a 3-inch male from Puerto Rico: olivaceous on the back with small pink dots; a salmon stripe along the side containing a row of green dots; body below stripe light green with some salmon markings on scales; head iridescent green with two narrow salmon bands beginning at mouth, the upper one running to eye and the other leading to an irregular network of salmon markings on gill cover; a black spot at upper pectoral base with a salmon band below, preceded by a turquoise band. Said to reach about 5 inches but few West Indian specimens have exceeded 3 inches. Tropical western Atlantic.

Taken by the author in the depth range of 25 to 180 feet; usually seen on sandy or weedy bottoms.

Emerald Parrotfish

Nicholsina usta (Valenciennes, 1839).

Figure 326

Pectoral rays 13; median predorsal scales 4 or 5; gill rakers 12 or 13; depth of body 3 to 3.2 in standard length; dentition similar to *Cryptotomus* but large teeth continuing along margin of lower dental plate nearly to posterior end of jaw; a small dermal cirrus at edge of anterior nostril (absent on *Cryptotomus*); gill membranes broadly attached to isthmus with a small free fold across; dorsal spines flexible; caudal fin slightly rounded. The illustrated specimen was mottled olive green on the back, the scales of the sides with reddish edges and bluish white centers; head below level of mouth yellow; two diagonal red-orange lines on cheek, the first running from corner of mouth to eye; median fins reddish; a blackish blotch at front of dorsal fin. Largest specimen examined, 11.5

Figure 326. Emerald Parrotfish (*Nicholsina usta*), 5.8 inches, Isla Cubagua, Venezuela.

inches, from South Carolina. New Jersey to Brazil. Known from the West Indies only from Cuba, Hispaniola and islands within the continental shelf. Appears to be most common in turtle grass beds; occurs at depths of a few feet to at least 240 feet. In 1968 a subspecies, *Nicholsina usta collettei*, was named from a series of specimens trawled in 20 to 50 meters off the Guinea coast of Africa.

Greenblotch Parrotfish

Sparisoma atomarium (Poey, 1861)
Figures 327 & 328

Pectoral rays x 13; median predorsal scales 4 (these two counts the same for all species of *Sparisoma);* a single median ventral scale posterior to base of pelvic fins; gill rakers 12 to 16; edges of dental plates scalloped and outer surface nodular (true of other *Sparisoma;* smoother in the species of *Scarus);* 1 to 3 prominent canine teeth on side of upper dental plate (in addition to interlocking canines at symphysis of jaw); gill membranes broadly joined to isthmus with no free fold across (also applies to other *Sparisoma);* interorbital space flat; anterior nasal tentacle simple; caudal fin slightly rounded; initial phase olive-brown, finely mottled with pale pink, with whitish stripes (most evident on ventral half of body); one changeable color phase with a broad dark stripe from snout, enclosing eye, and passing along upper side; ground color orange-red in deeper water; terminal males with a broad band of olive or red on upper side, finely flecked with other colors, the ventral half with iridescent light blue-green and wavy orange stripes; a bright green blotch as large as eye on shoulder region behind upper

Figure 327. Greenblotch Parrotfish (*Sparisoma atomarium*), male, at a depth of 70 feet, Rum Cay, Bahamas.

Figure 328. Greenblotch Parrotfish (*Sparisoma atomarium*), initial phase, Andros, Bahamas.

end of gill opening, sometimes containing one or two deep blue spots; an orange line from corner of mouth to and rimming lower edge of eye; a dark spot on first interspinous membrane of dorsal fin (sometimes present in large initial-phase fish). The smallest species of the genus, not exceeding 4 inches. Reported from Bermuda, Bahamas, Florida Keys and the Caribbean Sea; generally seen in seagrass beds or on reefs with thick algal cover.

Redband Parrotfish

Sparisoma aurofrenatum (Valenciennes, 1839). Figures 329 & 330

Gill rakers 11 to 16; body relatively deep, the depth 2.4 to 2.8 in standard length; interorbital space slightly concave to flat (slightly convex in young); tips of interspinous membranes of dorsal fin with a single small cirrus or none; flap on edge of anterior nostril taller than broad with about 4 to 8 cirri in adults; caudal fin slightly rounded in young, slightly emarginate at a length of 6 inches, and more emarginate in terminal-phase males (caudal concavity 6 in head length of a 9-inch male). The smaller color phase (first named *S. distinctum*) is brown or greenish brown with a dark blue cast on the back and sides, becoming red ventrally; a white spot on upper front part of caudal peduncle (the best underwater recognition marking); two broad dark brown stripes may be present, the uppermost at level of eye. The terminal-phase male is greenish gray on back, the sides with reddish tones; a yellow-orange spot about as large as eye on upper side above pectoral fin containing a black spot or spots in its upper portion; a yellow-orange band running on head from corner

Figure 329. Redband Parrotfish (*Sparisoma aurofrenatum*), terminal male, long Island, Bahamas.

Figure 330. Redband Parrotfish (*Sparisoma aurofrenatum*), initial phase, Andros, Bahamas.

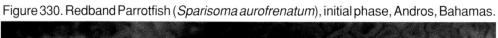

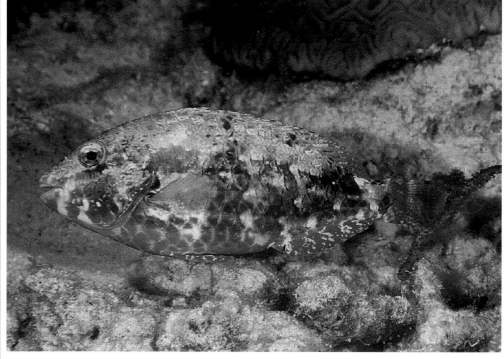

of mouth past lower edge of eye; tips of lobes of caudal fin black. A moderately common reef fish which attains a maximum length of slightly more than 10 inches. Tropical western Atlantic.

Redtail Parrotfish

Sparisoma chrysopterum (Bloch & Schneider, 1801).   Figures 331 & 332

Gill rakers 15 to 20 (juveniles less than 4 inches may have as few as 13); depth of body 2.7 to 2.9 in standard length; interorbital space flattish; membranes near tips of dorsal spines with a single cirrus; nasal flap small, often slender, with no more than about 6 cirri; caudal fin varying from slightly emarginate at lengths of 4 inches to lunate in terminal-phase males (caudal concavity 2.7 in head length of a 12-inch male). The smaller color phase is olivaceous tan, the exposed part of the scales brownish red dorsally; ventral part of body paler, the scales partly yellowish white and partly red; head with close-set round or oval pale spots, most evident on snout and interorbital space; median fins mottled brownish red; a prominent black spot at upper edge of pectoral fin base; rest of base and axil bright red. Terminal-phase males with centers of scales lavender brown, the edges green; head and body abruptly turquoise ventrally; a broad deep blue region beneath and posterior to pectoral fins; a large deep purple spot on upper half of pectoral fin base; lower half of base red-orange; pectoral fins with clear pinkish membranes and yellow rays; large crescentic central region of caudal fin orange-red. The young have three rows of white spots on the body. The red color phase attains a length of about 16 inches,

Figure 331. Redtail Parrotfish (*Sparisoma chrysopterum*), terminal male, Grand Bahama Island.

Figure 332. Redtail Parrotfish (*Sparisoma chrysopterum*), initial phase, Puerto Rico.

and the blue-green phase probably exceeds this in maximum size by a few inches. Tropical western Atlantic. Although often seen on reefs, this species also penetrates seagrass regions. Like other members of the genus, it takes on a mottled pattern when it comes to rest on the bottom and often matches the background closely. It can also display a color phase with broad dark stripes.

Bucktooth Parrotfish

Sparisoma radians (Valenciennes, 1839).
Figures 333 & 334

Two median ventral scales posterior to base of pelvic fins (one on *S. atomarium*); gill rakers 10 to 13; depth of body 2.4 to 3 in standard length; interorbital space flattish to slightly convex; membranes near tips of dorsal spines with cirri; flap on anterior nostrils without cirri; caudal fin slightly rounded; one to four canine teeth on side of upper dental plate at lengths as small as 1 inch standard length, the larger number of teeth generally in larger individuals (other species of *Sparisoma* all develop one or more canines on the outside of the upper dental plate, but only two have these at a size as small as the largest *radians*; one is *S. viride* which is easily distinguished by color and gill-raker counts, and the other is *S. atomarium*). Drab-phase fish are olivaceous to yellowish brown, finely speckled with pale dots, many of which are conjoined; base and axil of pectoral fins broadly blue-green; edge of opercle blue; chin crossed by two dark bands. Terminal-phase males are greenish brown with faint pale dots or a pale reticulum, some scales with reddish edges; a diagonal bicolored band of blue and orange running from corner of mouth,

Figure 333. Bucktooth Parrotfish (*Sparisoma radians*), terminal male, 3 inches, St. John, Virgin Islands.

Figure 334. Bucktooth Parrotfish *(Sparisoma radians)*, initial phase, Belize.

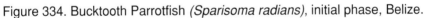

rimming lower edge of eye, and extending a short distance beyond eye; irregular orange-red markings on opercle; a blackish bar at pectoral base; a broad blackish border posteriorly on caudal fin; anal fin dusky. A small species, the largest specimen examined, 7.3 inches. Tropical western Atlantic. Lives mainly in seagrass beds. When frightened it swims away rapidly, then suddenly comes to rest in the seagrass and assumes a mottled color pattern which makes it very difficult to detect.

Yellowtail Parrotfish

Sparisoma rubripinne (Valenciennes, 1839).
Figures 335 & 336

Gill rakers 12 to 16; depth of body 2.5 to 2.9 in standard length; interorbital space slightly convex; anterior nasal tentacle palmate with 12 to 20 cirri (at lengths of 5 inches or more); interspinous membrane near tip of each dorsal fin with numerous cirri (may be reduced to one in very large adults); caudal fin slightly rounded in young, truncate to slightly emarginate in fish of intermediate size with drab color, and deeply emarginate in the large greenish terminal-phase males; juveniles and adults in drab phase (which may be either mature males or females) are light grayish brown, nearly white ventrally, the edges of the scales darker; alternate dark and pale bars (two of each) cross the chin; caudal peduncle and fin yellow (the most obvious color marking underwater); anal and pelvic fins red. Terminal-phase males (originally described as S. *axillare*) are primarily dull green or blue-green with a large black spot on

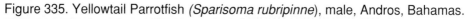

Figure 335. Yellowtail Parrotfish *(Sparisoma rubripinne)*, male, Andros, Bahamas.

Figure 336. Yellowtail Parrotfish (*Sparisoma rubripinne*), initial phase, Belize.

upper half of pectoral fin base; pectoral fins dark olive, the outer fifth abruptly pale; the living fish underwater may display a broad light yellowish region in the middle of the body. Largest female, 13.5 inches; largest terminal-phase male, 17.4 inches. Massachusetts to Rio de Janeiro; recently recorded from São Tomé off the coast of tropical west Africa. One of the most common reef fishes of the Caribbean; appears to occupy shallower water, generally, than most other parrotfishes. When pursued, it sometimes swims into the foaming swirl of waves striking a coral reef or rocky shore and disappears. Or it may come to rest upon the bottom where it rapidly assumes a mottled color pattern that matches the surroundings remarkably well.

Stoplight Parrotfish

Sparisoma viride (Bonnaterre, 1788).

Figures 337 & 338

Gill rakers 17 to 21 (one 2-inch juvenile with 14); body deep, the depth 2.3 to 2.6 in standard length; interorbital space very slightly convex; membranes near tips of dorsal spines with a single cirrus; flap on anterior nostril usually taller than broad with about 4 to 7 cirri; caudal fin truncate in young, emarginate in initial phase, and lunate in large adult males; initial-phase fish (originally described as *S. abildgaardi)* with a brown head, the scales of the upper two-thirds of the body with pale centers and dark brown edges, the lower third of body and fins bright red. Terminal-phase males are principally green with three diagonal orange bands on upper half of head, the posterior

Figure 337. Stoplight Parrotfish (*Sparisoma viride*), male, Bahamas.

Figure 338. Stoplight Parrotfish (*Sparisoma viride*), initial phase, St. Croix, Virgin Islands.

edge of the gill cover orange with a bright yellow spot near upper end, a large yellow spot basally on caudal fin and a narrow orange-yellow crescent posteriorly in fin. The basal third of the caudal fin of juveniles is white; the body has three lengthwise rows of about five pale spots; these persist as a color phase in red-bellied adults. This same pattern of spots also appears on other species of the genus, but to a lesser degree. Attains a length of at least 20 inches and a weight of 3.5 pounds. Tropical western Atlantic.

SCARINAE

Midnight Parrotfish

Scarus coelestinus Valenciennes, 1839.
Figure 339

Pectoral rays 16; median predorsal scales 6; third row of scales below eye usually consisting of two scales; inner gill rakers 46 to 58; caudal fin shape similar to that of the Rainbow Parrotfish; edges of scales broadly blackish, the centers bright blue; scaled portion of head blackish except for an irregular band of blue across interorbital space and blue centers of median predorsal scales; unscaled part of head bright blue; fins blackish with a bluish cast, the margins blue; dental plates blue-green. The young and adults of both sexes are essentially the same in color. Largest collected by author, 30 inches, 15.5 pounds, from Puerto Rico. Tropical western Atlantic. Not uncommon on reefs; sometimes schools with surgeonfishes.

Figure 339. Midnight Parrotfish (*Scarus coelestinus*), St. Croix, Virgin Islands.

Figure 340. Blue Parrotfish (*Scarus coeruleus*), male, 24.6 inches, 7.4 pounds, St. John, Virgin Islands.

Figure 341. Blue Parrotfish (*Scarus coeruleus*), Grand Bahama Island.

Figure 342. Blue Parrotfish (*Scarus coeruleus*), subadult, Bonaire.

Blue Parrotfish

Scarus coeruleus (Bloch, 1786).
Figures 340 to 342

Pectoral rays 14 or 15 (usually 15); median predorsal scales 6; outer gill rakers 31 to 50; inner gill rakers 44 to 52; reported to lack canine teeth on side of upper dental plate (present on adults of other western Atlantic *Scarus*); caudal fin of 8-inch fish truncate with the lobes slightly prolonged; lobes progressively longer in larger fish, the caudal concavity of an 18.5-inch specimen 3 in head length; forehead of large adults (perhaps only males) gibbous, the profile rising vertically from mouth; small to intermediate-sized individuals light blue, the basal part of the scales pale salmon; upper part of head yellow; a transverse salmon band on chin, edged in light blue; margins of fins blue. Large adults deep blue or greenish blue with a broad dark gray region on cheek and postorbital part of head. Reported to reach 3 feet; largest collected by author, a male of 24.6 inches, 7.4 pounds, from the Virgin Islands. Bermuda and Maryland to Rio de Janeiro. Young moderately common but large adults rare, at least in shallow water.

Rainbow Parrotfish

Scarus guacamaia Cuvier, 1829.
Figures 323 & 343

Pectoral rays 16; median predorsal scales 6; third row of scales below eye usually consisting of a single scale; inner gill rakers 51 to 64; caudal fin slightly rounded in 6-inch specimens, double emarginate in 10 to 15-inch individuals, the lobes greatly prolonged in large adults; principal colors green and orange; body scales of small to medium-sized fish with light green cen-

Figure 343. Rainbow Parrotfish (*Scarus guacamaia*), 22.5 inches, 7.1 pounds, St. John, Virgin Islands.

ters and narrow light brownish orange edges; scaled portion of head orange brown with short green lines around eye; unscaled part of head and chest dull orange; fins dull orange with tongues of green extending into the dorsal and anal; margins of median fins blue; dental plates blue-green; in large adults the colors are brighter, the green becoming restricted primarily to the upper posterior part of the body. There appears to be no obvious difference in color with sex. The largest recorded specimen measured 37 inches and weighed more than 20 kilograms (44 pounds); it was collected at the island of La Blanquilla, Venezuela. Tropical western Atlantic south to Argentina. The young are often found in mangrove areas; the adults are primarily reef fish.

Striped Parrotfish

Scarus iserti Bloch, 1789.

Figures 344 & 345

Pectoral rays 13 or 14 (usually 14); median predorsal scales 7 (rarely 8); scales in first row below eye 5 to 7 (usually 6), the last ending behind eye at level of center of eye; outer gill rakers 40 to 51; inner gill rakers 62 to 70 (58 to 62 on six 2- to 3-inch specimens); caudal fin truncate to slightly rounded; drab-phase fish with three dark brown stripes, the uppermost dorsally on back and the lowermost beginning beneath pectoral fin; region between dark stripes whitish; upper part of snout yellowish in life; terminal-phase males are blue-green and orange, the chest and head pink below a green band at lower edge of eye; a diffuse pink stripe posteriorly on head and on body above pectoral

Figure 344. Striped Parrotfish (*Scarus iserti*), terminal male, Bonaire.

Figure 345. Striped Parrotfish (*Scarus iserti*), initial phase, St. Croix, Virgin Islands.

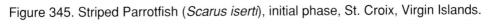

fins; median fins with blue borders, the broad central parts orange with linear blue markings. The smallest Atlantic species of *Scarus;* attains about 10 inches. Bermuda, southern Florida and Caribbean Sea. The most common species of the genus in the West Indies. *Scarus croicensis* is a junior synonym.

Princess Parrotfish

Scarus taeniopterus Desmarest, 1831.

Figures 346 & 347

Pectoral rays 13 or 14 (usually 14); median predorsal scales 7 (rarely 6); scales in first row below eye 6 to 8 (usually 7), the last ending behind eye at level of center of eye; outer gill rakers 40 to 52; inner gill rakers 54 to 67; caudal fin truncate to slightly rounded; drab-phase fish very similar to comparable phase of *iserti,* but not yellowish on snout and with upper and lower edges of caudal fin dark; terminal-phase males are principally blue-green and orange with a broad pale yellowish stripe on body beneath pectoral fin (and extending slightly above and posterior to fin); two narrow blue-green stripes on head, one through upper and the other through lower part of eye; caudal fin blue, the upper and lower margins broadly bright orange. Reaches a maximum length of about 1 foot. Bermuda, southern Florida and Caribbean Sea. Because this species has been confused with the striped parrotfish, the distribution of the two beyond what has been given herein is not certain; however, at least one of the species (and perhaps both) ranges south to Brazil and accidentally north to Massachusetts.

Figure 346. Princess Parrotfish (*Scarus taeniopterus*), terminal male, at a depth of 50 feet, Long Island, Bahamas.

Figure 347. Princess Parrotfish (*Scarus taeniopterus*), initial phase, Bonaire.

Figure 348. Queen Parrotfish (*Scarus vetula*), terminal male, Bonaire.

Figure 349. Queen Parrotfish (*Scarus vetula*), initial phase, Andros, Bahamas.

Queen Parrotfish

Scarus vetula Bloch & Schneider, 1801.

Figures 324, 348 & 349

Pectoral rays 14 (rarely 15); median predorsal scales 7; 4 rows of scales on cheek (horizontal rows below eye and above lower preopercular margin; the only parrotfish with this number of rows; other Atlantic *Scarus* have three); outer (lateral) gill rakers 50 to 62; inner (medial) gill rakers 71 to 84; depth of body 2.6 to 3 in standard length (body depth of other Atlantic *Scarus* too broadly overlapping to be useful in species separation); caudal fin truncate at lengths to about 7 or 8 inches; larger fish with fin emarginate; large terminal-phase males with the caudal lobes prolonged, thus forming a decidedly lunate fin. Drab-phase fish (originally given the name *S. gnathodus)* are reddish to purplish brown with a broad white stripe on lower side; terminal-phase males are gaudily colored with blue, green, rose and orange; the caudal fin is blue with broad submarginal bands of orange in the lobes. Largest specimen, 20 inches. A common parrotfish which is known from the coral reefs of Bermuda, southern Florida and the Caribbean Sea.

JAWFISHES
(OPISTOGNATHIDAE)

The jawfishes are carnivorous warm-water fishes that live in vertical burrows which they usually line with small stones or shell fragments. Normally they enter their burrows tail first. They keep their burrows clear by spitting out sand and debris with their mouth (Figure 350). Most species are small, those in the Atlantic not exceeding 8 inches. Twelve valid species have been

Figure 350. Yellow Jawfish (*Opistognathus gilberti*), female, at a depth of 55 feet, Roatan, Honduras.

named from the western Atlantic, and seven others remain to be described.

The family is characterized by its large head without spines or ridges, steep upper profile, and very short snout; the eyes are large, and the mouth very large, the maxilla extending to or well beyond posterior edge of eye; the body is moderately elongate; the scales are small and cycloid (none on head of *Opistognathus*); the lateral line runs near base of dorsal fin, ending at or slightly posterior to a vertical at middle of body; the dorsal fin is long and not deeply notched between spinous and soft portions; the pelvic fins are anterior to the pectoral fins, the rays I,5; moderate canine teeth are present in a single row along sides of jaws (anteriorly there may be one to several additional rows); there are no teeth on the palatines, and few or none on the vomer.

Most jawfishes are found in relatively shallow water, but several such as species of *Lonchopisthus* (*Lonchistium* is a synonym) have been collected from moderate depths. The males of at least some species incubate the eggs in the mouth.

Yellowhead Jawfish

Opistognathus aurifrons (Jordan & Thompson, 1905).   Figure 351

Dorsal rays XI,15 to 17; anal rays III,14 to 16 (rarely 14); pectoral rays 19 to 21 (rarely 21); lateral scale rows posterior to opercular flap 81 to 94; gill rakers increasing with age, those of lower limb varying from 17 in young to 37 for adults; pelvic fins long, 2.7 to 3.8 in standard length (4.5 to 6 in other Atlantic species of *Opistognathus*); body light bluish gray with numerous pale blue dots; head, nape and anterior part of dorsal fin yellow; a pair of black spots often present on chin; a pair of black lines may also be present posteriorly on chin beneath gill membranes, these lines sometimes ending in a second pair of black spots. Approaches 4 inches in maximum length. Florida Keys and the West Indies. Hovers with body obliquely vertical in the water above its burrow and feeds on zooplankton from the passing water mass. The most colorful of the jawfishes. Makes an interesting aquarium fish when given enough sand on the bottom to build a burrow and small stones with which to reinforce the walls.

Yellow Jawfish

Opistognathus gilberti Böhlke, 1967.
Figures 350, 352 & 353

Dorsal rays XI,12 to 14; anal rays II,13 or 14; pectoral rays 17 to 19; lower-limb gill rakers 21 to 28 (increasing, in general, with size of fish); body depth 4.2 to 4.5 in standard length; head length 2.9 to 3.1 in standard length; snout long for the genus, 5.0 to 5.7 in head; maxilla without a long flexible posterior extension; females gray, shading to whitish ventrally on head and abdomen, with a median yellow stripe in dorsal and anal fins (more evident posteriorly), and a large area of yellow in caudal fin; iris yellow except upper and lower edges; males with

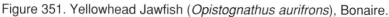

Figure 351. Yellowhead Jawfish (*Opistognathus aurifrons*), Bonaire.

Figure 352. Yellow Jawfish (*Opistognathus gilberti*), male, Roatan, Honduras.

Figure 353. Yellow Jawfish (*Opistognathus gilberti*), female, at a depth of 55 feet, Roatan, Honduras.

head and body reddish gray, darkening posteriorly to black, except abdomen which is whitish; iris and lips yellow; caudal fin black except for a wedge-shaped white marking dorsally and ventrally at fin base; dorsal and anal fins white, the dorsal with a round black spot between fifth and sixth dorsal spines. A small species, the maximum length about 2.8 inches. Known to date from the Bahamas, islands and reefs of the western Caribbean Sea, Jamaica, Mona Island and Puerto Rico (William F. Smith-Vaniz, pers. comm.).

Longjaw Jawfish

Opistognathus macrognathus Poey, 1860.
Figure 354

Dorsal rays XI, 16 (rarely 17); anal rays III, 16 (rarely 15); pectoral rays 19 to 21; lateral scale rows between end of opercular flap and base of caudal fin 97 to 110; gill rakers 12 to 16 + 24 to 28; depth of body 3.8 to 4.6 in standard length; head 2.7 to 3.1 in standard length; eye 2 to 3.5 in head; vomer with one or two teeth; maxilla with a supplemental bone; maxilla of some adults (probably just males) with a long posterior upcurved flexible extension, the underside of which has two black bands separated and bordered by white; body light brown with small pale blotches and two rows of seven large dark brown blotches, the first on mid-side, the second along back and extending into basal part of dorsal fin; blotches of the two rows sometimes conjoined; a black spot in outer half of dorsal fin between the sixth or seventh spines and the ninth. When the mouth of adult males is opened broadly, the alternate black and white bands of the underside of the maxilla and adjacent membranes make a striking display; perhaps these markings play a role in threat behavior. Females appear to lack the long double-banded maxilla, and there is only a single blackish band at the corner of the mouth. The largest specimen, from Isla Cubagua, Venezuela, is nearly 8 inches long. Known from the Atlantic and Gulf coasts of Florida, the Bahama Islands and the Caribbean Sea.

Figure 354. Longjaw Jawfish (*Opistognathus macrognathus*), 4.6 inches, St. John, Virgin Islands.

Figure 355. Mottled Jawfish (*Opistognathus maxillosus*), 3.3 inches, Antigua.

Mottled Jawfish

Opistognathus maxillosus Poey, 1860.
Figure 355

Dorsal rays XI, 15 (rarely 14); anal rays III, 15; pectoral rays 20 or 21; lateral scale rows posterior to opercular flap 89 to 100; gill rakers 8 to 10 + 19 to 22. Similar to *macrognathus*, differing in lacking a supplemental bone on the maxilla, having one fewer dorsal and anal rays, fewer gill rakers, a smaller eye, and in the position of the black spot in the dorsal fin; on *maxillosus* this spot is more in the lower half of the fin than the upper and is usually located between the sixth and ninth spines; there is some brown pigment at the corner of the mouth but no black and white bands inside the maxilla. Attains about 5 inches. Florida Keys and the West Indies. More common than the preceding species.

Dusky Jawfish

Opistognathus whitehurstii (Longley, 1931). Figure 356

Dorsal rays XI, 14 or 15; anal rays III, 13 or 14; pectoral rays 18 to 20;

Figure 356. Dusky Jawfish (*Opistognathus whitehurstii*), 2 inches, Puerto Rico.

lateral scale rows posterior to opercular flap 49 to 58; gill rakers 9 or 10 + 19 to 21. Differs from *maxillosus* in the lower scale counts, lower fin-ray counts, smaller maximum size and color. The dark spot (deep greenish blue in life) of the dorsal fin is usually found between the second and fourth or fifth dorsal spines; the body is densely mottled with dark brown and flecked with blackish; the caudal fin and posterior part of the dorsal fin are yellow with rows of small blackish spots. Largest specimen, 3.2 inches. Dry Tortugas and the West Indies.

COMBTOOTH BLENNIES
(BLENNIIDAE)

The Caribbean blennies are small blunt-headed benthic fishes that are most often found along rocky shores. They are characterized chiefly by the pelvic fins being anterior to the pectorals and having a reduced ray count of I,2 to I,4 (the spine is very short and difficult to see), no scales, and a single series of slender close-set teeth (a large curved canine tooth often present posterior to incisiform series in jaws). The mouth is low on the head and horizontal or directed slightly ventral. The upper jaw is not protractile, and the median part of the upper lip lacks a free margin. There is a continuous dorsal fin, typically with XII flexible spines; the number of dorsal rays is equal to or greater than the number of dorsal spines. All blenniids have two anal spines but the first is buried beneath genital tissues in females; in mature males these spines have knob-like fleshy protuberances.

Many blennies are primarily herbivorous, and some are mainly carni-

Figure 357. Redlip Blenny (*Ophioblennius atlanticus*), Bonaire.

Figure 358. Pearl Blenny (*Entomacrodus nigricans*), 2.4 inches, Puerto Rico.

vorous. Typically they lay demersal eggs that are aerated and guarded by the male.

Not included among the blennies below are a few species of *Hypleurochilus* and *Hypsoblennius* (the gill opening of these genera ends at the level of the base of the pectoral fin; the former has canine teeth at the ends of the jaws, the latter does not); these fishes are not common, particularly in the reef habitat.

Pearl Blenny

Entomacrodus nigricans Gill, 1859.
Figure 358

Dorsal rays XII,14 or 15; anal rays II,16 (rarely 15 or 17); pectoral rays 14; pelvic rays I,4; lateral line continuous, the pores difficult to count; gill rakers 15 to 19; body elongate, the depth 4.4 to 5.4 in standard length; nasal and supraorbital tentacles fringed; teeth in jaws numerous, comblike, with incurved tips; a very large canine tooth on each side of lower jaw inside main series; olivaceous with seven short dark brown double bars on side of body and rows of small pale blue spots. Attains a length slightly greater than 3 inches. Tropical western Atlantic. Occurs inshore on rocky bottom, often in a region of surf or swell; may be taken in tidepools. Feeds mainly on algae. *Salarichthys* is a synonym of *Entomacrodus.* The related *E. textilis* is restricted to the islands of Ascension and St. Helena in the South Atlantic.

Redlip Blenny

Ophioblennius atlanticus (Valenciennes, 1836).　　　　　Figures 357 & 359

Dorsal rays XII,19 to 21; anal rays II,20 or 21; pectoral rays 14 to 16 (usually 15); pelvic rays I,4 (the spine not visible externally); lateral line interrupted, the break about in middle of body; depth of body 3.4 to 4.1 in standard length; a group of cirri on margin of anterior nostril; a single small unbranched tentacle above each eye; a pair of cirri on either side of nape; lower jaw with large posterior canine teeth; ground color usually dark brown (but varies through olivaceous to light gray); small pale blotches sometimes present, especially on head; lower lip, lower edge of pectoral fins, and margin of dorsal fin orange-red (mar-

Figure 359. Redlip Blenny (*Ophioblennius atlanticus*), 4.5 inches, Tobago.

gin of dorsal much broader anteriorly); caudal fin pale pink with a broad median brown region and a dark lower margin. Largest specimen, 4.8 inches. The subspecies of the western north Atlantic ranges from North Carolina to the Caribbean Sea. One of the most abundant fishes on West Indian reefs. In one poison station on an inshore reef in St. John, Virgin Islands, 194 specimens were taken from an area of 297 square meters—more individuals than any other species of fish. Feeds almost exclusively on filamentous algae.

Seaweed Blenny

Parablennius marmoreus (Poey, 1875).
Figure 360

Dorsal rays XII, 17 or 18 (usually 18); anal rays II, 19 or 20; pectoral rays 14; pelvic rays I, 3; lateral line short, ending beneath rear of spinous portion of dorsal fin, with 11 to 13 pairs of pores; gill rakers 11 to 13; depth of body 4.2 to 4.6 in standard length; slender tentacle at

Figure 360. Seaweed Blenny (*Parablennius marmoreus*), 2.1 inches, Isla Cubagua, Venezuela.

edge of anterior nostril simple or branched; supraorbital tentacle fringed; a large canine tooth posteriorly in jaws; color variable, but often yellowish gray on back, bluish gray ventrally, with numerous small brown spots (orangish on head) which tend to intensify to form a broad stripe on upper side and dark bars; a small black spot at front of dorsal fin; edge of anal fin pale; paired fins yellow. Some individuals are almost entirely yellow. Rarely exceeds 3 inches. New York to Venezuela. Not common in the West Indies, in general, but may be locally abundant in areas of the southern Caribbean. Lives in shallow water, particularly on hard bottom with a good cover of algae. Backs into holes in rocks. Omnivorous, but feeds mostly on algae.

Molly Miller

Scartella cristata (Linnaeus, 1758).

Figure 361

Dorsal rays XII,14 or 15; anal rays II,16 or 17; pectoral rays 14; pelvic rays I,3; lateral line continuous but indistinct posteriorly (only about 16 pairs of pores can be counted in straight anterior part); gill rakers 17 to 21; depth of body 3.3 to 4 in standard length; a group of cirri on margin of anterior nostril; supraorbital tentacle fringed; a median band of cirri on top of head from interorbital space to origin of dorsal fin; one or two short canine teeth posteriorly in lower jaw at end of incisiform series but none on upper jaw; dull green or olive with dark bars on body which extend into lower part of dorsal fin (faint on some fish); pale spots often present, especially in dorsal fin; lower part of head pinkish tan. Rarely exceeds 4.5 inches. Both sides of the Atlantic; in the western part from Florida to Brazil, including the Gulf of Mexico. A common species usually found in rocky areas close to shore. Herbivorous.

Figure 361. Molly Miller (*Scartella cristata*), 3 inches, St. John, Virgin Islands.

SCALED BLENNIES
(LABRISOMIDAE)

Formerly classified as clinids, the labrisomids are now regarded as a New World family distinct from the Old World Clinidae. They are small bottom-dwelling carnivorous fishes. They share with the related comb-tooth blennies the forward position of the pelvic fins and fewer than I,5 pelvic rays (usually I,3). They differ in having many more spines than rays in the dorsal fin, stiff dorsal spines, and the upper edge of the upper lip entirely free. Often there are small villiform teeth behind the outer row of conical teeth in the jaws; there are no enlarged posterior canine teeth; the vomer and palatines often bear teeth. The body of all the Caribbean species except two species of *Stathmonotus* are scaled; the head is usually without scales. Those for which reproductive habits are known lay demersal eggs.

Forty-one species of seven genera are recorded from the West Indian region. Eight of the more common species are discussed below.

Puffcheek Blenny

Labrisomus bucciferus Poey, 1868.

Figure 363

Dorsal rays XIX to XXI, 10 to 12; anal rays II, 19 to 21; pectoral rays 12 to 14; lateral-line scales 45 to 48; gill rakers 11 to 14; body depth about 3.5 to 4.0 in standard length; maxilla ending below middle of eye; palatine teeth present, some of which are larger than teeth on vomer; prominent cirri on nasal and supraorbital tentacles and in a short transverse row on nape; first dorsal spine longer than fifth, about 2.2 in head; shortest pelvic ray 1.5 to 1.8

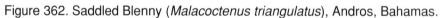

Figure 362. Saddled Blenny (*Malacoctenus triangulatus*), Andros, Bahamas.

Figure 363. Puffcheek Blenny (*Labrisomus bucciferus*), Belize.

in longest ray; brown with five irregular dark brown bars on body, the anterior three of which extend basally into dorsal fin; no black spot on opercle; two dark brown dots or short lines posterior to eye; peritoneum uniformly dusky to black; females with numerous dark dots in fins. Reaches 3.7 inches. Bermuda, Florida, Bahamas, and Caribbean Sea; occurs at depths less than 20 feet.

Hairy Blenny

Labrisomus nuchipinnis (Quoy & Gaimard, 1824).   Figure 364

Dorsal rays usually XVIII, 12; anal rays II, 17 to 19; pectoral rays 13 to

Figure 364. Hairy Blenny (*Labrisomus nuchipinnis*), 4.4 inches, Curaçao.

15; lateral-line scales 64 to 69; gill rakers 10 to 13; depth of body 3.4 to 4.1 in standard length; mouth relatively large, the maxilla usually ending beneath rear half of eye; an outer row of strong conical teeth and an inner band of villiform teeth in jaws; teeth present on vomer and palatines, those on the palatines not larger than those on vomer; a diagonal transverse row of cirri on a fleshy base on upper posterior part of each side of head; supraorbital and nasal flaps fringed with cirri; first dorsal spine 3.6 to 4.3 in head length, rarely longer than any other dorsal spine in adults; olivaceous with four irregular dark brown bars (fainter bars between these); a pale-edged black spot on opercle; often a dark spot at front of dorsal fin; adult males with red on lower part of head, chest and abdomen. Attains about 8 inches. Tropical Atlantic.

The largest and the most abundant inshore labrisomid fish in the West Indies. Feeds on crabs, other crustaceans, gastropod mollusks, brittle stars, sea urchins, fishes and polychaete worms; swallows its prey largely intact. *L. guppyi*, another common species with a black ocellus on the opercle, differs in having several palatine teeth larger than the vomerine teeth and 48 to 53 lateral-line scales.

Diamond Blenny

Malacoctenus boehlkei Springer, 1958.
Figure 365

Dorsal rays XXI to XXII, 11 to 13; anal rays II, 20 to 23; pectoral rays usually 15; lateral-line scales 58 to 66; gill rakers 8 to 11; body depth 4.0 to 4.3 in standard length; snout long and pointed, 3.2 to 3.4 in head; mouth not large, the maxilla ending beneath front edge of eye; a patch of

Figure 365. Diamond Blenny (*Malacoctenus boehlkei*), Long Island, Bahamas.

small teeth behind single row of large teeth at front of jaws (small teeth not present in following species); nasal, supraorbital, and nuchal cirri long; first dorsal spine shorter than all but tenth to last spines, about 2.6 in head; pelvic fins longer than head; shortest pelvic ray contained 4 or more times in longest ray; adults with predorsal and prepectoral scales; males light brown, finely spotted with white, with an upper row of seven irregular dark-edged brown blotches and a lower row of ten smaller brown blotches of irregular diamond shape with pale centers; top of head anterior to nuchal cirri dark brown; a black spot anteriorly in dorsal fin; females have brownish orange blotches instead of dark brown. Reaches about 2.7 inches. Known from the Bahamas, Virgin Islands, and islands of the western Carib-

bean; usually found at depths greater than 50 feet.

Rosy Blenny

Malacoctenus macropus (Poey, 1868).

Figure 366

Dorsal rays XXI to XXIII,8 to 11; anal rays II,18 to 22; pectoral rays 14 to 16; lateral-line scales 40 to 45; gill rakers 8 to 11; body depth 3.6 to 4.2 in standard length; snout not long, 3.6 to 4.2 in head; mouth not large, ending below front edge of eye; teeth in jaws in two rows; first dorsal spine longer than second to fifth spines, 5.3 to 8.8 in standard length; shortest pelvic ray contained 2.0 to 3.2 in longest ray; no median predorsal scales; prepectoral scales present; female with irregular brown blotches dorsally on body (may be faint and reddish ventrally), uniformly speckled with small whitish spots, the dorsal fin with many small

Figure 366. Rosy Blenny (*Malacoctenus macropus*), Belize.

dark reddish spots; postorbital head and body of males covered with small red spots and blotches; no dark spots in dorsal fin. Maximum length about 2.2 inches. Bermuda, Bahamas, Florida, and Caribbean Sea; generally found in less than 20 feet, often in substrata with turtle grass. A common species, but not often seen.

Saddled Blenny

Malacoctenus triangulatus Springer, 1959.
Figures 362 & 367

Dorsal rays XIX to XXI,11 to 13; anal rays II,20 to 22; pectoral rays 13 to 15; lateral-line scales 52 to 61; gill rakers 11 to 14; depth of body 3.4 to 4.3 in standard length; snout moderately pointed; mouth not large, the maxilla ending approximately beneath front edge of eye; conical teeth in jaws in a single close-set row; a few teeth on vomer but none on palatines; cirri on head similar to *M. boehlkei* but shorter; first dorsal spine 2.4 to 3 in head length, always longer than the next three and the last three spines of

fin; length of shortest pelvic ray contained 2.1 to 3.1 times in longest ray; at least one predorsal scale, and prepectoral region with scales (absent in young); color variable but usually pale yellowish with five or six dark saddle-like triangular bars on back with a large spot between each bar ventrally on body; head with a few small dark spots; bars on body sometimes not very dark but outlined by dark dots; scattered dots then often present elsewhere on the body. The related *M. gilli* has a prominent ocellated black spot at rear base of spinous portion of dorsal fin. Attains about 2.5 inches. Known from Florida, Mexico and throughout the Caribbean Sea.

Banded Blenny

Paraclinus fasciatus (Steindachner, 1876).
Figure 368

Dorsal fin entirely spinous, the spines XXVIII to XXXI; anal rays II,17 to 20; pectoral rays 12 to 14; pelvic rays I,2; lateral-line scales 32 to 38; depth of body about 4.2 in standard length; mouth moderately

Figure 367. Saddled Blenny (*Malacoctenus triangulatus*), 2.1 inches, St. John, Virgin Islands.

Figure 368. Banded Blenny (*Paraclinus fasciatus*), 1.8 inches, Trinidad.

large, reaching to or beyond rear edge of eye in large adults; teeth in jaws and on vomer, but none on palatines; a broad dark brown or black transverse flap on each side of nape; supraorbital tentacle of one to four (usually two) slender filaments; a long cirrus at edge of anterior nostril; pectoral base with two or three rows of scales; color varies from uniform dark brown to light brown with dark bars; the nuchal lappets are always darker than the body; a black ocellus usually present in dorsal fin between the 22nd to 25th spines. Attains about 2 inches.

Southern Florida, Bahamas and throughout the Caribbean. Two other species of the genus have the dorsal entirely spinous, *P. cingulatus* and *P. naeorhegmis*. Both have palmate flaps with cirri on the nape, and the former lacks scales at the pectoral base. The five other western Atlantic species have a single soft ray in the dorsal fin following the long series of spines.

Spotted Blenny

Starksia guttata (Fowler, 1931).

Figure 369

Dorsal rays XX to XXII,8 or 9;

Figure 369. Spotted Blenny (*Starksia guttata*), 1.4 inches, Tobago.

anal rays 17 to 18 (usually 18); pectoral rays 13 or 14 (usually 14); lateral line interrupted, the scales 15 to 18 + 20 to 22; body depth 4.3 to 4.9 in standard length; mouth moderately large, the maxilla ending slightly posterior to rear edge of eye; an outer row of stout canines in jaws with a patch of small teeth inside at front; teeth on vomer and palatines; a single slender cirrus on each side of nape, on top of eye, and at edge of anterior nostril; abdomen without scales; first anal spine modified to an intromittent organ in the male; pale with irregular dark brown spots which are larger dorsally than ventrally, none on lower head or abdomen. Reaches 1.8 inches. Grenadines to Trinidad and Curaçao. Greenfield (1979) divided what was once regarded as a single variable species, *Starksia ocellata,* that ranged from North Carolina to Brazil, into six allopatric species of which *guttata* was one. The others: *ocellata* (Florida to North Carolina), *occidentalis* (western Caribbean), *variabilis* (Colombia), *culebrae* (Haiti to St. Vincent), and *brasiliensis* (Brazil).

Seagrass Blenny

Stathmonotus stahli (Evermann & Marsh, 1899).   Figure 370

Dorsal fin entirely spinous, the spines XLII to XLIV; anal rays II,23 to 25; pectoral rays 8 or 9; pelvic rays I,2; body elongate, the depth 7.1 to 7.8 in standard length; body scaled; maxilla reaching below center of eye; two rows of conical teeth at front of jaws and one along sides; teeth on vomer but none on palatines; preopercle without a free margin; supraorbital cirrus flap-like; a simple cirrus usually present on each side of nape and at edge of anterior nostrils; usual color, green. Attains about 1.3 inches. Dry Tortugas and the West Indies. Usually collected from seagrass beds. Two other species are known from the Caribbean, *S. gymnodermis* and *S. hemphilli.* Neither of these have scales, and *S. hemphilli* lacks cirri on the head.

FLAG BLENNIES
(CHAENOPSIDAE)

The chaenopsid blennies are closely related to the labrisomids,

Figure 370. Seagrass Blenny (*Stathmonotus stahli*), 1.3 inches, Puerto Rico.

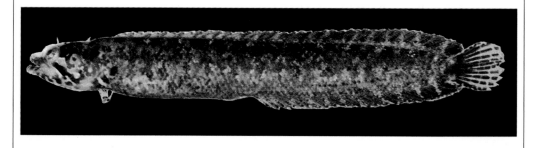

Figure 371. Secretary Blenny (*Acanthemblemaria maria*), Bonaire.

and some authors have regarded them as a subfamily of the Labrisomidae. They are small fishes with no scales and no lateral line. The body is moderately to very elongate. There are only two bones in the circumorbital series. The pelvic rays are I,3 (but usually only two rays are visible without careful dissection). The dorsal fin is continuous, with at least half as many soft rays as spines; the spines are flexible. The spinous portion of the dorsal fin of males is often elevated. Frequently observed with head protruding from small holes.

Caribbean genera include *Protemblemaria*, *Ekemblemaria*, *Emblemaria*, *Acanthemblemaria*, *Coralliozetus*, *Emblemariopsis*, *Hemiemblemaria*, *Lucayablennius* and *Chaenopsis*. The one species of *Hemiemblemaria*, *H. simulus*, is remarkable in its role of mimicking the wrasse *Thalassoma bifasciatum*.

Three representative chaenopsid species are discussed below.

Yellowface Pikeblenny

Chaenopsis limbaughi Robins & Randall, 1965.   Figure 372

Dorsal rays XVIII-XXI,31 to 36; anal rays II,33 to 37; pectoral rays 12 or 13; body very elongate, the depth at anal origin 15 to 20 in standard length; snout long and pointed ("U"-shaped when viewed from above, the sides parallel for most of its length); gape of mouth very large, the maxilla reaching well beyond eye; outer row of teeth conical at front, compressed with blunt tips along sides of jaws; an inner patch of small teeth at front and an inner row of small teeth continuing posteriorly on the upper jaw for nearly half its length; teeth on vomer and palatines; no cirri on head; spinous portion of dorsal fin of males about three times as high as that of

Figure 372. Yellowface Pikeblenny (*Chaenopsis limbaughi*), male, 2.9 inches, St. John, Virgin Islands.

females, the longest spines about 2.2 in head; light brown with pale dots and a narrow mid-lateral brown stripe, sometimes broken into blotches; faint bars on body; a yellowish cast anteriorly; a small black spot at front of dorsal fin; mature males with more yellow on head, gill membranes black, the branchiostegal rays blue; black dorsal spot edged in white with an area of bright orange above. Attains 3 inches. West Indies. The most common of the four western Atlantic species; usually found in clear water on coral rubble bottoms or sandy areas near reefs in the depth range of 10 to 70 feet. Feeds mainly on small crustaceans. The related *C. ocellata* lives in old worm tubes in shallow seagrass beds; its snout when viewed from above is more converging toward the tip, and it attains a greater length (nearly 5 inches).

Sailfin Blenny

Emblemaria pandionis Evermann & Marsh, 1900.   Figure 373

Dorsal rays XXI, 16; anal rays II, 23 or 24; pectoral rays 13; depth of body about 5.5 in standard length; head blunt, the snout very short, about one-fourth length of maxilla; teeth on vomer and palatines; top of head not spinous (as in many *Acanthemblemaria*); supraorbital cirrus trifid at tip; a simple cirrus at edge of anterior nostril; dorsal fin

Figure 373. Sailfin Blenny (*Emblemaria pandionis*), female, 1.5 inches, Curaçao.

origin closer to eye than end of gill cover; anterior part of dorsal fin very elevated in the male, the length of the first five spines about 2.7 in standard length; pelvic fins long; female light tan with scattered small pale spots and dark flecks; dorsal fin with diagonal broken dark lines anteriorly; males darker in general, especially the outer half of the spinous portion of the dorsal fin. Attains a length slightly greater than 2 inches. Florida, Bahamas, Gulf of Mexico and the Caribbean Sea.

Arrow Blenny

Lucayablennius zingaro (Böhlke, 1957).
Figure 374

Dorsal rays XVIII to XX, 19 or 20; anal rays II, 22 or 23; pectoral rays 13; pelvic fins I,3; no branched rays in any fins; no scales; body slender, 9.3 to 9.6 in standard length; head pointed, the lower jaw prolonged into a fleshy projection; maxilla extending to below anterior edge of pupil; small teeth in three or four rows anteriorly in jaws, in one row along side of jaws where slightly enlarged; villiform teeth on vomer and palatines; translucent gray, the vertebral column showing through as light yellow; abdomen dark purplish red; a black stripe from tip of lower jaw through eye to end of operculum; a median dorsal light yellow line on head; dorsal fin and adjacent back with three large black spots, and two on anal fin. Reaches a maximum length of about 1.6 inches. Reported from the Bahamas, Grand Cayman Island, Jamaica, Barbados, Belize and Honduras at depths of 20 to 140 feet. Maintains its body in a curved position and swims with its pectoral fins. Four specimens were found with gobiid fishes in their stomachs, one of which was identified as *Coryphopterus hyalinus*.

Figure 374. Arrow Blenny (*Lucayablennius zingaro*), at a depth of 60 feet, Long Island, Bahamas.

TRIPLEFINS
(TRIPTERYGIIDAE)

This blennioid fish family has often been grouped as a subfamily of the Clinidae, but it is now clearly recognized as a family. The most obvious distinction is the three separate dorsal fins. Five western Atlantic species are known, all in the genus *Enneanectes*. These fishes are small, rarely exceeding 1.5 inches. One species is discussed below as an example of the family.

Redeye Triplefin

Enneanectes pectoralis (Fowler, 1941).

Figure 375

Dorsal rays III-XI or XII-6 to 8; anal rays II,14 to 16; pectoral rays 15 or 16; lateral line interrupted, the anterior scales 12 to 14; depth of body 3.7 to 4.1 in standard length; no palatine teeth; mouth moderately large, the maxilla reaching posterior to center of eye; no palatine teeth; upper margin of preopercle and edge of circumorbital bones serrate; first two dorsal spines about equal in height, the third slightly shorter, and all much shorter than longest spine of second dorsal fin; body completely scaled; ctenoid scales on opercle and on upper cheek behind eye; supraorbital tentacle about as broad as long; five dark bars on body, the last at base of caudal fin almost black; a narrow dark bar running ventrally from eye; anal fin evenly pigmented. Largest specimen, 1.6 inches. Florida, Bahamas and the Caribbean. The closely related *E. jordani* lacks scales on the opercle and has six or seven dark bars on the anal fin. Three other species are known from the West Indian region, all described as new by Rosenblatt (1960).

GOBIES
(GOBIIDAE)

The gobies are the largest family of fishes of tropical seas, and they are also well represented in temperate waters. They are among the smallest of fishes; indeed the small-

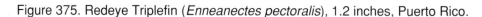

Figure 375. Redeye Triplefin (*Enneanectes pectoralis*), 1.2 inches, Puerto Rico.

est recorded vertebrates are gobies. One from the Philippines is mature at 6 millimeters. Typically they are bottom-dwelling and carnivorous. Most have the pelvic fins joined to form a sucking disc. Usually there are two dorsal fins (although they may be connected basally), the first of two to eight slender flexible spines; often the spacing between the last two spines is greater than that between preceding spines. The second dorsal and anal fins have an initial weak spine. The fins are not scaled except the basal portions of the caudal and pectorals. The caudal fin is usually rounded, sometimes lanceolate, and rarely emarginate. There is no lateral line and usually no swimbladder. There are no spines on the opercle, and the preopercle is smooth or has small spines. The skin may be naked or scaled; the skin of the head is continuous with

the covering of the eyes. The gill membranes are united to the isthmus, thus restricting the gill opening to the sides. The mouth is usually oblique; the dentition is variable but the teeth in the jaws are usually small; teeth are usually not present on the roof of the mouth.

Gobies generally live in direct contact with the substratum, but a few such as *Coryphopterus personatus* and *Microgobius carri*, a pale fish with a yellow stripe on the side, swim freely just off the bottom. Many species penetrate brackish or even fresh water. Some live in close association with other animals. *Evermannichthys metzelaari*, a slender species about an inch long, the equally short but more robust *Risor ruber*, and *Gobiosoma chancei*, a larger species which is dark with a yellow stripe, are commensals of sponges. The small, colorful

Figure 376. Nassau Grouper (*Epinephelus striatus*) and cleaning goby (*Gobiosoma oceanops*), Belize.

Gobiosoma multifasciatum and Ginsburgellus novemlineatus (the latter dark with blue vertical lines), may be found hiding beneath sea urchins inshore. The slender Nes longus shares a burrow in the sand with an indefatigable snapping shrimp. Species of Gobiosoma of the subgenus Elacatinus appear to feed primarily on ectoparasites or mucus of other fishes.

The closely related sleepers (Eleotridae), sometimes classified in the same family as the gobies, are usually larger, lack the pelvic sucking disc, and often occur in brackish or fresh water.

The following 15 species have been selected as common representatives of the Gobiidae in the Caribbean Sea. Many more are known from the region.

Frillfin Goby

Bathygobius soporator (Valenciennes, 1837).
Figure 377

Dorsal rays VI-I,9 or 10; anal rays I,7 to 9; pectoral rays 18 to 21, the upper four to six slender, flexible and free (gobies of other genera with all pectoral rays joined by membranes); lateral scale rows 37 to 44; gill rakers 9 to 11; head broader than deep, its length 3 to 3.3 in standard length; body cylindrical anteriorly, becoming progressively more compressed posteriorly, the greatest depth 3.8 to 5.3 in standard length; caudal fin relatively short, its length 3 to 4 in standard length; pelvic fins forming a sucking disc; scales ctenoid; head not scaled except for occipital region; small conical teeth in bands in jaws; tongue bilobed; color variable, usually drab; tidepool specimens from western Puerto Rico had olive spots, most of which were interconnected, and alternating orange-yellow and dotted pale blue lines; there was a blue spot at the upper end of the gill opening. Attains 6 inches. Both sides of the Atlantic and the tropical eastern Pacific. Has been divided into subspecies, the West Indian one being Bathygobius soporator soporator. Jordan and Evermann referred to this species as the com-

Figure 377. Frillfin Goby (*Bathygobius soporator*), 6.2 inches, Puerto Rico.

Figure 378. Colon Goby (*Coryphopterus dicrus*), Long Island, Bahamas.

monest of shore fishes of tropical America. Variable in habitat; may be found on mud bottom in rivers or in fully saline seawater on rocky bottom in tidepools. The related *B. curacao* has 31 to 36 lateral scale rows and 15 to 18 pectoral rays.

Colon Goby

Coryphopterus dicrus Böhlke & Robins, 1960.   Figure 378

Dorsal rays VI-I,9; anal rays I,9; pectoral rays 18 to 20; longitudinal scale series 26; lower-limb gill rakers usually 7; body depth 3.9 to 5.0 in standard length; no prolonged dorsal spines; pelvic fins broadly joined by membrane; no pelvic frenum; fourth pelvic ray clearly longer than fifth; translucent gray with numerous small brown spots, the largest a series of six along lower side, and small pale blue-green flecks; horizontal dark lines on head,

the most prominent posterior to eye; two small black spots, one above other, at base of pectoral fins; a vertical blackish line or two blackish spots at base of caudal fin. Largest specimen, 2 inches. Florida Keys, Bahamas, Puerto Rico, Virgin Islands, and western Caribbean Sea; depth range 3 to 50 feet. The similar *Coryphopterus thrix* has a single large dark spot on the upper half of the pectoral-fin base, a filamentous second spine of the first dorsal fin, and a pelvic frenum.

Pallid Goby

Coryphopterus eidolon Böhlke & Robins, 1960.   Figure 379

Dorsal rays VI-I,9 to 11 (usually 10); anal rays I,8 to 9 (usually 9); pectoral rays 18 to 20 (rarely 18); longudinal scales series 25 or 26; lower-limb gill rakers 6 or 7; body depth 3.85 to 4.3 in standard length;

Figure 379. Pallid Goby (*Coryphopterus eidolon*), Long Island, Bahamas.

no elongate dorsal spines; pelvic fins fully joined by membrane along edge of fifth rays; fourth pelvic ray notably longer than fifth; pelvic frenum well developed; translucent gray with a narrow yellow stripe, faintly edged with dusky pigment, extending posteriorly from eye, and small yellow or dusky yellow spots or short bands on snout, cheek, and anteriorly on body; a row of small faint yellow spots dorsally on body; internal black dashes along vertebral column; a narrow vertical blackish line at base of caudal fin. Reaches 2.2 inches. Florida, Bahamas, Haiti, Virgin Islands and Belize; collected from 10 to 85 feet; found on sand near or within reefs.

Bridled Goby

Coryphopterus glaucofraenum Gill, 1863.
Figure 380
Dorsal rays VI-I,9; anal rays I,9; pectoral rays 17 to 20; lateral scale rows 26 to 28; gill rakers 11; depth of body 3.5 to 4.7 in standard length; width of body 1.3 to 1.6 in depth; caudal fin 3.4 to 3.7 in standard length; pelvic fins forming a sucking disc, the fifth (innermost) ray not notably shorter than the fourth; second spine of first dorsal fin not filamentous; a low fleshy mid-dorsal ridge running from just behind interorbital space to origin of dorsal fin; scales of body ctenoid; head and nape not scaled; teeth in bands in jaws, the inner and outer rows enlarged as slender canines, the outer row of lower jaw confined to anterior half of jaw; tongue truncate to rounded; color variable; individuals from white sand bottom and clear water are pale with two rows of faint yellow spots on side of body; a horizontal orange streak extending posteriorly from middle of eye to above pectoral fin, this streak containing a prominent dusky spot (sometimes

Figure 380. Bridled Goby (*Coryphopterus glaucofraenum*), Belize.

bilobed) above opercle; a second fainter orange line from lower edge of eye; a pale bluish line under eye; a vertical dusky bar at base of caudal fin; a row of dusky spots at base of dorsal fins; about six black dots at top of iris; individuals from darker bottom and more turbid water are more darkly pigmented; there are two rows of dark spots on side of body and one mid-dorsally, most of the spots on the side X-shaped; base of caudal fin with two blackish spots connected by a dusky bar; a dark blotch or streak behind corner of mouth; fins dusky. Attains 3 inches. Known from Bermuda and North Carolina to Brazil, but not yet recorded from the Gulf of Mexico. A very abundant goby in southern Florida and the West Indies from the shore to a depth of about 80 feet.

Bluenose Goby

Coryphopterus lipernes Böhlke & Robins, 1962.   Figure 381

Dorsal rays VI-I,9; anal rays I,9; pectoral rays 16 to 18 (usually 17); longitudinal scale series 26; lower-limb gill rakers 8; a single median interorbital pore; body slender, the depth 4.2 to 5.0 in standard length; no elongate dorsal spines; pelvic fins nearly separate, without a frenum; translucent yellowish gray with iridescent blue markings on snout and upper part of eye; alternating yellow and narrow blue lines extending posteriorly from eye onto anterior body; a black ring around anus. Maximum length 1.3 inches. Florida Keys, Bahamas and Caribbean Sea, generally at depths of at least 40 feet; often seen perched on live coral.

Figure 381. Bluenose Goby (*Coryphopterus lipernes*), Bonaire.

Figure 382. Masked Goby (*Coryphopterus personatus*), Belize.

Masked Goby

Coryphopterus personatus (Jordan & Thompson), 1905.   Figure 382

Dorsal rays VI-I,9 or 10; anal rays I,9 or 10; pectoral rays 14 to 16; lateral scale rows 24 to 28; gill rakers 9 to 12; depth of body 3.7 to 4.7 in standard length; width of body 1.4 to 1.7 in depth; caudal fin slightly emarginate, its length 3.4 to 3.7 in standard length; pelvic fins nearly completely divided; second dorsal spine prolonged in adults, especially in males; a narrow fleshy mid-dorsal ridge on occipital region of head and nape; body scaled (most scales finely ctenoid); head and nape without scales; teeth in bands in jaws, the outer row enlarged, especially those at front of lower jaw; translucent orangish gray dorsally shading to violet gray ventrally, with a lengthwise row of six rose spots (the largest but most obscure one anteriorly); a conspicuous black ring around anus; snout, upper lip and region just below eye darkly pigmented; two diffuse orange lines running posteriorly from eye; an iridescent pale blue spot behind and adjacent to upper part of eye; an elongate iridescent pale blue spot at pectoral base; eye with iridescent reflections, especially blue-green; dorsal fin rays red. Probably does not exceed 1.5 inches in length. Bermuda, southern Florida and the West Indies. A common free-swimming species which usually occurs in small aggregations; rarely ventures more than a few feet from the live coral substratum with which it is usually associated; collected by the author in the depth range of 10 to 140 feet. The closely related Glass Goby *(Coryphopterus hyalinus)* also has divided pelvic fins, a black ring around the anus, and an elongate second dorsal spine in adults. It is said to differ in having a transverse pair of large pores anteriorly in the interorbital space (compared to a single large median pore in *personatus*); however, Kathleen S. Cole (pers. comm.) questions the validity of C. *hyalinus*.

Goldspot Goby

Gnatholepis thompsoni Jordan, 1902.
                    Figure 383

Dorsal rays VI-I,11; anal rays I,11; pectoral rays 17; lateral scale rows 30 to 32; gill rakers 4 or 5; head compressed, the width about 1.2 in depth at end of operculum; depth of body 4.4 to 5 in standard length; width of body 1.2 to 1.4 in depth; caudal fin 2.8 to 3.3 in standard length; scales of body ctenoid; head with cycloid scales except interorbital, snout, and ventrally; pelvic fins forming a sucking disc; upper jaw with a narrow band of villiform teeth and an outer row of well-separated curved slender canines, those on sides of jaw curving forward; lower jaw with an inner row of small canines and an outer row of long protruding curved canines anteriorly; tongue distinctly bilobed. The illustrated specimen was whitish, blotched with orange-brown, with two indistinct brownish orange stripes, the first running from behind eye to above pectoral base where it expands to a "U"-shaped blackish blotch containing a bright yellow spot, then continues dorsally and posteriorly; second stripe beginning at front of opercle and running to pectoral base, com-

Figure 383. Goldspot Goby (*Gnatholepis thompsoni*), Belize.

mencing again in axil of pectoral; a vertical brownish orange line at top of iris and running ventrally from eye. Attains about 2.5 inches. Bermuda, Bahamas, southern Florida, and the Caribbean Sea. A common goby on sand patches in and about reefs; collected by the author from several West Indian localities in the depth range of 2 to 160 feet.

Dash Goby

Gobionellus saepepallens Gilbert & Randall, 1968. Figure 384

Dorsal rays VII-I,11; anal rays I,12; pectoral rays 15 to 17; longitudinal scale series 29 to 34; no scales on head or nape; mouth terminal, the maxilla ending below middle of eye; teeth in two rows in jaws, those of outer row larger (especially in males), with three recurved canines on side of jaw; body depth 4.8 to 6.4 in standard length; third dorsal spine of adult males (and occasionally adult females) prolonged, sometimes extending beyond base of second dorsal fin; caudal fin pointed, 1.9 to 2.9 in standard length; mottled light gray dorsally, shading to white ventrally, with a midlateral row of blackish dashes, often alternating with small black spots; a vertical black line through eye, extending a short distance below; a black spot on opercle. Reaches 2 inches. Florida, Bahamas, and Caribbean Sea from the shallows to at least 145 feet. Occurs on sand or silty sand.

Sharknose Goby

Gobiosoma evelynae Böhlke & Robins, 1968. Figure 385

Dorsal rays VII-I,10 to 12 (usually 11); anal rays I,10 to 12 (rarely 12); pectoral rays usually 16 or 17; no scales; gill rakers 7 to 9; body

Figure 384. Dash Goby (*Gobionellus saepepallens*), Bonaire.

Figure 385. Sharknose Goby (*Gobiosoma evelynae*), St. Croix, Virgin Islands.

slender, the depth about 6 in standard length, and moderately compressed; caudal fin rounded, its length about 5 in standard length; pelvic fins forming a cup-like sucking disc; mouth distinctly ventral, the snout overhanging upper lip; upper lip not separated by a distinct groove from front of snout; a single row of close-set slender conical teeth in upper jaw and two or three rows anteriorly in lower; a distinct canine medially near front of lower jaw in males, none in females; a black stripe beginning on snout, passing through lower part of eye, across upper end of gill opening onto body where it broadens and continues along lower side to end of caudal fin; a mid-dorsal blackish band commencing at front of interorbital space, bifurcating as it passes posteriorly on head, thence on either side of base of dorsal fins, merging as a single band dorsally on caudal peduncle and ending as a narrow slightly diagonal streak in upper part of caudal fin; pale region between lateral and mid-dorsal black bands on head and anterior part of body yellow, shading posteriorly to light gray; pale region between mid-dorsal and lateral black bands on snout appearing as a continuous "V" when viewed from the front. Attains about 1.5 inches. Known from the Bahamas, Puerto Rico, Lesser Antilles and islands of the southern and western Caribbean Sea. Feeds on ectoparasites of fishes. Often seen in pairs resting on a prominent coral head. Fishes in the vicinity visit such sites, and the gobies swim up from the coral and attach with their pelvic disc to the surface of the host fishes and skit-

ter over them. Sometimes they enter the mouth or gill chamber, ostensibly in search of parasites. This species is one of 12 of the subgenus *Elacatinus* in the western Atlantic.

Genie's Cleaning Goby

Gobiosoma genie Böhlke & Robins, 1968.
Figure 386

Dorsal rays VII-I,10 or 11 (usually 11); anal rays I,10 or 11 (usually 10); pectoral rays 16 to 18 (rarely 18); no scales; gill rakers 7 or 8; mouth distinctly inferior (hence snout overhanging upper lip); upper lip separated from snout by a deep groove; teeth in upper jaw uniserial; body depth 5.0 to 6.2 in standard length; whitish with two black stripes, one middorsal and the other lateral on head but passing to lower side on body, both ending in caudal fin; pale band separating two black stripes bright yellow on head, this band narrowing as it passes anteriorly, forming a V on top of snout with band of other side. Attains 1.8 inches. Known from the Bahamas and the Cayman Islands; reported to hybridize with *G. evelynae* in the southern Bahamas.

Yellowline Goby

Gobiosoma horsti Metzelaar, 1922.
Figure 387

Dorsal rays VII-I,11; anal rays I,10 or 11; pectoral rays 18 or 19; no scales; mouth slightly inferior; a deep groove separating upper lip from snout; upper jaw with two rows of teeth, those of outer row small at the front but with three or four as curved canines posteriorly in jaw; dentition of the sexes similar; body depth 4.0 to 5.0 in standard length; black, shading to whit-

Figure 386. Genie's Cleaning Goby (*Gobiosoma genie*), Bahamas.

Figure 387. Yellowline Goby (*Gobiosoma horsti*), Bahamas.

ish ventrally, with a narrow yellow stripe beginning at upper edge of eye and extending into base of caudal fin. Attains 2.2 inches. Bahamas, Gulf of Mexico and Caribbean Sea. Commensal in tubular sponges.

Neon Goby

Gobiosoma oceanops (Jordan, 1904).

Figure 388

Dorsal rays VII-I,10 to 13; anal rays I,9 to 12 (rarely 9); pectoral rays 16 to 19 (usually 16 or 17); no scales; gill rakers 8 to 10; mouth distinctly inferior; no deep groove between upper lip and snout; teeth in upper jaw in one row, none enlarged; teeth in lower jaw in three or four rows anteriorly, narrowing to a single row posteriorly, the males with two or three large recurved canines in an inner row posteriorly; body depth about 5.0 to 5.5 in standard length; translucent gray with a middorsal black stripe and a lateral black stripe, both extending into caudal fin; a narrow blue stripe within light gray zone separating the two black stripes, the anterior part of which is white. Attains 1.6 inches. Florida, Texas and western Caribbean (no records from the Bahamas or Antilles); depth range 3 to 130 feet. Florida fish differ from western Caribbean ones in having the pale zone between the two black stripes entirely blue.

Yellownose Goby

Gobiosoma randalli Böhlke & Robins, 1968.

Figure 389

Dorsal rays VII-I,11; anal rays I,10; pectoral rays 17 or 18 (usually 18); no scales; gill rakers 7; mouth slightly inferior; upper lip separated from snout by a deep groove; males

Figure 388. Neon Goby (*Gobiosoma oceanops*), Belize.

Figure 389. Yellownose Goby (*Gobiosoma randalli*), at a depth of 20 feet, Bonaire.

with four or five recurved canine teeth in an outer row at front of upper jaw (females have a smaller mouth and lack canines); body depth 5.0 to 5.9 in standard length; head and body with two black stripes, one middorsal and one lateral, the two separated by a narrow bright yellow stripe which commences on upper part of eye; all three stripes continuing into caudal fin; a median dorsal yellow band on snout. Reaches 1.5 inches. Ranges from Puerto Rico south through the Lesser Antilles to islands of the southern Caribbean and coast of Venezuela; it may share the same coral head with *G. evelynae*.

Atlantic Shrimp Goby

Nes longus (Nichols, 1914).   Figure 390
   Dorsal rays VII-I,13; anal rays I,12; no scales on head or body; no pores on head; mouth terminal or with lower jaw slightly projecting; mouth large, the maxilla extending slightly posterior to a vertical at rear of eye; upper jaw with two rows of teeth, the teeth of outer row larger; lower jaw with a narrow band of small teeth; body very elongate, the depth 6.0 to 7.5 in standard length (larger individuals more elongate, in general); first dorsal spine of adults prolonged; caudal fin narrowly rounded, about equal to head length; whitish with a row of five dark yellowish brown double spots on lower side of body; head and dorsal part of body with irregular yellowish brown spots of variable size; caudal fin with chevron markings. Attains 3.5 inches. Florida, Bahamas and Caribbean Sea. Lives symbiotically with a snapping shrimp in sand or silty sand; the shrimp (generally a pair of shrimps), builds and maintains the burrow

Figure 390. Atlantic Shrimp Goby (*Nes longus*), and alpheid shrimp (*Alpheus floridanus*), Bonaire.

Figure 391. Rusty Goby (*Priolepis hipoliti*), Belize.

into which the goby dashes when alarmed; the goby serves as the sentinel.

Rusty Goby

Priolepis hipoliti (Metzelaar, 1922).
Figure 391

Dorsal rays VI-I,9 (rarely 8 or 10); anal rays I,8 (rarely 7 or 9); pectoral rays 17 to 19; lateral scale rows 27 to 32; gill rakers 15 or 16; depth of body 3.4 to 4.3 in standard length; width of body 1.3 to 1.7 in depth; caudal fin 3.2 to 3.6 in standard length; pelvic fins largely divided (united basally by a membrane); second dorsal spine prolonged; scales of body ctenoid; head not scaled except for occipital region; teeth in bands in jaws, the inner and outer rows enlarged, those of inner row of upper jaw only slightly enlarged and confined to front of jaw and those of outer row of lower jaw restricted to front of jaw; usual color dull orange with narrow light bluish gray bars (eight on body including one at caudal base); it could also be stated that the fish is gray with broad orange bars; median fins with rows of small orange spots. Attains about 1.5 inches. Florida Keys and Caribbean Sea. A common reef fish known from the shore to 420 feet. but rarely seen.

DARTFISHES AND WORMFISHES
(MICRODESMIDAE)

This family formerly included just the wormfishes such as those of the genera *Microdesmus* and *Cerdale*. A recent study by the author and Douglass F. Hoese showed that the dartfishes (also known as hover gobies) are more closely related to the

Figure 392. Helen's Dartfish (*Ptereleotris helenae*), Puerto Rico.

wormfishes than to the gobies. However, they clearly remain in the suborder Gobioidei.

Dartfishes are classified as a separate subfamily, Ptereleotrinae, of which the only Atlantic genus is *Ptereleotris* (*Ioglossus* is a synonym). There are two species of *Ptereleotris* in the western Atlantic, compared to 13 in the Indo-Pacific region.

The microdesmid fishes have elongate bodies (extremely elongate in some wormfishes) with small, embedded, usually nonoverlapping scales; the scales are cycloid, but may be ctenoid posteriorly on some fishes of the Ptereleotrinae. There is no lateral line. The mouth is strongly oblique with the lower jaw projecting. Microdesmids are small fishes, none exceeding 12 inches.

Helen's Dartfish

Ptereleotris helenae (Randall, 1968).

Figures 392 & 393

Dorsal rays VI-I,22 to 24; anal rays I,21 to 23; pectoral rays 20 to 22; pelvic rays I,4; lateral scale rows about 135 to 166; gill rakers 6 to 9 + 17 to 20; body elongate, the depth 5.6 to 6.7 in standard length, and moderately compressed, the width 1.5 to 1.9 in depth; caudal fin emarginate in juveniles, rounded in adults, the longest rays in upper half of fin (length of fin 2.7 to 3.6 in standard length); pelvic fins divided for at least seven-eighths of their length; a low median fleshy ridge (light blue in color) running from interorbital to origin of first dorsal fin; scales ctenoid posteriorly on body, cycloid elsewhere, those anteriorly on body embedded (hence difficult to count); no scales on head; mouth very oblique, opening dorsally; teeth in two rows in upper jaw, the inner row small except for a pair of large incurved canines anteriorly; two rows of teeth at front of lower jaw and one row on side, the largest consisting of one to four canines antero-laterally in inner row; light bluish gray with two horizontal metallic blue or violet lines on opercle; a yellow line midventrally on gill membranes; median fins primarily yellowish with blue margins; juveniles are more colorful, the body more blue and the fins more yellow, than adults. Largest specimen, 4.7 inches. South Florida and the West

Figure 393. Helen's Dartfish (*Ptereleotris helenae*), 4.3 inches, Puerto Rico.

Figure 394. Lancer Dragonet (*Callionymus bairdi*), male, 1.7 inches, St. John, Virgin Islands.

Indies. Lives in "U"-shaped burrows on sand or silty sand bottoms; often seen in pairs near reefs at depths of about 40 to at least 200 feet. Juveniles are not uncommon over sand or coral rubble in less than 40 feet. Feeds on zooplankton. Descends near its burrow with the approach of danger, darting in head first with further provocation. The related *Ptereleotris calliurus* from Florida has a pointed caudal fin and a black margin on the dorsal fins.

DRAGONETS
(CALLIONYMIDAE)

The dragonets are small bottom-dwelling fishes which are characterized as follows: body moderately elongate, not scaled; head usually broad and depressed; gill opening small; two dorsal fins, the first of three or four flexible spines; mouth small, protruding, the upper jaw protractile; teeth very small, only in jaws; eyes high on head, partially directed upward; pelvic fins I,5, broadly separated.

Lancer Dragonet

Callionymus bairdi Jordan, 1887.
Figure 394

Dorsal rays IV-9; first ray of soft dorsal fin not branched; anal rays 8; pectoral rays 19 or 20; caudal rays 15; a prominent stout bony process on preopercle, commonly ending in one forward-directed spine at the bottom and three upturned spines at the top (but there may be as many as nine upper spines, especially on older individuals from deeper water); males have an elevated first dorsal fin. Largest specimen 4 inches, but few exceed 2.5 inches. Tropical western Atlantic. Usually associated with reefs or coral rubble areas. Only one other shallow-water species of the genus is known from the western Atlantic, *C. pauciradiatus*. It has fewer soft rays in the fins (6 dorsal and 4 anal) and lacks the lower spine on the bony preopercular process; typically it lives in seagrass beds.

SURGEONFISHES
(ACANTHURIDAE)

The surgeonfishes, sometimes called "tangs," are readily distinguished by their possession of one or more spines or tubercles along the side of the caudal peduncle. They are high-bodied and compressed and have small scales. The eye is high on the head, and the small mouth is low; the upper jaw is not protractile; the preorbital is very deep. The bones of the pelvic girdle are long and curved. There is a continuous dorsal fin of IV to IX spines with no notch between spinous and soft portions. Pelvic rays are I,5 (I,3 in two Indo-Pacific genera).

There are six genera; only one, *Acanthurus*, is known from the western Atlantic. The caudal spine of this genus is lancet-like and folds into a horizontal groove. The "hinge" is toward the back of the spine, thus the sharp inner edge faces forward when the tail is bent to the opposite side. Surgeonfishes are able to slash other fishes with this spine. More often they merely exhibit a warning side-sweep of the tail toward an intruding fish who almost invariably withdraws. In an aquarium a surgeonfish can utilize its spine or the threat of same to gain domi-

Figure 395. Surgeonfishes (*Acanthurus chirurgus* & *A. coeruleus*), Roatan, Honduras.

Figure 396. Ocean Surgeon (*Acanthurus bahianus*), Bonaire.

nance over resident fishes. An unwary human who tries to handle surgeonfishes risks being badly cut.

The teeth of *Acanthurus* are spatulate, close-set and denticulate on the edges. They are specialized for grazing on filamentous algae (there are, however, a few deeper-water species in the Indo-Pacific which feed on zooplankton). The very long digestive tract is also indicative of plant-feeding.

Surgeonfishes may form feeding aggregations, occasionally as mixed schools of more than one species (Figure 395) which, by virtue of their numbers, overcome the territorial damselfishes (*Stegastes* spp.) trying to protect their private pastures of benthic algae.

The late postlarval stage is called the "acronurus." It is orbicular and transparent with silvery over the abdomen. It can be dipnetted at night lights at the surface.

Four species of *Acanthurus* are known from the western Atlantic. One appears to be confined to southern and western Florida.

Ocean Surgeon

Acanthurus bahianus Castelnau, 1855.
Figures 396 & 397

Dorsal rays IX,23 to 26; anal rays III,21 to 23; pectoral rays 15 to 17; outer gill rakers 20 to 22; inner gill rakers 17 to 19; a 9-inch fish with 14 upper and 16 lower teeth; depth of body about 2 in standard length; caudal fin moderately emarginate, the caudal concavity contained 5 to 12 times in standard length; light yellowish brown to grayish brown with pale greenish gray to pale bluish longitudinal lines on body; throat pale grayish blue; caudal fin olive-yellow to olive brown, the posterior margin bluish white (broader to-

Figure 397. Ocean Surgeon (*Acanthurus bahianus*), juvenile, at a depth of 20 feet, Long Island, Bahamas.

ward central part of margin); dorsal fin with alternating narrow lengthwise bands of dull orange and light bluish green; anal fin with bands of grayish blue and dark gray, the border blue; pectoral rays dusky orange, the membranes clear; pelvic rays pale blue, the membranes black; a narrow violet area around caudal spine, the inner edge blackish, the sheath dark brown; opercular membrane purple and black; a purplish gray area adjacent to posterior edge of eye, this crossed by six or seven narrow yellow lines which radiate from eye; a short blue line in front of eye; base of caudal fin often abruptly paler than body. Largest specimen examined, 14 inches, from Rio de Janeiro. Bermuda and Massachusetts to Brazil; also recorded from Ascension and St. Helena. A recent record from the Seychelles, Indian Ocean is probably a locality error.

Doctorfish

Acanthurus chirurgus (Bloch, 1787).
Figures 395 & 398

Dorsal rays IX,24 or 25; anal rays III,22 or 23; pectoral rays 16 or 17; outer gill rakers 16 to 19; inner gill rakers 15 to 18; adults with 18 to 20 teeth in jaws; depth of body about 2 in standard length; caudal fin slightly emarginate, the caudal concavity 14 to 18 in standard length; varies in color from light grayish brown to dark brown, the sides of the body with about ten narrow dark bars, most of which are posterior to pectoral fin; median fins often bluish with faint longitudinal bands, the borders of the dorsal and anal blue (better defined on anal); base of caudal fin usually abruptly paler than body; pectoral rays dark brown except outer fourth; pelvics pale bluish, the membranes dark brown; opercular membrane black; edge of caudal spine socket nar-

Figure 398. Doctorfish (*Acanthurus chirurgus*), St. Croix, Virgin Islands.

Figure 399. Blue Tang (*Acanthurus coeruleus*), Andros, Bahamas.

Figure 400. Blue Tang (*Acanthurus coeruleus*), juvenile, Long Island, Bahamas.

rowly black, surrounded by pale blue, the sheath of the spine dark brown. Largest specimen, 13.5 inches, from Venezuela. Both sides of the Atlantic; on the western side from Massachusetts to Rio de Janeiro. Both this species and *bahianus* have a thick-walled gizzard-like stomach and often ingest sand with their algal food. Probably there is some grinding of the algae in the stomach.

Blue Tang

Acanthurus coeruleus Bloch & Schneider, 1801.   Figures 395, 399 & 400

Dorsal rays IX,26 to 28; anal rays III,24 to 26; pectoral rays 16 or 17; outer gill rakers 13 or 14; inner gill rakers 13; large adults with 14 upper and 16 lower teeth; body deep, the depth about 1.7 in standard length; color of adults varying from blue to purplish gray, with gray longitudinal lines; dorsal and anal fins blue with orange-brown diagonal-lengthwise bands; sheath of caudal spine white. The young are bright yellow. Largest specimen, 14.4 inches, from Venezuela. Bermuda and New York to Rio de Janeiro. A common reef fish.

TRIGGERFISHES
(BALISTIDAE)

The triggerfishes are one of several families of the order Tetraodontiformes (Plectognathi). They are distinctive and often colorful shore fishes of tropic seas which appear to be derived from the surgeonfishes or acanthurid-like stock. The body is relatively deep and moderately compressed; the eye is high on the head and the preorbital deep. The snout is long but not attenuate, and the mouth is terminal or directed slightly upward. The jaws are short but strong; there are eight long close-set protruding incisiform teeth in each jaw, the upper with six inner reinforcing teeth. The gill opening is restricted to a short slit. There are two dorsal fins, the first of two or three spines; the first spine is the longest and is very stout. The pelvic fins are replaced by a single small spinous knob (here termed the pelvic terminus) which is articulated to the long pelvis. The skin is tough; the scales are modified to plate-like structures with small spines or tubercles.

The triggerfishes are usually solitary. They swim by undulating the soft dorsal and anal fins, bringing their tail into action only if they wish to move rapidly. When pursued, however, they usually seek shelter in a small cave in the reef with restricted entrance, raise their first dorsal spine, and lower their pelvis, thus wedging themselves firmly in place. The triggerfishes are named for the interlocking arrangement of the bases of the three dorsal spines, such that the first can be fixed in the erect position; if one depresses the second or "trigger" spine with a finger, the first spine is no longer locked in the vertical position.

In spite of their small mouths, many triggerfishes feed on relatively large and well-armored invertebrates such as crabs, mollusks, echinoderms, and in some species, even coral; they use their powerful jaws and sharp teeth to render the hard portions of these various animals into small pieces. Some

Figure 401. Queen Triggerfish (*Balistes vetula*), St. Croix, Virgin Islands.

balistids are therefore incompatible with certain animals in an aquarium.

In general, triggerfishes are good to eat; however, some of the large species such as *Balistes vetula* have on rare occasions caused illness when consumed.

Gray Triggerfish

Balistes capriscus Gmelin, 1788.

Figure 402

Dorsal rays III-27 to 29; anal rays 23 to 26; pectoral rays 15; lateral scale rows 57 to 63; gill rakers about 31 to 35; depth of body at anus about 2.2 in standard length; head length 2.7 to 3 in standard length; pectoral fins about 2.7 in head; soft dorsal and anal fins elevated anteri-orly, but no rays prolonged as filaments; third dorsal spine relatively long, extending well above contour of back when fin raised; caudal fin slightly rounded in the middle, the lobes very prolonged in adults; olivaceous gray dorsally with large squarish dark blotches along back; three faint irregular broad dark bars on body; a narrow pale transverse band on chin; small light blue spots on upper half of body and median fins, and whitish spots and irregular short lines ventrally; upper edge of eye blue. Said to reach a little more than 1 foot in length. Tropical and temperate Atlantic; on the western side from Nova Scotia to Argentina; rare in the West Indies.

Figure 402. Gray Triggerfish (*Balistes capriscus*), 5.3 inches, Puerto Rico.

Figure 403. Queen Triggerfish (*Balistes vetula*), Bonaire.

Queen Triggerfish

Balistes vetula Linnaeus, 1758.

Figures 401 & 403

Dorsal rays III-29 to 31 (usually 30); anal rays 26 to 28; pectoral rays 15 or 16 (usually 15), the uppermost very short; lateral scale rows from upper end of gill opening to caudal fin base 56 to 63; gill rakers about 35 to 38; depth of body at anus 1.8 to 2.4 in standard length; head length to upper end of gill opening 2.7 to 2.9 in standard length; pectoral fins 2.3 to 2.7 in head length; soft dorsal and anal fins elevated anteriorly, the fifth or sixth dorsal ray and adjacent rays prolonged as a filament; third dorsal spine relatively long, extending well above contour of back when fin elevated; caudal fin slightly emarginate in young, becoming very lunate with prolonged lobes in adults; greenish or bluish gray on back, orange-yellow on lower part of head and abdomen, with two broad diagonal curved bright blue bands running from snout to below and in front of pectoral fins, the lowermost continuous with a blue ring around lips; dark blue lines with yellow edges radiating from eye and one from snout to gill opening which parallels the blue bands on the cheek; a broad blue bar across caudal peduncle, and blue submarginal bands in median fins. Largest collected by author, 22.5 inches in fork length (length not including long caudal filaments), from the Virgin Islands. Both sides of the Atlantic; on the western side from Massachusetts to Brazil. Common on reefs but ventures into adjacent sand, rubble or seagrass habitats. Adults feed on a great variety of invertebrates but most heavily on sea urchins, particularly *Diadema*, when available. The scientific name *vetula* is derived from the common name "old wife" that is often used in the West Indies for this fish.

Ocean Triggerfish

Canthidermis sufflamen (Mitchill, 1815). Figure 404

Dorsal rays III-26 or 27; anal rays 24; pectoral rays 16; lateral scale rows 53 to 58; gill rakers about 32 to 36; depth of body at anus 2.1 to 2.3 in standard length; head about 3.2 in standard length; pectoral fins about 2.3 in head; soft dorsal and anal fins very elevated anteriorly, the longest rays nearly as long as head; third dorsal spine short, barely visible above contour of back when fin elevated; caudal fin double-emarginate, the lobes of adults slightly to moderately prolonged; brownish gray with a large dark brown spot at base of pectoral fins. Attains a length of at least 22 inches and a weight of nearly 10 pounds. Known in the western Atlantic from Bermuda and Massachusetts to the Caribbean Sea; probably much more broadly distributed. Pelagic. Very rare inshore, but common on offshore reefs in clear water near drop-offs to deep water. Usually observed in loose aggregations well above the bottom; appears to feed principally on the larger animals of the zooplankton. The related *C. maculatus* is more elongate, has a very rough skin, and is dark with pale spots; it apparently occurs only well offshore.

Black Durgon

Melichthys niger (Bloch, 1786). Figure 405

Dorsal rays III-32 to 34; anal rays 28 to 31; pectoral rays 16 or 17, the uppermost very small; lateral scale rows 54 to 60; keels along center of posterior scales, thus forming lon-

Figure 404. Ocean Triggerfish (*Canthidermis sufflamen*), Bonaire.

Figure 405. Black Durgon (*Melichthys niger*), at a depth of 80 feet, Puerto Rico.

gitudinal ridges; gill rakers about 36 or 37; depth of body at anus about 2.4 in standard length; head about 3.5 in standard length; pectoral fins about 3.2 in head; dorsal and anal fins moderately elevated anteriorly; third dorsal spine short, not visible above upper contour of back when fin elevated; caudal fin with lobes somewhat prolonged; black, sometimes with a dark green cast; edges of scales at front of head may be orangish; a narrow pale blue band at base of dorsal and anal fins. Attains fourteen inches. Circumtropical. Most common in clear outer-reef areas at depths of about 50 feet or more. Often seen well above the bottom. Omnivorous, but more inclined to ingest plant than animal life. Grazes on benthic algae or will rise to the surface to feed on floating plant material. Animals that are consumed are principally plank-tonic, such as pteropods, crab larvae, siphonophores and salps. *Melichthys radula* and *M. piceus* are synonyms.

Sargassum Triggerfish

Xanthichthys ringens (Linnaeus, 1758).
Figure 406

Dorsal rays III-26 to 29; anal rays 23 to 27; pectoral rays 13 (rarely 14); lateral scale rows 39 to 44; gill rakers 36 to 40; depth of body 2.6 to 2.9 in standard length; head 3.1 to 3.3 in standard length; chin protruding anterior to mouth; pectoral fins about 3 in head length; soft dorsal and anal fins moderately elevated anteriorly; third dorsal spine small, not extending above contour of back when fin elevated; caudal fin emarginate; three prominent slightly diagonal grooves running from below and behind mouth nearly to gill opening; light brownish gray

Figure 406. Sargassum Triggerfish (*Xanthichthys ringens*), Puerto Rico.

with rows of dark brown spots on body; grooves on head dark brown; scaly base of soft dorsal and anal fins and membranes of spinous dorsal fin dark brown; caudal fin pale with orange-red upper and lower borders and a large orange-red crescent posteriorly. Attains a maximum length of about 10 inches. Western Atlantic only from South Carolina and Bermuda to Brazil at 4° S. The young, which are variable in color, have often been collected near floating *Sargassum*. Adults are rarely encountered in less than about 100 feet of water, but beyond this depth they become one of the most abundant West Indian reef fishes.

FILEFISHES
(MONACANTHIDAE)

The filefishes are closely related to the triggerfishes; in fact, some authors have combined the two as a single family. Still others, however, have divided the monacanthids into two families, one of which consists of the bizarre *Aluterus* and its relatives.

The filefishes differ from the triggerfishes in having more compressed bodies, a spinous dorsal fin with a single long spine and usually a second rudimentary spine, six sharp incisor-like teeth in the jaws, the upper jaw with an inner reinforcing row of four teeth, and small poorly differentiated scales which bear small spinules (thus giving the skin a sandpaper-like texture). The spinules on the side and in front of the caudal peduncle of several species are elongate, forming a bristle-like patch; these patches are generally better developed or only present on males. Males of some species also have a few recurved spines on

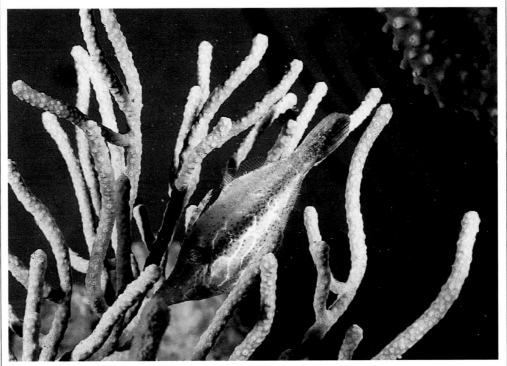

Figure 407. Slender Filefish (*Monacanthus tuckeri*), Grand Bahama Island.

the side of the caudal peduncle which are lacking or poorly developed on females.

Many of the filefishes are secretive; they swim slowly and tend to hide among plants, gorgonians, etc. Some species vary in color to match their surroundings; they may have scattered small fleshy projections on the body.

Filefishes are very generalized in their food habits. Some seem to ingest just about any form of benthic life they encounter, including such seemingly unwholesome things as sponges, gorgonians, hydroids and stinging coral. The ripe eggs of several West Indian species are green.

The Monacanthidae is represented by more species in Australia than any other major region of the world. These fishes are called leatherjackets in Australia.

Unicorn Filefish

Aluterus monoceros (Linnaeus, 1758).

Figure 408

Dorsal rays II-46 to 50; anal rays 47 to 52; pectoral rays 14 or 15; gill rakers of one specimen from Puerto Rico 31; depth of body between origins of second dorsal and anal fins 2.3 to 2.9 in standard length; eye to dorsal spine distance 11 to 17 in standard length; ventral contour of head concave below chin, followed by a prominent convexity; caudal fin short, 3.8 to 5.6 in standard length, rounded in young, emarginate or double emarginate in adults; caudal peduncle longer than deep; pelvic terminus rudimentary in young, absent in adults; gray to brown, mottled with dark, with scattered small dark spots. Attains at least 2 feet. Cosmopolitan; rare in the West Indies.

Figure 408. Unicorn Filefish (*Aluterus monoceros*), 18.4 inches, Isla de Margarita, Venezuela. Photo from Fernando Cervigon.

Orange Filefish

Aluterus schoepfii (Walbaum, 1792).

Figure 409

Dorsal rays II-32 to 39; anal rays 35 to 41; pectoral rays 11 to 14; gill rakers 21 to 27; depth of body variable (the smaller individuals more slender), the depth between origins of second dorsal and anal fins 2.1 to 5.3 in standard length; eye to dorsal spine distance variable, 7.4 to 26 times in standard length; caudal fin rounded, 1.9 to 4.8 in standard length; depth of caudal peduncle varying from slightly longer to slightly shorter than its length (measured to rear base of anal fin); pelvic terminus always absent; ground color varying from pale gray to dark gray or brown, the head and body with numerous small round orange or orange-yellow spots; lips often blackish. Attains about 20 inches. Nova Scotia and Bermuda to Brazil. Not common in the West Indies; usually encountered over bottoms of seagrass, sand or mud. Appears to feed mainly on algae and seagrasses. *Aluterus punctatus* is a synonym.

Scrawled Filefish

Aluterus scriptus (Osbeck, 1765).

Figure 410

Dorsal rays II-43 to 49; anal rays 46 to 52; pectoral rays 13 to 15; gill rakers 32 to 42; body elongate, the depth between origins of second dorsal and anal fins 2.9 to 4.6 in standard length; snout long, prominently projecting and slightly upturned (upper head profile concave); eye to dorsal spine distance relatively small, 15 to 20 in standard length; gill opening oblique, forming an angle of about 45 degrees to the horizontal in specimens of about 40 mm standard length or more (true of *Aluterus* in general; other filefishes discussed herein have gill openings that are more nearly vertical); caudal fin rounded and long, its length 1.6 to 3 in standard length; caudal peduncle deeper than long;

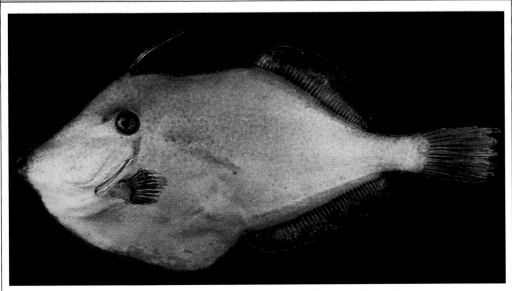

Figure 409. Orange Filefish (*Aluterus schoepfii*), 17 inches, Puerto Rico.

first dorsal spine slender and long (when not broken), inserted over middle of posterior part of eye, and not followed by a deep groove (applies also to other *Aluterus)*; pelvic terminus rudimentary or absent; skin finely velvety; ground color varying from light bluish gray to olive or brown; body and head with blue or blue-green spots and irregular lines and scattered small black spots. Said to reach a length of 3 feet; largest collected by author, 28.5 inches, 5.5 pounds, from the

Figure 410. Scrawled Filefish (*Aluterus scriptus*), Bonaire.

Virgin Islands. Cosmopolitan in tropical and subtropical seas but usually not common. Very diverse in its food habits; West Indian adults have been found with hydrozoans, algae, gorgonians, seagrass, colonial sea anemones and tunicates in their stomachs. One fish may have almost entirely plant material in its gut, and another nearly all stinging coral *(Millepora)*. The related *A. heudelotii (A. ventralis* is a synonym) has been confused with *A. scriptus*. It was described from West Africa but also occurs in the western Atlantic from Massachusetts to Brazil (but is not yet recorded from the West Indies). It differs from *scriptus* in having 36 to 41 soft dorsal rays, 39 to 44 anal rays and a greater average body depth (depth at origins of second dorsal and anal fins 2.1 to 3.6 in standard length).

Whitespotted Filefish

Cantherhines macrocerus (Hollard, 1854).

Figure 411

Dorsal rays II-34 to 36; anal rays 29 to 32; pectoral rays 13 or 14 (usually 14); gill rakers 29 to 35. Similar to the following *(C. pullus)*, differing in lower gill-raker counts, higher average pectoral-ray count, two or three pairs of enlarged spines on side of caudal peduncle (not visible on juveniles), and in color. Adults are brown, with or without many prominent white spots on body and head; body suffused with orange except upper anterior part and regions along base of second dorsal and anal fins; caudal fin black with an obscure curved median white bar and two indistinct white basal spots. Largest specimen, 16.5 inches, from Cuba. Tropical western Atlantic; not common. Usually

Figure 411. Whitespotted Filefish (*Cantherhines macrocerus*), at a depth of 70 feet, Bonaire.

Figure 412. Tail-Light Filefish (*Cantherhines pullus*), St. Croix, Virgin Islands.

seen in pairs; limited data suggest that such pairs consist of one member of each sex. Males are readily distinguished from females of about the same size by the larger spines on the caudal peduncle (a large female, however, could have larger spines than a notably smaller male) and by the orange color of the patch of setae anterior to the peduncular spines on males. Feeds mainly on sponges, but also eats hydroids, stinging coral, gorgonians and algae.

Tail-Light Filefish

Cantherhines pullus (Ranzani, 1842).
Figure 412

Dorsal rays II-33 to 36; anal rays 29 to 32; pectoral rays 12 to 14 (usually 13); gill rakers 34 to 46; depth of body at origin of anal fin 2.3 to 2.6 in standard length; first dorsal spine originating over center or front part of eye and followed by a deep groove into which the spine can fold; no enlarged spines on side of caudal peduncle; males with a dense setous patch along side of and slightly anterior to caudal peduncle; the most common color phase has indistinct dark and light stripes which converge toward the tail; body with small scattered orange spots, many of which have brown centers, and whitish spots of the same size or smaller; a prominent white spot dorsally on caudal peduncle immediately posterior to second dorsal fin, and a similar but smaller spot ventrally on caudal peduncle (these two spots are the most obvious color markings when this species is viewed underwater); dull yellow lines on head which run towards snout, those near eye alternating with bluish lines. Largest male specimen, 7.8 inches; largest

Figure 413. Fringed Filefish (*Monacanthus ciliatus*), 3.8 inches, St. John, Virgin Islands.

female, 7 inches. Massachusetts and Bermuda to Rio de Janeiro; also recorded from West Africa. The most common filefish on West Indian reefs. Late postlarval stages may occur at the surface far from land and are commonly found in the stomachs of predaceous pelagic fishes. Adults feed mainly on benthic algae and sponges.

Fringed Filefish

Monacanthus ciliatus (Mitchill, 1818).

Figure 413

Dorsal rays II-29 to 37; anal rays 28 to 36; pectoral rays usually 11; gill rakers 15 to 23; scales with one to eight unbranched spinules, each arising independently from scale base; depth of body between origins of soft dorsal and anal fins 1.8 to 2.5 in standard length; pelvic flap well developed (when fully expanded in large adults it may increase the aforementioned depth by as much as 1.7); head relatively short, the length in adults 3 to 3.45 in standard length; snout prominently projecting but not very elongate, its length in adults 3.9 to 4.5 in standard length; first dorsal spine originating above posterior part of eye and bearing two rows of prominent recurved spines along its posterior edge; no deep groove behind first dorsal spine; pelvic terminus movable; adult males with two pairs of enlarged recurved spines on each side of caudal peduncle and two or more lesser enlarged spines associated with each larger pair (spines of females only slightly larger than other scale spinules of caudal peduncle); small fleshy projections may be present on body; color variable. Largest specimen, 5.2 inches. Both sides of the Atlantic; on the western side from Newfoundland and Bermuda to Argentina. Lives in close association with benthic plants such as turtle grass; has been observed hiding head-down among clumps of algae on coral rubble or sand bottoms. Feeds mainly on algae, organic detritus and small planktonic crustaceans.

Slender Filefish

Monacanthus tuckeri Bean, 1906.
Figures 407 & 414

Dorsal rays II-32 to 37; anal rays 31 to 36; pectoral rays usually 11; gill rakers 19 to 24. Similar to *ciliatus*, but body more slender, the depth between origins of soft dorsal and anal fins 2.6 to 3.2 in standard length, and the head longer, its length 2.4 to 3 in standard length; snout prominently projecting, angling slightly upward, and moderately elongate, its length in adults 3.5 to 4 in standard length. The illustrated male specimen was yellowish brown in life with small yellowish brown to brown spots, those in a region running from below posterior part of eye to base of caudal fin the darkest, thus forming an indistinct longitudinal dark band; a coarse whitish reticulum on body, dividing it into large brown-spotted blotches which tend to have straight sides; posterior edge of pelvic flap broadly yellow with interconnected rows of blue dots, those of outer row forming a well-defined submarginal blue line. A small species which matures at a total length of less than 2.5 inches. Largest specimen collected by author, 3.4 inches, from Puerto Rico. Bermuda and the Carolinas to southern Florida and the West Indies. Sometimes seen hiding among gorgonian fronds.

Speckled Filefish

Stephanolepis setifer (Bennett, 1830).
Figure 415

Dorsal rays II-27 to 32; anal rays 26 to 32; pectoral rays 11 to 13; gill

Figure 414. Slender Filefish (*Monacanthus tuckeri*), 3.4 inches, Puerto Rico.

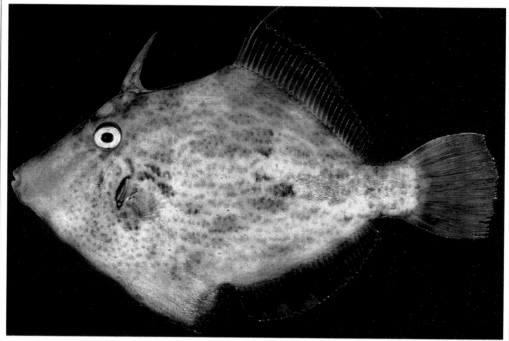

Figure 415. Speckled Filefish (*Stephanolepis setifer*), 7 inches, Puerto Rico.

rakers 22 to 31; scales with one to eight close-set spinules (progressively more in larger individuals), each branched many times in fish larger than about 2 inches; body relatively deep, the depth between origins of second dorsal and anal fins 1.7 to 2.1 in standard length; pelvic flap not well developed; head length 2.5 to 3.2 in standard length; snout 3.7 to 5.4 in standard length; first dorsal spine originating over hind part of eye and bearing two posterior rows of spines which are relatively smaller on larger specimens; no deep groove behind first dorsal spine; second ray of second dorsal fin of males elongate; pelvic terminus movable; no enlarged spines on caudal peduncle, but males with an elongate patch of bristle-like spinules; color variable but usually with short horizontal dark streaks or rows of small dark spots on body; small dark spots on head below eye and on chest; caudal fin with two dark bars, the first usually darker. Largest collected by the author, 7 inches, from Puerto Rico. Belize, throughout the Caribbean Sea, to Brazil. In addition, the pelagic young are known from the Gulf of Mexico and along the Atlantic seaboard from Florida to North Carolina. Not common in the West Indies. Often classified in the genus *Monacanthus*. The closely related *S. hispidus* is known from Nova Scotia to Brazil; it is differentiated by having 29 to 35 dorsal rays, 30 to 35 anal rays, 30 to 41 gill rakers, and a color pattern in which small dark spots, if present, are obscure (none are visible ventrally on head or on chest).

TRUNKFISHES
(OSTRACIIDAE)

The trunkfishes are a small family of bottom-dwelling fishes of tropical and subtropical seas. Usually they are found in relatively shallow water. They are unique in possessing a bony carapace over most of the head and body (gaps exist for the mouth, nostrils, anus, gill opening, caudal peduncle and fins). The carapace, which is made up of strong hexagonal or polygonal plates, is approximately triangular, square or pentagonal in cross-section. Adults of all Atlantic species belong to the triangular category. Small tubercles may impart a slight roughness to the carapace. There is a single dorsal fin, which is posterior in position, and no pelvic fins. None of the fins have spines; the dorsal, anal and caudal fins of Atlantic species all have 10 rays. The mouth is small and low on the head, and the lips are fleshy; the teeth are yellowish brown, moderately long, subconical to nearly incisiform, and occur in a single close-set row in the jaws; among Atlantic species there are 8 to 12 upper and 6 to 10 lower teeth; there are none on the palate. The gill opening is a short near-vertical slit immediately in front of and above the base of the pectoral fin.

These fishes are slow-swimming. Their normal progression is accomplished by a sculling action of the dorsal and anal fins and by the pectoral fins; greater speed is attained by bringing the caudal fin into play. Still, it is evident that they rely upon their bony armor to give them their principal protection from predation. The larger species are found over open bottoms of sand and seagrass far from the protection of reefs.

These fishes secrete a poisonous substance which can kill other fishes, and even themselves, in a crowded aquarium or live well. This

Figure 416. Smooth Trunkfish (*Lactophrys triqueter*), St. Croix, Virgin Islands.

Figure 417. Honeycomb Cowfish (*Acanthostracion polygonius*), Bonaire.

toxin appears to be exuded in greatest quantity when the trunkfishes are under duress (as when one tries to net them from a tank). Glands in the skin, especially in the mouth region, have been shown to be responsible for the production of the toxin in *Ostracion.* Possibly the toxic substance provides an additional deterrent to predators. However, the author has found ostraciontids in the stomachs of the Tiger Shark, Nassau Grouper, and Cobia; therefore they do not enjoy complete protection from predation.

Trunkfishes are highly esteemed as food. The muscle tissue of the back is eaten; it is tender and has a delicate flavor. In Puerto Rico, where these fishes are called "chapin," the fishermen are so fond of them that they often keep them for themselves and their families. A former fisheries officer in the Bahamas reported that improper cleaning of trunkfishes can lead to illness when these fishes are eaten. He was not aware of the epidermal origin of the toxin. It would seem possible, however, that contamination of the flesh with material from the mouth or skin could result in the ingestion of some toxin.

Trunkfishes were well known to early naturalists, for they are often dried and saved as curios.

Honeycomb Cowfish

Acanthostracion polygonius Poey, 1876.
Figure 417

Pectoral rays usually 12; gill rakers 11 to 14; shape of carapace and its spines similar to *A. quadricornis,* but only rarely with a very small postdorsal spine and a small plate on upper surface of caudal peduncle (no comparable postanal spine or plate); width of carapace 1.4 to 1.7

in depth; caudal fin rounded; olivaceous with dark polygonal or hexagonal rings submarginally in plates on body (rings incomplete dorsally) and a dark reticulate pattern on head; centers of dorsal rings yellow; a wash of purplish blue, especially on sides and ventrally; large individuals develop irregular dark markings inside the dark rings. Largest specimen, 15.3 inches. New Jersey to Brazil, but not the Gulf of Mexico. The least common of western Atlantic trunkfishes. Appears to be primarily a reef species. Stomachs of three specimens contained tunicates, alcyonarians, sponges and shrimps.

Scrawled Cowfish

Acanthostracion quadricornis (Linnaeus, 1758).   Figure 418

Pectoral rays usually 11; gill rakers 13 to 17; a latero-posterior spine on each ventral ridge of carapace and another extending anteriorly in front of each eye; upper part of carapace continuous posterior to dorsal and anal fins, often with a spine projecting backward from end of carapace posterior to these fins; a small isolated dorsal and a comparable ventral plate often present on caudal peduncle posterior to carapace; carapace relatively narrow, the width 1.6 to 1.9 in depth; caudal fin slightly rounded to truncate (sometimes with lobes slightly projecting); yellowish with blue spots and irregular blue markings on body, caudal peduncle and fin, and two to four approximately horizontal (sometimes broken) blue bands on cheek between eye and mouth. Attains about 18 inches. Massachusetts and Bermuda to Brazil; two unusual records from South Africa. In the Caribbean region found

Figure 418. Scrawled Cowfish (*Acanthostracion quadricornis*), Bonaire.

mainly in seagrass beds. Analysis of the gut contents of a few specimens revealed feeding on sponges, tunicates, colonial sea anemones, hermit crabs and other crustaceans, gorgonians and marine plants. *A. tricornis* is a synonym.

Spotted Trunkfish

Lactophrys bicaudalis (Linnaeus, 1758).
Figure 419

Pectoral rays 12; gill rakers 12 to 14; a backward-directed spine from the ventral ridge on each side of carapace, the tip reaching anus; no preorbital spines; upper part of carapace continuous posterior to dorsal fin; width of carapace about 1.2 in depth; whitish with numerous small black spots on carapace, caudal peduncle and caudal fin; lips whitish; bases of dorsal, anal and pectoral fins blackish; large adults with black spots missing from three small

areas in a diagonal row anteriorly on body at level of eye, thus appearing as three white spots. Reaches at least 16 inches. Florida Keys to Brazil; also recorded from Ascension Island. Limited data indicate that *L. bicaudalis* feeds mainly on tunicates, sea cucumbers, brittle stars and sea urchins, but it also ingests seagrasses, algae, starfishes and crabs. This species and *triqueter* are sometimes classified in the genus *Rhinesomus*, leaving only *trigonus* in *Lactophrys*.

Buffalo Trunkfish

Lactophrys trigonus (Linnaeus, 1758).
Figures 420 & 421

Pectoral rays 11 to 13 (usually 12); gill rakers 17 or 18; a lateroposterior spine on each ventral ridge of carapace, as in *bicaudalis;* no preorbital spines; a gap usually present in carapace just behind

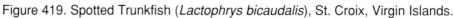

Figure 419. Spotted Trunkfish (*Lactophrys bicaudalis*), St. Croix, Virgin Islands.

Figure 420. Buffalo Trunkfish (*Lactophrys trigonus*), St. John, Virgin Islands.

dorsal fin, followed by a small isolated mid-dorsal bony plate (which may on occasional individuals be followed by a still smaller plate); width of carapace about 1.1 in depth in adults (width greater than depth in juveniles in spite of their being much deeper-bodied than adults); caudal fin rounded in young, emarginate in adults (rounded on other Atlantic trunkfishes except *A. quadricornis)*; olivaceous with small diffuse white spots; two areas where the hexagonal plates are dark-edged, thus forming chain-like markings, one on the pectoral region of the body and the other approximately half way between gill opening and posterior end of carapace; large indi-

Figure 421. Buffalo Trunkfish (*Lactophrys trigonus*), 12.8 inches, Bimini, Bahama Islands.

Figure 422. Smooth Trunkfish (*Lactophrys triqueter*), Long Island, Bahamas.

viduals lose the pale spots and chain markings and develop an irregular dark reticulate pattern over the entire carapace and caudal peduncle (although individuals as small as 13 inches may have the reticulate pattern, it usually does not appear until a length of about 15 inches). Attains at least 18 inches. Massachusetts and Bermuda to Brazil. Primarily a resident of the seagrass habitat. Feeds on crabs, pelecypod mollusks, polychaete worms, sea urchins, tunicates and other invertebrates, and marine plants.

Smooth Trunkfish

Lactophrys triqueter (Linnaeus, 1758).
Figures 416 & 422
Pectoral rays 12 (discounting the short upper rudimentary ray); gill rakers 8 or 9; no spines on carapace; upper part of carapace continuous posterior to dorsal fin; carapace nearly as wide as deep, the width about 1.1 in depth; carapace and caudal peduncle blackish with numerous small white spots; lips and bases of fins blackish; terminal edge of caudal fin narrowly white with a blackish submarginal band. The smallest of Atlantic trunkfishes; attains about 12 inches. Massachusetts and Bermuda to Rio de Janeiro. Usually found in reef areas. Feeds on a great variety of invertebrate animals such as polychaete worms, peanut worms, crabs, shrimps, tunicates, sponges and acorn worms. Has been observed to eject a current of water from its mouth into the sand, thus exposing burrowing forms which form a major part of its diet.

PUFFERS
(TETRAODONTIDAE)

The puffers are bizarre fishes of warm seas which are well known for the capacity, when provoked, to greatly inflate themselves by drawing water (or air, if removed from the sea) into the abdomen. They are slow-swimming, apparently relying on their ability to increase their volume through inflation to discourage predators.

Puffers are characterized morphologically as follows: skin tough, usually without normal scales and often with spinules, giving it a prickly texture; each jaw armed with a sharp beak-like dental plate with a median suture; gill opening small, immediately anterior to pectoral fin; no pelvic fins; no spines in fins; a single dorsal fin posterior in position; anal fin similar to dorsal and located approximately beneath it; one or two lateral lines; no ribs.

The viscera of puffers, especially the liver, may be very toxic and can cause a serious illness known as tetraodon poisoning when eaten; not infrequently this illness terminates in death. The toxin has been isolated by Japanese biochemists. The amount present in a fish, and hence the virulence, varies with the species.

Of the Caribbean tetraodontids only *Canthigaster rostrata* is consistently found in the reef habitat; a few other species are usually seen in adjacent habitats but may on occasions be observed on reefs. Some are found in turbid brackish environments (at times even fresh water). Examples are the large *Lagocephalus laevigatus*, an elongate species with 13 or 14 dorsal rays and a deeply emarginate cau-

Figure 423. Bandtail Puffer (*Sphoeroides spengleri*), St. Croix, Virgin Islands.

dal fin, and *Sphoeroides testudineus*, a moderately large and distinctively marked species (dark brown on the back, with pale bands enclosing circular and elliptical areas, and black spots on the sides).

Sharpnose Puffer

Canthigaster rostrata (Bloch, 1782).

Figure 424

Dorsal rays 10; anal rays 9; pectoral rays 16 to 18 (including uppermost rudimentary ray); gill rakers 6 or 7; no lateral line; beak-like dental plates with a median suture; each nostril a single aperture surrounded by a fleshy rim; body moderately compressed (when not inflated), the width about 1.7 in depth (body of tetraodontids nearly cylindrical); snout somewhat pointed; skin smooth except lower parts of head and abdomen which have spinules (with two lateral roots) that fold into small sockets; gill opening very short, not extending below mid-base of pectoral fin; pectoral fins about 2.6 in head, their posterior margin concave; caudal fin slightly rounded to slightly emarginate; back brown, the sides white with faint blue dots, the abdomen and side of head with a yellowish cast; upper and lower edges of caudal peduncle and fin black; vertical light blue lines on side of caudal peduncle which become broadly reticulate on the lower black edge; a broad yellow-orange region around eye; blue lines radiating from lower half of eye; some blue lines on snout behind mouth and on chin. Attains 4.5 inches. Both sides of the Atlantic; on the western side from Bermuda and Florida to the Caribbean Sea. A common reef fish which ranges into other habitats such as beds of seagrass. Feeds on seagrasses (78%

Figure 424. Sharpnose Puffer (*Canthigaster rostrata*), Guadeloupe.

Figure 425. Caribbean Puffer (*Sphoeroides greeleyi*), 3.4 inches, Puerto Rico.

of the stomach contents of four specimens from Puerto Rico consisted of the tips of manatee grass), sponges, crabs and other crustaceans, mollusks, polychaete worms, sea urchins, starfishes, hydroids and algae. Some authors place *Canthigaster* in a family by itself, but recent studies indicate it is best classified as a subfamily of the Tetraodontidae.

Caribbean Puffer

Sphoeroides greeleyi Gilbert, 1900.
Figure 425

Dorsal rays 8, the first ray about one-third to one-half as long as the second; anal rays 7; pectoral rays 15 or 16 (count includes uppermost rudimentary ray); gill rakers 7 or 8; skin with small scales (overlapping like normal scales but not ossified), scattered membranous flaps, and a dorsal patch of small spinules running from interorbital space nearly to dorsal fin; pectoral fins not short, 2.1 to 2.3 in head; terminal edge of caudal fin slightly rounded or slightly obtusely angular, the apex at middle ray; olivaceous, shading to whitish ventrally, the upper two-thirds of head and body with groups of small dark brown spots (many of the spots within groups conjoined, especially on lower sides); caudal fin with a dusky bar basally and a second but fainter dark bar in outer-middle part of fin. Attains about 6 inches. Caribbean Sea to Brazil. Common in shallow turbid water over mud bottoms; occasionally seen along sandy shores. *S. eulepidotus* appears to be a synonym. The similar *S. dorsalis* is more characteristic of clear water, but it is not a common species. It has a transverse pair of very small black membranous flaps on the back near the mid-line approximately above the center of the pectoral fins; it is yellowish brown on the upper two-thirds of the body with scattered small black spots and numerous pale blue-green dots; tongues of blackish, broadly edged in dull yellow, extend into the lower whitish ventral part of the head and body.

Figure 426. Bandtail Puffer (*Sphoeroides spengleri*), 4.6 inches, St. John, Virgin Islands.

Bandtail Puffer

Sphoeroides spengleri (Bloch, 1785).

Figures 423 & 426

Dorsal rays 8, the first ray very short, especially on adults; anal rays 7, the first ray very short; pectoral rays 14 (count includes uppermost ray which is just a nubbin in adults); gill rakers 9 or 10; a single nasal tube on each side with a medial and a lateral opening near tip (true of other *Sphoeroides*); body moderately elongate; skin relatively smooth, usually with a few slender membranous flaps and a dorsal patch of tiny spinules running from slightly in advance of gill opening to about half the distance to the dorsal fin; lower part of head and abdomen with small spinules (applies to other western Atlantic *Sphoeroides*); pectoral fins short, 2.7 to 3.1 in head (measured to upper end of gill opening); terminal edge of caudal fin slightly rounded; dark green to yellowish brown on back, with scattered small spots, and whitish ventrally, with a single row of about 12 to 14 round black spots on lower side of head and body; caudal fin with broad proximal and distal dusky bars, the two separated by a broad pale region. Reported to reach a length of more than 1 foot; however, the author has collected none in the Caribbean Sea larger than 5 inches. Eastern and western Atlantic; on the western side from Massachusetts and Bermuda to Brazil. Moderately common on bottoms of seagrass, sand, and coral rubble. Feeds on crabs and other crustaceans, mollusks, polychaete worms, sea urchins, brittle stars, algae and seagrass (plants less than 10% of diet).

PORCUPINEFISHES AND BURRFISHES
(DIODONTIDAE)

The porcupinefishes and burrfishes are similar to the puffers, differing notably in having prominent spines that cover the head and body except the mouth region and caudal peduncle. Also they have large eyes, and their beak-like dental plates lack a median suture. The caudal fin is rounded, and the pectoral fins are broad, the posterior edge often emarginate.

In the Caribbean Sea the family includes *Chilomycterus*, whose spines are three-rooted and rigidly erect, and the wide-ranging *Diodon*, the long quill-like spines of which are mostly two-rooted and hence movable. Normally the spines of *Diodon* lie nearly flat against the body, the sharp tips directed posteriorly. After inflation they are fully erect and present a formidable appearance to enemies.

The skin of porcupinefishes is often dried in an inflated state and used as an ornament, sometimes with a light source inside.

The diodontids feed mainly on invertebrate animals which rely on protection from shells, spines, or hard exoskeletons. The dermal armor of these animals is readily crushed by the powerful beak-like jaws of these fishes. Because of their large size, the porcupinefishes are able to feed on some of the larger hard-shelled invertebrates that are denied as food to most fishes.

The fin-ray counts given for the four diodontids discussed below are based on only five or six West Indian specimens of each species.

Bridled Burrfish

Chilomycterus antennatus (Cuvier, 1818).
Figures 427 & 428

Dorsal rays 11 to 13; anal rays 11 or 12 (dorsal and anal counts of 10 have also been recorded); pectoral rays 23 to 26; spines on head and body short, fixed, and with a fleshy sheath, those on sides and top of body more vertically erect; 10 to 12 spines in an approximate row from snout to dorsal fin; a prominent short spine in middle of forehead; a long fleshy tentacle above eye (sometimes with small branches), with a

Figure 427. Bridled Burrfish (*Chilomycterus antennatus*), night photo, Roatan, Honduras.

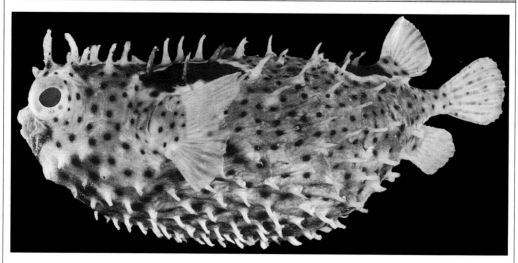

Figure 428. Bridled Burrfish (*Chilomycterus antennatus*), 5.4 inches, St. John, Virgin Islands.

spine on supraorbital ridge on either side; nostrils terminating in a slender hollow tentacle with a pair of holes at tip; a large elongate dark blotch above pectoral fin and another mid-dorsally on back, enclosing base of dorsal fin in its posterior part; a mid-dorsal dark blotch on postorbital portion of head; small black spots on head and body but not on fins; ventral part of body anterior to anal fin may be blackish, but the spines remain white; a curious red secretion may color large regions of the body, especially ventrally. Largest collected by author, 10 inches, from Puerto Rico. Caribbean Sea; also recorded from the Cape of Good Hope. Relatively rare; most often taken from seagrass beds.

Web Burrfish

Chilomycterus antillarum Jordan & Rutter, 1897.   Figure 429

Dorsal rays 11 to 13; anal rays 10 to 12; pectoral rays 22 or 23; spines short, especially those ventrally on body, and rigidly erect; 12 spines in an approximate row from front of head to dorsal fin; spines with a thin sheath, those along side at level of lower pectoral base with a tentacle extending from sheath; a row of six to eight tentacles on chin not associated with spines; a short tentacle over eye; nostrils terminating in a slender hollow tentacle with a pair of holes at tip; dorsal, anal and caudal fins small, the dorsal and anal fins very posterior on body; a coarse reticulum of dusky olive or blackish on head and body, the enclosed round, oblong, or hexagonal spots white except a bar below eye and ventral part of body where yellow predominates; a large black spot above pectoral fin and a smaller one beneath and posterior to fin, each surrounded by white which in turn is enclosed in a dusky ring; a black blotch at base of dorsal fin; pectoral fins grayish; median fins light bluish gray; supraorbital tentacle yellow; iris mainly yellow, pupil blue-green. Largest specimen, 10 inches, from Venezuela. Tropical

Figure 429. Web Burrfish (*Chilomycterus antillarum*), Curaçao.

Figure 430. Spiny Puffer (*Diodon holocanthus*), St. John, Virgin Islands.

Figure 431. Porcupinefish (*Diodon hystrix*), Bonaire.

western Atlantic, but not Bermuda. Collected by the author in Puerto Rico and Curaçao from shallow water to 80 feet. Not common.

Spiny Puffer

Diodon holocanthus Linnaeus, 1758.
Figure 430

Dorsal rays 13 or 14; anal rays 13 or 14; pectoral rays 22 or 23; spines on head and body long and movable, 14 to 16 in an approximate row between snout and origin of dorsal fin; spines mid-dorsally at front of head longer than longest spines beneath or posterior to pectoral fins; a short cylindrical loop of skin over nasal opening; light brown dorsally, shading to white ventrally, with a large brown bar above and below each eye; a broad transverse brown bar on occipital region of head; a large brown blotch above pectoral fin, one mid-dorsally in front of dorsal fin, and one surrounding base of dorsal fin; scattered dark brown spots on about upper half of postorbital part of head and body, some approaching size of pupil; fins light yellowish gray without spots; iris yellowish, pupil blue-green. A smaller species than the following; probably does not exceed 20 inches. Circumtropical. Although it may be seen on reefs, it appears to occur more often in other habitats such as mangrove channels. Feeds on mollusks (especially gastropods), sea urchins, hermit crabs and crabs.

Porcupinefish

Diodon hystrix Linnaeus, 1758. Figure 431

Dorsal rays 15 to 17; anal rays 15 or 16; pectoral rays 25; spines on head and body moderately long and movable, about 20 in an approximate row between snout and dorsal fin; spines mid-dorsally at front of head not long, 1.6 to 2.2 in longest spine posterior to pectoral fins; a short cylindrical loop of skin over nasal aperture; olivaceous on back, shading to white ventrally, with numerous small black spots on head, body and fins; no large distinct brown blotches or bars; a diffuse transverse dusky band on lower head which ends beneath pectoral fins. Said to attain a length of 3 feet; largest collected by author, 22.4 inches. Cosmopolitan in warm seas; ranges north to Massachusetts in the western Atlantic. Not uncommon on reefs of the Caribbean Sea. Feeds on sea urchins, mollusks (especially gastropods), crabs and hermit crabs, all of which it crushes with its strong jaws.

GLOSSARY OF ICHTHYOLOGICAL TERMS

Adipose eyelid: an immovable transparent outer covering or partial covering of the eye of some groups of bony fishes, such as mullets and jacks, which serves protective and streamlining functions.

Adipose fin: a small fleshy fin without rays found on the back behind the dorsal fin of some primitive teleost fishes such as the lizardfishes.

Anus: the posterior external opening of the digestive tract from which wastes are voided; sometimes called the vent.

Axil: the acute angular region between a fin and the body; usually used in reference to the underside of the pectoral fin toward the base. Equivalent to the armpit of man.

Bar: an elongate color marking of vertical orientation, the sides of which are usually more-or-less straight (although they need not be parallel).

Barbel: a slender tentacle-like protuberance of sensory function which is often seen on the chin of some fishes such as goatfishes and some of the croakers.

Bifid: divided into two equal parts or lobes; often used in reference to the distal ends of cirri or teeth of fishes.

Branchiostegal rays: slender bones which support the gill membranes; sometimes referred to simply as branchiostegals.

Canine: a prominent slender sharp-pointed tooth.

Carnivore: a flesh-eating animal.

Caudal concavity: the horizontal distance between the shortest and longest fin rays of an emarginate, lunate or forked caudal fin.

Caudal fin: the tail fin. The term tail alone generally refers to that part of a fish posterior to the anus.

Caudal peduncle: the part of the body between the posterior basal parts of the dorsal and anal fins and the base of the caudal fin. The usual vertical measurement is the least depth; the length measurement herein is horizontal, and the fin of reference (*i.e.* rear base of dorsal or anal) is designated.

Circumorbital bones: the series of small dermal bones that rim the eye; those along the lower edge are termed suborbitals, the first of which is the preorbital.

Circumpeduncular: around the caudal peduncle; usually used in reference to scale counts.

Cirrus: a small slender flexible fleshy protuberance; the plural is cirri.

Compressed: laterally flattened; often used in reference to the shape of the body—in this case deeper than wide.

Conical: resembling a cone in shape; a descriptive term for teeth.

Ctenoid scales: scales of bony fishes which have tiny tooth-like projections along the posterior margin and part of the exposed portion. Collectively these little teeth (or ctenii) impart a rough texture to the surface of the scales.

Cycloid scales: scales of bony fishes, the exposed surfaces and edges of which lack any small tooth-like projections; they are therefore smooth to the touch.

Depressed: dorso-ventrally flattened. The opposite in body shape of compressed.

Depth: a vertical measurement of the body of a fish; most often employed for the maximum height of the body excluding the fins.

Distal: outward from the point of attachment; the opposite of proximal.

Dorsal: toward the back or upper part of the body; the opposite of ventral.

Dorsal fin: a median fin along the back which is supported by rays. There may be two or more dorsal fins, in which case the most anterior one is designated the first.

Double emarginate: biconcave; used to describe the shape of the posterior edge of the caudal fin in which there are two curved indentations separated by a convexity.

Emarginate: concave; used to describe the posterior border of a caudal fin which is inwardly curved.

Finlets: small separate fins, each consisting of one soft ray, which occur singly or in series behind the dorsal and anal fins. They are most characteristic of the tunas and mackerels.

Fork length: the horizontal measurement of a fish from the front of the upper lip to the posterior end of the middle caudal rays. This measurement is used in lieu of standard length in those fishes on which it is difficult to ascertain the end of the vertebral column.

Forked: inwardly angular; used in describing the shape of a caudal fin which is divided into two equal lobes, the posterior border of each of which is relatively straight.

Fusiform: spindle-shaped; used in reference to the body shape of a fish which is cylindrical or nearly so and tapers toward the ends.

Gill arch: the bony support for the gill filaments and gill rakers. Normally there are four pairs of gill arches in bony fishes.

Gill membranes: membranes along the ventral and posterior margin of the operculum (gill cover) which function in respiration; they are supported by the branchiostegal rays.

Gill opening: the opening posteriorly and often also ventrally on the head of fishes where the water of respiration is expelled. Bony fishes have a single such opening on each side whereas cartilaginous fishes (sharks and rays) have five to seven. The gill openings of sharks and rays are called gill slits.

Gill rakers: stout protuberances of the gill arch on the opposite side from the red gill filaments which function in retaining food organisms. They vary greatly in number and length and are important in the classification of fishes.

Head length: the straight-line measurement of the head taken from the front of the upper lip to the membranous posterior end of the operculum.

Herbivore: a plant-feeding animal.

Illicium: the "fishing pole" and "lure" of lophiiform (pediculate) fishes which is used to attract prey close to the mouth of these fishes.

Incisiform: chisel-like; used to describe teeth which are flattened and truncate with sharp edges like the front teeth of some mammals such as man.

Interopercle: one of the bones comprising the operculum; bordered antero-dorsally by the preopercle and postero-dorsally by the opercle and subopercle.

Interorbital space: the region on the top of the head between the eyes; measurements may be taken of the least width, either fleshy (to the edges of the orbits) or bony (between the edges of the frontal bones which rim the orbits).

Isthmus: the throat region of a fish which extends forward from the ventral part of the chest and narrows anteriorly.

Jugular: denotes the position of the pelvic fins in the throat region—the most anterior position of these fins in bony fishes. The blennies are a typical group with pelvics at this location. Other pelvic fin positions are thoracic and abdominal.

Keel: a lateral strengthening ridge posteriorly on the caudal peduncle or base of the caudal fin; typically found on swift-swimming fishes with a narrow caudal peduncle and a broadly lunate caudal fin.

Labial: referring to the lips.

Lanceolate: lance-shaped, hence gradually tapering to a point; used to describe a caudal fin with very long middle rays. An unusual fin shape most often seen among the gobies.

Lateral: referring to the side or directed toward the side; the opposite of medial.

Lateral line: a sensory organ of fishes which consists of a canal running along the side of the body and communicating via pores through scales to the exterior; functions in perceiving low frequency vibrations, hence provides a sense which might be termed "touch at a distance."

Lateral-line scales: the pored scales of the lateral line between the upper end of the gill opening and the base of the caudal fin. The count of this series of scales is of value in the descriptions of fishes. So also at times is the number of scales above the lateral line (to the origin of the dorsal fin) and the number below the lateral line (to the origin of the anal fin).

Lateral scale rows: the number of near-vertical scale rows between the upper end of the gill opening and the base of the caudal fin; sometimes called vertical scale rows. This count is taken on fishes which lack a lateral line or on which the lateral-line scales are difficult to enumerate.

Leptocephalus: the elongate highly compressed transparent larval stage of some primitive teleost fishes such as the tarpon, bonefish and eels.

Lower limb: refers either to the horizontal margin of the preopercle or to the number of gill rakers on the first gill arch below and including the one at the angle.

Lunate: sickle-shaped; used to describe a caudal fin which is deeply emarginate with narrow lobes.

Maxilla: a dermal bone of the upper jaw which lies posterior to the premaxilla. On the higher fishes the maxilla is excluded from the gape, and the premaxilla bears the teeth.

Medial: toward the middle or median plane of the body; opposite of lateral.

Median fins: the fins in the median plane, hence the dorsal, anal and caudal fins.

Median predorsal scales: the number of scales running in a median row anteriorly from the origin of the dorsal fin.

Molariform: shaped like a molar, hence low, broad and rounded.

Naked: scaleless.

Nape: the dorsal region of the head posterior to the occiput.

Narial: referring to the nostrils.

Occiput: the region of the head above the cranium and posterior to the eye.

Ocellus: an eye-like marking with a ring of one color surrounding a spot of another.

Omnivore: an animal which feeds on both plant and animal material.

Opercle: the large bone which forms the upper posterior part of the operculum; often bears one to three backward-directed spines in the higher fishes.

Operculum: gill cover; comprised of the following four bones; opercle, preopercle, interopercle and subopercle.

Orbital: referring to the orbit or eye.

Origin: the beginning; often used for the anterior end of the dorsal or anal fin at the base. Also used in zoology to denote the more fixed attachment of a muscle.

Paired fins: collective term for the pectoral and pelvic fins.

Palatine: a paired lateral bone on the roof of the mouth lying between the vomer and the upper jaw; the presence or absence of teeth on this bone is of significance in the classification of fishes.

Pectoral fin: the fin usually found on each side of the body behind the gill opening; in primitive fishes this pair of fins is lower on the body than in more advanced forms.

Pelvic fin: one of a pair of juxtaposed fins ventrally on the body in front of the anus; varies from abdominal in position in primitive fishes such as herrings to the more anterior locations termed thoracic or jugular in advanced fishes. Sometimes called ventral fin.

Pelvic terminus: the small external spinous knob generally found at the end of the long pelvic girdle of trigger-fishes and filefishes; it is unpaired and usually movable.

Peritoneum: the membranous lining of the body cavity.

Pharyngeal teeth: opposing patches of teeth which occur on the upper and lower elements of the gill arches. They vary from sharp and piercing to nodular or molariform; they may be modified into a grooved grinding apparatus (or pharyngeal mill), such as seen in the parrotfishes.

Premaxilla: the more anterior bone forming the upper jaw. In the higher fishes it extends backward and bears all of the teeth of the jaw. It is this part of the upper jaw which can be protruded by many fishes.

Preopercle: a boomerang-shaped bone, the edges of which form the posterior and lower margins of the cheek region; it is the most anterior of the bones comprising the gill cover. The upper vertical margin is sometimes called the upper limb, and the lower horizontal edge the lower limb; the two limbs meet at the angle of the preopercle.

Preorbital: the first and usually the largest of the suborbital bones; located along the ventro-anterior rim of the eye. Sometimes called the lacrymal bone.

Principal caudal rays: the caudal rays which reach the terminal border of the fin; in those fishes with branched caudal rays, the count includes the branched rays plus the uppermost and lowermost rays which are unbranched.

Proximal: toward the center of the body; the opposite of distal.

Ray: the supporting bony elements of fins; includes spines and soft rays.

Rhomboid: wedge-shaped; refers to a caudal fin shape in which the middle rays are longest and the upper and lower portions of the terminal border of the fin are more-or-less straight; essentially the opposite of forked. An uncommon fin shape most often found in the croakers and flatfishes.

Rounded: refers to a caudal fin shape in which the terminal border is smoothly convex.

Rudiment: a structure so deficient in size that it does not perform its normal function; often used in reference to the small nodular gill rakers at the ends of the gill arch.

Scute: an external bony plate or enlarged scale.

Serrate: notched along a free margin, like the edge of a saw.

Sexual dichromatism: a condition wherein the two sexes of the same species are of different color.

Simple: not branched.

Snout: the region of the head in front of the eye. Snout length is measured from the front of the upper lip to the anterior edge of the eye.

Soft ray: a segmented fin ray which is composed of two closely joined lateral elements. It is nearly always flexible and often branched.

Spine: an unsegmented bony process consisting of a single element which is usually rigid and sharp-pointed. Those spines which support fins are never branched.

Spinule: a small spine. Term generally not used in reference to the small spines of fins.

Spiracle: an opening between the eye and the first gill slit of sharks and rays which leads to the pharyngeal cavity.

Standard length: the length of a fish from the front of the upper lip to the posterior end of the vertebral column (the last element of which, the hypural plate, is somewhat broadened and forms the bony support for the caudal–fin rays).

Stripe: a horizontal straight-sided color marking.

Subopercle: an elongate flat dermal bone which is one of the four comprising the operculum; lies below the opercle and forms the ventro-posterior margin of the operculum.

Suborbital depth: the distance from the lower edge of the eye to the nearest edge of the upper lip.

Supplemental bone: a slender bone lying along the upper edge of the maxilla; also called the supramaxilla.

Supraorbital: the region bordering the upper edge of the eye.

Swimbladder: a tough-walled gas-filled sac lying in the upper part of the body cavity of many bony fishes just beneath the vertebral column, the principal function of which is to offset the weight of the heavier tissues, particularly bone. In some fishes such as the croakers it also functions in sound production, and in a few others such as the tarpon it is important in respiration. Primitive fishes tend to have a connection between the swimbladder and the esophagus. The organ is also called the air bladder or the gas bladder.

Symphysis: an articulation, generally immovable, between two bones; often used in reference to the anterior region of juncture of the two halves of the jaws.

Synonym: an invalid scientific name of an organism proposed after the accepted name.

Teleost: refers to the Teleostei, the highest superorder of the ray-fin bony fishes, including all those of the present book. The others are the Chondrostei (the sturgeons and paddlefishes are the living representatives) and Holostei (the bowfin and gars are the contemporary forms). The Teleostei and Holostei may be polyphyletic (of multiple origin), so these superordinal group names, though often heard, are usually omitted from recent formal classifications.

Thoracic: referring to the chest region.

Total length: the length of a fish from the front of whichever jaw is most anterior to the end of the longest caudal ray.

Trifid: branched into three approximately equal parts; usually used in reference to the divided end of a cirrus or tooth.

Truncate: square-ended; used to describe a caudal fin with a vertically straight terminal border and angular or slightly rounded corners.

Upper limb: refers either to the vertical free margin of the preopercle or to the number of gill rakers on the first gill arch above the angle.

Ventral: toward the lower part of the body; the opposite of dorsal.

Villiform: like the villi of the intestine, hence with numerous small slender projections. Used to describe bands of small close-set teeth, particularly if slender. If the teeth are short, they are often termed cardiform.

Vomer: a median unpaired bone toward the front of the roof of the mouth, the anterior end of which often bears teeth.

INDEX OF SCIENTIFIC NAMES

INDEX OF COMMON NAMES